SILK ROAD COOKING
A Vegetarian Journey

Najmieh Batmanglij

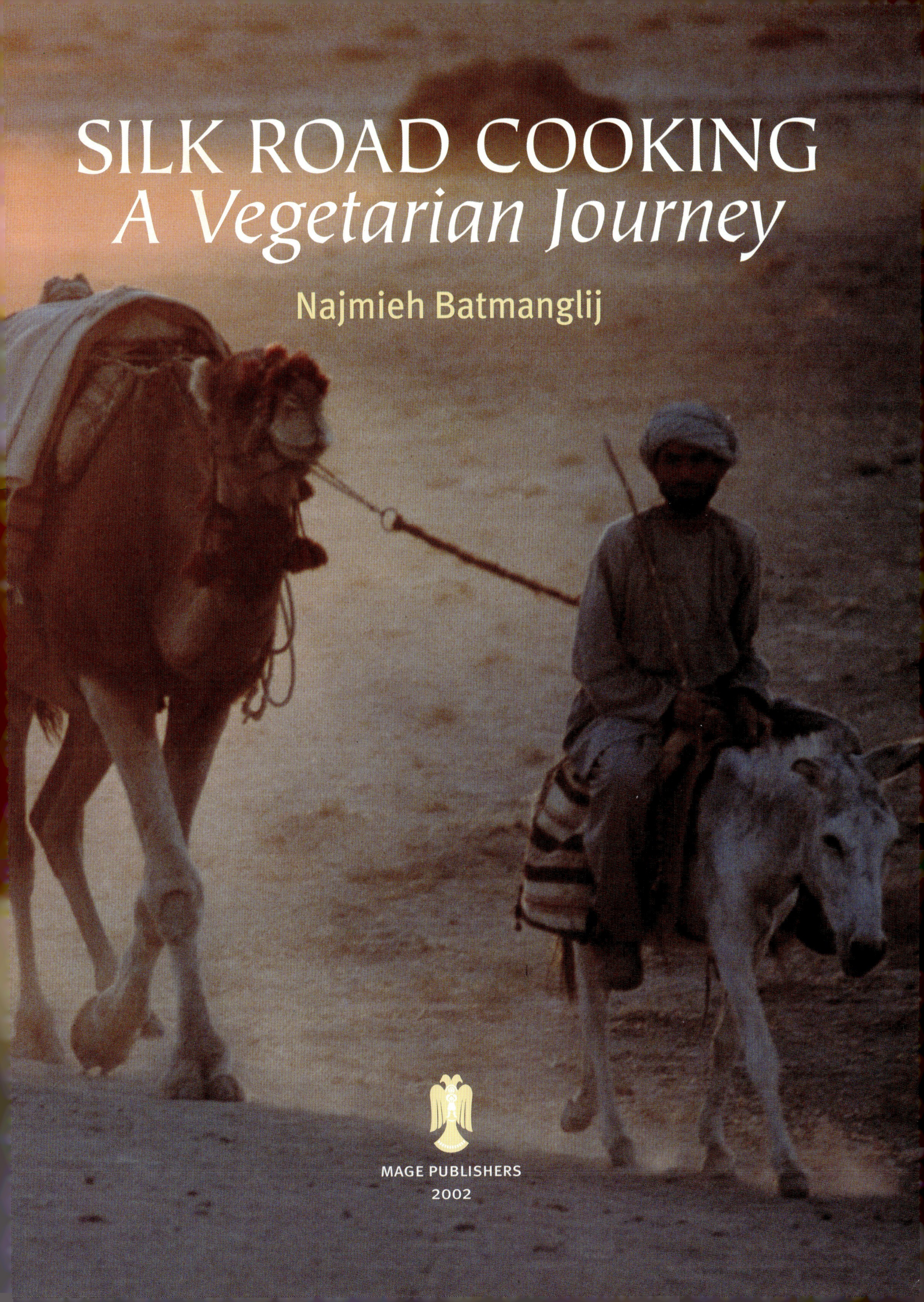

MAGE PUBLISHERS
2002

Copyright © 2002 Mage Publishers, Washington, DC
Designed by Najmieh Batmanglij

Full credits on page 329

All rights reserved.
No part of this book may be reproduced
or retransmitted in any manner whatsoever,
except in the form of a review, without the
written permission of the publisher.

LIBRARY OF CONGRESS
CATALOGING-IN-PUBLICATION DATA
Batmanglij, Najmieh
Silk road cooking: a vegetarian journey / Najmieh
Batmanglij. p. cm. ISBN 0-934211-63-9
(alk. paper)
1. Vegetarian cookery. 2. Silk Road. I. Title.
TX837. B3385 2002
641.5'636--dc21

FIRST EDITION
ISBN 0-934211-63-9

Printed and manufactured in Korea

An Uzbek woman offers fresh figs in the Tashkent market. This black variety has been cultivated since at least the fourth millennium BCE in Egypt; by 800 BCE the tree was domesticated throughout the Middle East and Greece. From there, it spread north and east.

Mage books are available at bookstores or directly from the publisher: Mage Publishers, 1032-29th Street, NW, Washington, DC 20007.
To receive our latest catalogue, call toll free 1-800-962-0922 or visit Mage online at www.mage.com

CONTENTS

9   Introduction
A Traveler's Tale
The Era of Caravans
New Foods—East & West
Toward a Silk Road Cuisine

59   Salads

95   Soups

119   Eggs

135   Rice

173   Fruit & Vegetable Braises

197   Pasta, Pizza & Bread

239   Pastries, Desserts & Candies

273   Teas, Coffee & Sherbets

293   Preserves, Pickles & Spices

306   Silk Road Glossary & Resources

329   Credits & Acknowledgments

331   Index

To my mother, who was a natural herbalist

Our guest's the sun that rises in the east—tonight,
That glowing heavenly disk will share our feast—tonight!
Play us, sweet singers, songs that tell love's secrets, till
Our souls rise up, enraptured and released—tonight.

Jalal al-Din Rumi / Dick Davis

INTRODUCTION

Come join me on a voyage of culinary discovery, along a path that stretches through the ages and across half the world, from China in the east to the Mediterranean in the west. The path is the ancient network of trading routes known today as the Silk Road.

Cooking traditions are often defined in geographic terms; a cuisine may be associated with a particular province, for instance, or a country or perhaps a wider region such as the Mediterranean. To speak of Silk Road cooking is to invoke spaces and distances far greater, continental in scope. But while the unity is more elusive, it is very real, created by exchanges so slow and subtle as to be almost imperceptible. For centuries—along with the silk, ivory, incense and other trade goods flowing over the vast network—vegetables, fruits, grains and cooking techniques passed from one civilization to another, to be absorbed and transformed into local specialties. This process of mutual enrichment shaped the cuisines of far-flung cultures in profound ways, especially their vegetarian dishes. It is one of the great stories of cooking—yet one of the least known.

I was born in Iran, a country positioned at the center of the ancient trading nexus, looking both east and west. Some of my happiest childhood memories are linked to Silk Road cooking, although of course I had no notion of such a thing at the time. On certain school half-days, when I arrived home early in the afternoon, I would hear distant echoes of a setar and my mother singing verses by the thirteenth-century poet Rumi, a great favorite of hers:

Oh listen to the flute as it complains

The sweet, sad tones drew me to the brightest room in our house, where, sitting on the Persian carpet striped with light and color from the sunshine that seeped through bamboo shades, I found my mother and four or five old

Opposite: A farmer in southwest China embraces rice, the "Golden Harvest." The staff of life for half of humanity, rice is sacred throughout Asia.

This page: The Western staff of life is wheat, here being winnowed by an Afghan farmer *(top)*. In a sixteenth-century Persian miniature *(bottom),* a woman is shown rolling wheat dough for noodles using a technique handed down through the generations.

Introduction / 9

ladies, all distant relatives. From the crisply ironed white cotton cloths being spread over the carpet and the captivating aroma of fresh dough, I knew it was noodle-making day. "Come on in," said the old ladies, tearing off a piece of dough for me to play with.

They were kneading dough and rolling it into rectangles on large wooden boards. When they had rolled it thin, they folded each sheet twice; then, with one hand as a guide and working with fast, confident strokes, they used sharp knives to cut their dough sheets into quarter-inch strips. The room would fall silent as they concentrated on the task, joyfully competing to see who could cut the most even strips in the shortest time.

Every so often, as if reminded by something, my mother would stop cutting, put down her knife and continue to sing her poem from where she had left off:

> *In anguished tales of separation's pains;*
> *Since they have torn me from the reedbed I*
> *Make men and women heartsick with my sigh . . .*

Everyone would stop working, some still kneading the dough, some with finished strips in hand. All would lean back from their work and join in the refrain:

> *Oh listen to the flute as it complains*

Just as quickly as it had started, the singing would stop. Tea would appear, and there would be some gossip, a few new jokes, lots of laughing. Then, as if on cue, everyone would go back to work. One of the old ladies would give me some strands of the fresh noodles to arrange, carefully separated for drying, on the floured cotton sheets.

I found myself as delighted by the cheerful ceremony of preparation as by the reward for the work. The next day, convivial crowds of relatives would come to our house for a glorious lunch of noodle soup garnished with fried garlic, onion, mint and sun-dried yogurt.

This page: The hand that cut them holds fresh Persian noodles in a bunch; they are destined for a soup garnished with garlic, onion, mint and sun-dried yogurt *(opposite),* a favorite *Nowruz* or New Year's dish. Eating the noodles signifies unravelling the strands of the year ahead.

Introduction / 10

Such pleasurable memories inspired me years later, when I turned to a more serious study of cookery. I began with Persian foods and dishes, and the traditions behind them. Later, in France and America, I learned techniques from other cuisines. Later still, I traveled to such countries as China, Uzbekistan, Afghanistan, India, Turkey and Italy, growing ever more intrigued by commonalities and connections in their cooking.

One universal rule seems to be something I first noticed in Iran: The food in restaurants—the food that visitors see as characteristic of a culture—often is only a small sampling of the dishes people eat at home. When contemplating the cookery of Iran or of the Middle East, for example, most Westerners think of meat kabobs, which certainly are popular fare, especially as street food and for celebrations. But Persians eat meat sparingly at home and, as in every other culture, save extravagant meat dishes for special occasions and grand festivities. On the other hand, they prepare a wide range of grain, vegetable and fruit dishes, delicious creations barely known outside of the country. I found the same contrast between restaurant and home cooking in every place I visited.

In Iranian home cooking, a meal always begins with bread, cheese, and whatever vegetables and herbs are freshest in the garden or market that day. They are spread out for the family or any guests who may appear, and to them may be added salads and various yogurt-based dips for the bread. Then there are stuffed vegetables; fragrant kukus, or vegetable omelets; and soups.

Vegetable markets and vegetarian dishes in all the countries once traversed by the Silk Road offer the same painterly displays, varied fragrances and intense tastes. In markets in Uzbekistan, I found huge melons of surpassing sweetness and vibrant orange carrots unlike any others. I saw nan, the familiar flat bread of Iran, cooked in a tandoor (clay oven) or on a saaj or taveh (a convex cast iron plate placed over a fire). Sold from wooden carts, the flat loaves—known as nan there, too, as well as in India, Pakistan, Afghanistan, much of central Asia and western China—are scented with onion, garlic and sesame, cumin or nigella seeds. Across the world in Xian I reveled in the vast outdoor market, its stalls groaning under bright persimmons, pomegranates, big red jujubes, aromatic ginger, onions and leeks. Such cornucopias are also to be found in Istanbul, Genoa—indeed, almost everywhere—and the wonderful produce, fresh from the earth, stalk, vine or branch, has come to the markets of America, too.

The foods made from this bounty appear in infinite variety. Consider only meze, that tempting assembly of little dishes found throughout the Middle East and into Spain (where they are called tapas). Appealing arrays

Bread, fresh cheese, onions, herbs, and fruit welcome guests to Iranian homes. To these will be added a variety of little dishes, ancestors of Turkish meze, Greek mezedes, and Spanish tapas.

Introduction / 12

of this kind are also spread out in the unpretentious cafés, or *lokantas* (from the Italian *locanda,* meaning "inn"), that one finds in every Turkish town. In the warm weather people sit outside, helping themselves to dolmas (stuffed vine leaves), vegetable tempuras, the marvelous pastries called boreks and—my favorite, which also made the imam faint, as its name says— imam bayaldi. There is something about stuffing an eggplant with onion, garlic and tomato that endows its flesh with a most subtle sweetness.

The story of Silk Road cooking has a strong vegetarian focus, partly because various early religions that spread along the trade routes encouraged vegetarian diets (see pages 221–223), but chiefly for economic reasons: vegetables, fruits, nuts and other vegetarian ingredients were more affordable than meat. This has a happy corollary: As we are now frequently told by doctors, a diet that includes plenty of vegetables and fruits is a healthy way to eat. For that reason alone, the cuisines that evolved along the Silk Road offer rich rewards to modern-day cooks.

Ingredients are only part of the story, of course. Ideas for preparation naturally accompanied the constituents themselves. The noodles of my childhood are a case in point. In the course of my journeys, I found them everywhere—and in China I saw the making and serving of noodles elevated to art. A noodle master of northern China, in what looks like sleight of hand, can stretch and swing a lump of dough into perfect individual strands in 15 minutes. And the sauces and soups that enhance these noodles exist in as rich a variety in China as they do in Italy.

Such mastery would seem to support the old legend that Marco Polo brought noodles from China to Italy in the thirteenth century. Recent archeological and linguistic scholarship shows, however, that the transfer was much earlier, and in both directions, east and west. Today, food scholars agree that pasta probably originated in Persia. The first pasta dish is recorded in a tenth-century Arab cookery book, *Kitab al tabikh va islah al-aghdhiya al makulat,* which calls it by the Persian

Silk Road market treasures *(counterclockwise from opposite top):* piping hot beets sold on the street in Tehran; a woman sells herbs in Bokhara; an Uzbeki woman and her granddaughter in Tashkent sell stacks of nan, or hot bread rounds; a vendor shows just one of the olive varieties available in an Istanbul market.

word *lakhsha* (which means "slippery") presumably because of the slipperiness of noodles. In eastern Iran, Afghanistan, Uzbekistan, Tajikistan, parts of western China, and Indonesia, they still use a variation of the name lakhsha to refer to a dish that uses wide, flat strips of dough. The same book also mentions that the dish was invented by the Persian Sasanian king Khosrow (Khosrow I, 531–579). It was probably the Arabs who introduced noodles, and the hard durum wheat necessary for making it, to Italy in the ninth century via Sicily and Genoa.

No one knows exactly how the technique for making pasta reached China. What can be said with certainty is that before the Han dynasty (202 BCE-220 CE), that country lacked the mills for large-scale flour grinding. Such mills appeared as China expanded to the west via the newly explored Silk Road, and Han cooks soon adapted or invented a vast array of "noodle foods," as they were called by writers of the time. By the end of the dynasty, China already had developed the technique for swinging dough into individual strands. These were boiled and served with a range of seasonings, and although they were generally considered common food, they were so delicious that even the emperor ate them. Other pasta foods of China include dumplings, steamed buns and little wheat cakes. Some were invented by ordinary people, a third-century chronicler reports, and some came from foreign lands. The many types and many names of Chinese noodle foods offer the sorts of clues that delight linguistic scholars, who find hints of food origins in the wanderings of words. Among the Chinese favorites, for example, is man t'ou, a steamed, sweetened, bread-like bun. The term appears in Iran and Afghanistan as mantu; in Japan as manzu, a steamed dough with a filling; and in Korea as mandu, a kind of ravioli filled with beef. Tibetans make stuffed dumplings in a variety of shapes and call them momo. In central Asia, manti is a small steamed pasta that may contain meat, vegetables, or cheese and is served with yogurt or vinegar; in Turkey and Armenia the same word refers to a small stuffed pasta shell poached in broth or steamed. Although some suggest a Central Asian origin for such dishes, no one knows for sure. What is more important than the origin is that the dishes and their names are all related. They form a culinary bond—a sign of early and peaceful communication—that links distant and sometimes hostile cultures.

Young chefs in Tashkent and Beijing demonstrate the ancient art of swinging noodles by hand. The dough is first rested to strengthen the gluten in the flour; then rolled into a tube; then rhythmically stretched, folded and twisted; and finally, with special hand holds, swung to split it into noodles. As shown counterclockwise from top left, the chef splits the dough, swings it, and folds it, doubling the strands each time until he has made 256 strands. The result of the 15-minute process, which may take two years to learn, is the finest and silkiest of noodles.

A grandmother in Yuanyang, southwest China, helps her grandson learn the polite way to eat with chopsticks. The rice bowl—or as here, noodle bowl—should be held close to the chin with one hand so that food may be scooped into the mouth without waste or mess.

It is a curious fact that the noodles that reached culinary heights in China and Japan, not to mention Italy, occupy only a humble place in the cookery of their Iranian home. Rice, on the other hand, is the same story in reverse. The grain, cultivated in China and India for at least 5,000 years seems to have reached Persia only in the fourth century BCE. It did not begin to play an important part in Iranian cookery, however, until the eighth century. Since then, rice has become something special in Iran. It is not the anchor of a meal as it is in China but the basis of festive and elaborate dishes called polows. As you will see in the rice chapter (pages 135-171), a polow may be cooked with a golden crust; it may be flavored with tart cherries, quinces, pomegranates, barberries or candied bitter orange peel; it may include pistachios, almonds, walnuts or rose petals. Like other good dishes, polow has spread far beyond its Persian source. Under such related names as pullao, pilavi, pilaf, and pilau, and with such additions as chickpeas and raisins or onions and carrots, it graces celebrations from Afghanistan to Albania, and from India to Turkey.

Similar tales linking east and west, north and south, could be told for rice pudding, bread, bulgur and dozens of other preparations based on vegetables, grains, fruits, herbs and spices. It is this rich mosaic—each piece related but distinct—that I have explored during the last 25 years.

But let us begin at the beginning and tell a traveler's tale...

Opposite: Street vendors offer two kinds of stuffed pastries found under different names throughout the Silk Road region. The Uzbeki boy at top sells samsa, crisp baked or fried pies that may be half-moon shaped, as here, or triangular. Similar dishes are called sanbusek by Arabs, sambosa by Afghans and samosa by Indians—all versions of the original Persian name sanbosag. In Xian, below, a woman sells the steamed buns called man t'ou in China and by similar names throughout Asia.

Right: Open-air rice cookery involves a range of styles. In China, the grain is usually steamed and served plain, as in the market at Chengdu, top. In Central Asia, rice is the basis for elaborately flavored festive dishes such as the Uzbeki pavlov shown below.

A TRAVELER'S TALE

The centuries just before the Common Era were an age of empire, west and east. In the west, the vast but short-lived empire of Alexander the Great had fragmented into different states and kingdoms. Mauryan kings reclaimed their Indian territories. The kingdom then known as Iran rose again with the Parthians of its eastern regions, who came to dominate most western trade routes. Egypt remained the kingdom of the Ptolemys, descendants of one of Alexander's generals. Its chief city, Alexandria, was the jewel of the Western world.

Egypt soon was to become a possession of the fastest-growing empire of all. Rome. Still a republic, but evolving toward imperial government, Rome sent its legions to rule all of Europe, all the Mediterranean ports, and much of Asia Minor. The city itself was an entrepot for foods and treasure throughout the known world.

Five thousand miles to the east, another empire grew, larger than Rome, better governed, more refined and utterly unknown to the west. After centuries of civil strife, China was united in 202 BCE by the Han dynasty. At its peak, under the "martial emperor" Wu Di, the Han empire encompassed almost all of modern China, south to what is now northern Vietnam, north into Korea and west into Tibet. The vast land was organized down to the level of the smallest hamlet and governed by a trained bureaucracy, which standardized its writing, weights and measures, and even the wheel gauge of its vehicles. Its capital, Chang'an (modern Xian), the largest city on earth, centered on a royal palace of surpassing splendor set among gardens adorned with exotic plants and animals. The city was crossed by boulevards 140 feet wide and divided by walls into 60 wards. Nine markets, their thousands of stalls grouped by product—food, furs, lacquerware and so on—served the people who lived in the wards and the traders who came from abroad.

China's northern border was shielded by garrisons stationed along the recently completed Great Wall, 1,500 miles in length—a bastion against nomad tribes that regularly descended from the northern steppes to kill and plunder. The Chinese called these people the Xiungu; other cultures called them Huns.

As a further defense, Emperor Wu conceived the idea of an alliance with a people called the Yuezhi, who had been driven far west by the nomads. But first the Yuezhi had to be found. A commander of the palace guard named Zhang Qian volunteered for the job and set off to the west with a company of 100 men. The year was 138 BCE.

Introduction / 24

Zhang was a brave man indeed, for he had to traverse some of the most harrowing terrain on earth. Beyond the west end of the Great Wall, near Dunhuang, lies the Tarim Basin, some 1,200 square miles in area. It is flanked in the south by the Himalayas, in the north by the Tian Shan mountains and the wastes of Siberia, and blocked in the west by the 25,000-foot peaks of the Pamirs. The basin itself consists of five deserts, of which the most famous is probably the Taklimakan, whose name means in the local dialect, "You may go in, but you won't come out."

No one knows what route Zhang followed. In the wilds of western China, the Huns captured his little band and held him for ten years. Eventually, with some of his companions—and with the yak tail banner that proclaimed him an ambassador—he escaped and marched doggedly west until he reached Khokand in the Ferghana valley between the Pamirs and the Tian Shan. Here he discovered peaceful people living not in nomads' tents but in houses surrounded by fields of waist-high alfalfa, which supplied fodder for the prince of Ferghana's

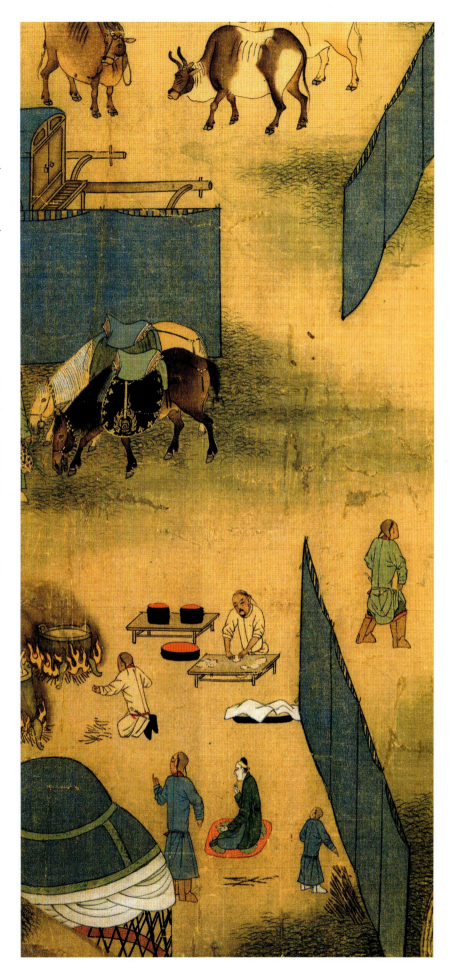

Opposite: A seventh-century wall painting from the caves of Dunhuang in western China portrays a monk returning from India with sacred Buddhist texts. Such pilgrims were among the earliest to write about the hazards of the Silk Road.

Right and overleaf: Details of nomad life appear in fourteenth-century illustrations of the true story of Lady Wen-chi, a Chinese aristocrat held captive for 12 years by the Huns of Inner Mongolia in the second century. At right, camp cooks prepare the nomads' unleavened bread and boiled mutton, producing odors the lady despised.

Overleaf: Concealed by the panels of her camel cart and flanked by nomad and Chinese outriders, the newly ransomed Wen-chi begins the long journey home to China.

Introduction / 26

"Heavenly Horses," magnificent, swift mounts capable of carrying men in full armor. They were heavenly indeed, compared to the ponies of China.

Taking note, Zhang pushed on, until at last he arrived at the land of the Yuezhi—pleasant, green country watered by the Amu Darya in what is now south-central Uzbekistan. Here his primary mission met defeat: The Yuezhi had no wish for an alliance with China. The Huns were close; the emperor was far away.

On the other hand, Zhang acquired valuable information. He was told of 36 rich, walled cities. He learned that a powerful nation called Parthia lay to the west and heard that north of Parthia was a rich nation he named Li-chien, which we now think probably meant Rome. In the places he visited he found delightful foods, wines and other items of interest to emperors. (His reports on these no doubt inspired the legend that it was Zhang himself who introduced such exotica as grapes, pomegranates, walnuts, sesame, beans, coriander and cucumber to China; they would arrive within a couple of decades of his adventure, but Zhang could hardly have carried them.) And he met merchants of Bactria, now Afghanistan, eager for trade. Finally, there were the Heavenly Horses.

So Zhang headed for home, eventually reaching Chang'an with one companion, 13 years after he had left and long after he had been given up for dead. When Emperor Wu received Zhang's report, he made his faithful soldier a prince.

Ever the visionary, the emperor saw the value of the horses of Ferghana: Possession of these fabulous creatures was a mark of Heaven's grace, not to mention a powerful asset to Wu's armies. He also saw the benefits of trade, and he realized that to secure trade routes he must control the northern nomads. He therefore mounted successive military campaigns so effective that by 101 BCE he

Introduction / 27

had conquered not only Ferghana but all the small kingdoms that lay along the route west; he manned them with garrisons and colonists, making travel possible. He also acquired breeding herds of the famed horses and imported alfalfa to feed them.

Sometime during this period, Wu sent his first embassy to Parthian Persia, which was approaching its peak as an empire that extended from the Euphrates across Afghanistan to the Indus and from the Amu Darya to the Indian Ocean. The embassy's purpose was commercial, and it was highly successful. The Parthians presented the emperor with an ostrich egg and some conjurors, according to the Chinese annals. To the Parthians, the Chinese presented bolts of silk.

This fabric—the strongest of all natural fibers, light, warm and beautiful—was intrinsic to Chinese civilization. Although its origins are lost in legend, archeological evidence dates it to the neolithic era, and its manufacture became a major Chinese industry. Women raised the silkworm, *Bombyx mori,* feeding it on mulberry leaves, keeping it warm and quiet as it spun its cocoon. Then they unraveled the cocoon strand for weaving and dying. For the rich there were silk gauzes and brocades, silks woven with tiny bird feathers and silks embroidered with gold. Other silks were used for musical instrument strings and fishing lines, for padding winter clothing and making rag paper. Silk could even be fashioned into waterproof containers. Bolts of silk were used as money.

The secret of silk making remained in China for centuries: Foreigners thought it grew on trees. It was certainly greatly coveted in the West. The Parthians used it to make shimmering battle banners and thereby introduced it to the Romans during one episode among their long hostilities. It was only a matter of time before the wondrous fabric became the rage of luxury-loving Rome. Romans were willing to pay its weight in gold; within a century, the Roman emperor Augustus, dismayed by the gold drain, tried to restrict its use to women and angrily observed that in exchange for such trifles, Roman coin was sent even to Rome's enemies.

Servants attend to camels, luggage and cooking in this sixteenth-century Persian miniature. It illustrates a pilgrimage scene from a famous love story, *Layli and Majnun,* by the twelfth-century poet Nizami.

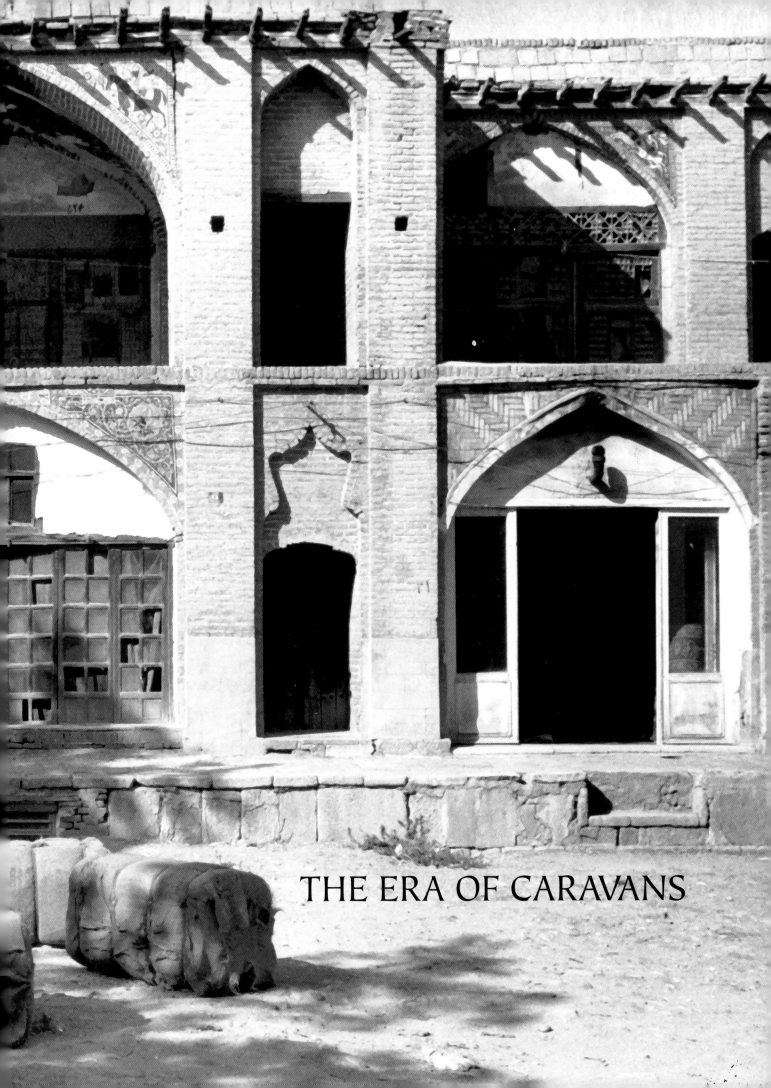

THE ERA OF CARAVANS

With the establishment of the trading route, a long and enlightening commerce between east and west began, one that was to continue for more than a thousand years, through the rise and fall of many empires. After the thirteenth-century Mongol conquests of most of Asia and large sections of Europe, the Silk Road enjoyed a last great efflorescence. For a hundred years, a Pax Mongolica lay over the trade routes; and Europeans such as Marco Polo could travel to the Far East. Then the Mongols declined in their turn and with them overland trade, which was transferred to sea routes. Central Asia sank into the shadows of history.

Through these centuries, not always without interruption, the trade caravans plodded to and fro. Flanked by outriding guards, moving in trains of thousands of burdened beasts—dromedaries in the west, yaks for the icy passes of the Pamirs, sturdier Bactrian camels in the east—they left tracks so deep that some may still be seen.

It was never easy; it was often cold and lonely, as the ninth-century poet Li Ho's "On the Frontier" suggests:

> *A Tartar horn tugs at the north wind,*
> *Thistle Gate shines whiter than the stream,*
> *The sky swallows the road to Koko Nor,*
> *On the Great Wall, a thousand miles of moonlight.*

Once past the Chinese frontier, a hostile wilderness tested the travelers. "Beyond the Jade Gate in the Great Wall is a desert belt, the home of malevolent spirits who stir up hot winds," wrote the itinerant Buddhist priest Fa Hsien, in 399. Yet there were respites at green oases here and there. As often as not, even as far east as Turfan, the oases were watered by snowmelt, brought down from the mountains using the ancient qanat system of underground conduits. This allowed for fields of wheat or cotton, for orchards, for the shade-giving poplars and willows that made the oases refuges from the desert. Most had caravansaries, great courtyard buildings with animals for hire, stables, warehouses, rooms for rent and—depending on the period—temples, churches, shrines or mosques for the devout.

Merchants weigh jujubes, also known as Chinese dates, in the courtyard of a caravansary at Tashkurgan, Afghanistan, on the eastern slopes of the Pamirs. Tashkurgan, which means "tower of stone," is a favorite choice among archeologists as the ancient entrance to the central Asian Silk Road.

Opposite: A woman carries freshly picked cotton on the road between Samarkand and Bokhara. The bolls will become fabric; the seeds produce cooking oil.

This page, clockwise from top left: Delicacies from east and west, sold in the Tashkent market. White mulberries, originally from China, are delicious; their leaves provide the only sustenance for silkworms. Peaches are from China, too, but reached their peak in central Asia, hence "the golden peaches of Samarkand." In Afghanistan, a woman prepares Seville orange peels for marmalade.

There were also bazaars—seductive markets laden with produce: "Crimson peaches, apricots, mulberries, enormous bunches of black and white grapes and purple and yellow figs," wrote a nineteenth-century visitor to Kashgar. "Enormous watermelons, almost too heavy to lift, with their red flesh and black seeds; melons green all the way through and intensely sweet; melons with pink insides, and others pure white, or apricot colored when cut open." The bazaars were the meeting and trading places for folk of every culture—Persians, Jews, Kushans, Chinese, Uighurs. In the early centuries, priests of all the religions of Asia were to be found: Zoroastrians, Manicheans, Christians, Buddhists, Hindus and, from the seventh century, Muslims (see pages 221–223).

Some of these oases became great cities. There was Khotan, for instance, on the southern fringe of the Taklimakan. Now no more than sand-buried ruins, it was famed for its jade, washed down from the Kunlun Mountains. In the west lay Samarkand, a rich provincial city even in Alexander's day; by the seventh century it was a major trading town, ringed by warehouses bulging with silk, rugs and spices. And in the fourteenth century, the Mongol Tamerlane made Samarkand golden. Captured Persian, Arab, Indian and Chinese artists built his city of palaces, mosques and schools, cultivated his tree-shaded gardens, melon fields and vineyards.

Opposite: A caretaker picks grapes from a school garden in Samarkand.

This page: On the coast of the Caspian Sea, a boy carries a watermelon home. A different species from other melons, much valued for its liquid, this fruit originated in Africa and spread east and west along ancient trade routes.

Introduction / 37

NEW FOODS—EAST AND WEST

Trade spread wealth. Among China's goods were silk, porcelain, paper, iron and steel; among the riches from the west: gold, ivory and the incense of Arabia. For imperial courts at either end of the Silk Road, trade brought new and exotic foods.

Few cultures were as enthusiastic as China about culinary imports, but then, few cultures were as food-oriented as China's. The Chinese always maintained an encyclopedic knowledge of their plants, partly for medicinal purposes. On a more rarefied level, as comments in the sixth-century-BCE Confucian analects specify, a Chinese gentleman was expected to be knowledgeable and discriminating about food and wine.

While the central philosophy of eating, in early periods as now, was that a meal should consist of fan, or grain, as the primary food and ts'ai—vegetables and/or meat and fish, cut small, carefully blended and flavored, and quickly cooked—the possibilities for variation were infinite, especially at imperial courts, which had their own granaries and markets, not to mention kitchen staffs numbering in the thousands.

In Han China, for instance, grains included various millets and wheat grown in the north, barley, soybeans and rice; the last, a southern crop, became the grain of choice among prosperous northerners. As we have seen, noodle food from the west was popular; this, too, counted as fan. Soldiers and travelers, rich or poor, kept supplies of boiled, dried grain, which could be reconstituted in water on the road.

The possibilities for ts'ai were great before the opening of trade routes. The rich enjoyed every kind of meat, including panther breast and baked owl, and a wide variety of fish. Ordinary people (as well as the rich) ate such vegetables as bamboo shoots, water mallow (something like spinach), turnips, yams, radishes, lotus root, scallions, shallots, and mushrooms. During the Han and later dynasties, new vegetables arrived from western Asia and Persia—among them, spinach, rhubarb, onions, cucumbers, broad beans, peas and melons. The Chinese classified them, developed them and found new ways to cook them.

It was the same with fruits and nuts. China was blessed with superb produce, including peaches, plums, apricots and persimmons, and from the south came mangoes, bananas and citrus. The Chinese also carefully cultivated new fruits arriving from the Silk Road—figs and dates, cherries, melons, pomegranates, grapes, almonds, pistachios, walnuts, caraway, coriander and sugarcane. The soybean was as central to Chinese cuisine as ginger, and it still is. It provided bean curd and soy sauce, among other preparations. Then there were fermented and pickled foods,

Scenes from Chengdu and Xian display the infinite variety of delicacies sold at Chinese markets. At left, herb and spice grocers offer a range of dried mushrooms and fruits. At right *(top to bottom)*: vegetables and fruit on sticks sold for the vegetarian version of Mongolian hot pot (similar to fondue); in an intimate gathering of friends and family, each person cooks their choice of ingredients in the simmering broth in the Mongolian pot, seasons it with dipping sauce and finishes off the meal by sharing the flavorful broth as a soup; fried persimmon patties sold on the street; and fresh ginger.

used for flavoring, but also useful to travelers because they didn't spoil.

Such abundance and such traditions led to legendary extravagances. We hear of banquets of 30 courses with 100 dishes in twelfth-century Song dynasty palaces. There was a vibrant restaurant trade as well: Such Song cities as Kaifeng and Suchow boasted hundreds of restaurants, noodle shops, and street vendors. For Buddhists who chose to be vegetarian, the Chinese invented "temple food" restaurants that served vegetable dishes cunningly disguised to resemble meat.

Still, the first rule of Chinese dining, for those who could afford it, was "nothing to excess"; even children were admonished to eat only until they were 70 percent full. Thus gourmets developed the fashion for "natural foods," which fit China's Taoist roots as well as Buddhist precepts. What was natural food? It was food gathered in the mountains or woods—edible plants, herbs, mushrooms and the like—cooked as simply as possible so as to reveal its unique flavor: "Plain and elegant," as the Song poet Su Shih put it, "showing its clarity." It was the kind of culinary philosophy good cooks advocate today.

Left: A salad bar in the streets of the Sichuan city of Chengdu is the latest version of an old tradition: Chinese cities have had street vendors and restaurants for more than 2,000 years.

Opposite: A bean curd seller displays her wares—doufu in Chinese—on a Shanghai street. Bean curd may be sold fresh and white, flavored with spices and pressed into cubes, or in a number of fermented or pickled versions.

And what of cuisine on the other side of the world? Although there are a couple of "Parthian" recipes in what was once thought to be the earliest Western cookbook, that of the Roman Apicius, perhaps from the fourth century, we have few records of Persian and Parthian food. According to the Roman historian Justin—hardly a friendly commentator—the Parthians were very fond of palm wine and ate lightly of grains, vegetables, a little fish and game. The Persians, however, reported the Greek historian Xenophon, kept the recipes from their past and had special cooks for devising new ones. They had inherited a millennia-old tradition of Mesopotamian cookery from the empires of Sumeria, Babylon, Assyria and Akkad, to name a few. The cuneiform texts of these civilizations reveal a rich vocabulary for classifying beers and wines, for instance. And although these texts concern the diet of court and temple, and are therefore focused on a bewildering catalogue of meat and game, they also reveal cultures blessed with the abundance of pasture and field. Sumerian tablets record about 20 kinds of cheese, 100 soups, 300 breads. Their cooks dried grains, beans, dates, grapes and figs; they preserved fruits in honey; they flavored their various stews with garlic, onions, leeks and possibly mint, mustard, cumin and coriander. The various Mesopotamian kingdoms borrowed dishes from one another, as recorded in their names.

The imperial courts of the Persians were as renowned for their elaborate banquets and inventive dishes as for their interest in new foods. We may suppose that the later Parthians, originally nomadic horsemen, ate such dairy products as clarified butter (ghee, which keeps well in hot climates) and yogurt (often fermented with cracked wheat and still very popular in Kurdistan where it is called tarkhineh). As the prime middlemen controlling the Silk Road, they taxed and no doubt enjoyed exotica arriving from east and west.

All these elements converged in the court cooking of the second Persian empire of the Sasanians, whose magnificent capital, Ctesiphon, not far from what is now Baghdad, was a bustling entrepôt of Silk Road trade. From the Sasanian court come accounts of the elegant dining by those with discriminating tastes. A fourth-century poem, "Khosrow and his Knight," outlines the most favored dishes; among them are desserts such as almond and walnut pastries, coconuts from India, and Persia's own dates stuffed with walnuts or pistachios.

Indeed, it was Persian cooking, already international, that helped to influence the conquering Arabs of the seventh century and the Mongols of the thirteenth century. In medieval Arab cookbooks appear the Persian foods and preparations that were to travel with the conquerors far beyond Persia's borders. The herbs and spices are familiar. They include Iran's mint, coriander, saffron and caraway, as well as cinnamon and ginger from Ceylon and China, and cloves from the East Indies. The cuisine of the court was meat based, but it emphasized nuts and fruits. Ground almonds and walnuts thickened the rich sauces. Pomegranates, quinces, cherries and limes, combined with dates, honey and sugar, produced the sweet and sour contrasts that characterize Persian cuisine today. Arabs adopted the braises, salads, breads, cheeses and omelets of Iran, and created magnificent polows from rice that had been imported for cultivation centuries before from the east.

Such classic Persian preparations spread throughout western Asia and into Europe from Baghdad with the Arab diaspora. Later, the Mongols, like the Arabs before them, combined their own nomad traditions with those of the Persian court and exported the new cuisine. It was the Mongols' descendants who helped shape the cuisines of India as we know them today.

Opposite, top: This 3,700-year-old cuneiform recipe for turnip soup comes from Babylonia. The Assyriologist and gourmet cook Jean Bottéro provides a translation for those of us not fluent in cuneiform: "Garden-variety turnips. Meat is not used. Prepare water; add flat onion, arugula, coriander, samidu, and turnips. At the end add coriander and cake crumbs...as well as mashed leeks and garlic."

Opposite and right: Carved on the massive ceremonial staircase at Persepolis, subjects of Darius the Great's far-flung empire bring him tributes of spices and perfumes. Representatives of more than 20 nations paid homage to the sixth-century-BCE Great King at annual New Year festivals.

India is unique among nations in having not just vegetarian dishes, but several vegetarian cuisines. This vast country, larger than Europe, was home to civilizations as ancient as those of Mesopotamia or China; archeologists place the earliest known plowed field in Rajasthan. Successive waves of settlement as well as trade gave India early access to the fruits, vegetables and spices of cultures both east and west. The Aryan invaders who came from central Asia to India in 1500 BCE, for instance, left in their Sanskrit language a number of linguistic clues to the origins of different foods. Foods native to India—the eggplant, for instance—often have names derived from pre-Aryan languages. Imports are given prefixes that indicate their origins; that for Chinese imports, for example, is chini, as in chinani for peach. The names of later imports are often versions of the names from their home countries. Thus the stuffed pastries known as samosa in India are named (like Arab sanbusaq, Turkish samsa and central Asian sambusai varaqi) for their medieval Persian originals, sanbosag. And,

especially in the southwest, there are dishes adapted from and named after those of the Portuguese, who ruled a colony at Goa for 400 years. Indian cooks gave their recipes complexity by adding such spices as cardamom, mustard seeds, cloves, cumin and ginger, not to mention generous lacings of chili peppers. These, imported by the Portuguese from the New World in the sixteenth century, were enthusiastically received: India grows more chilies than any other nation.

Such a cosmopolitan past inspired as many cuisines as there are states in India. As in China, a broad division lies between rice eaters in the south and wheat eaters in the north; in the poorest states, the grain is

Vegetable and flower merchants work among the water lilies on Kashmir's Lake of Srinigar. The floating market began in 1875, when the maharajah of Kashmir, concerned that British officials would crowd his lovely country, forbade Europeans to own land there. The British then constructed houseboats for holidays on the lake, and the merchants took to the water to serve them.

often millet. Southern cuisine emphasizes the bounty of the tropics: Cooks there use many varieties of rice and protein-rich pulses; the cooking oil is coconut, sesame or mustard seed; the vegetables are fresh; fruit, such as mangoes and bananas, plays an important role; and the spicing is subtle. Northern cuisine centers on a variety of breads; because of the north's long communication with central Asia, the cooking fat is usually ghee, and yogurt plays a greater part in the cuisine. Northern fruits are those, such as peaches, that thrive in temperate to cold climates; dried fruits and vegetables flavor many dishes.

These general differences aside, there remains a characteristic Indian style: A meal consists of a central platter of grain surrounded by smaller dishes of savories. Complex spicing is the rule, although in the north it is more intense. And thanks to India's long vegetarian history, protein-rich beans, lentils and chickpeas appear on every table.

India's vegetarianism was first encouraged in the ninth-century-BCE Hindu sacred texts the *Upanishads*, which emphasized non-violence, the unity of all being and a belief in reincarnation. Although it was not so strictly vegetarian, fifth-century-BCE Buddhism also stressed non-violence and reincarnation. And the Jainism arising at the same time prohibited the taking of even the smallest forms of life, including even the roots that gave life to plants. Devout Jains abstain from root vegetables such as onions, garlic and ginger.

Until the sixteenth century, Indian food consisted of boiled grains and pulses, fried bread, and stewed vegetables. With the advent of the Islamic Moghul empire, however, came the Persian-based cuisine of western Asia. The Muslims were meat eaters, and even today the north of India, where they were dominant, is known for its meat dishes. But Moghul innovations—including polows, pastries, stuffed vegetables, baked bread, sherbet and such sweet confections as halvah—transformed Indian cookery. To suit their own tastes, Indian cooks adapted the luxurious creations for vegetarian dining.

A wonderful assortment of dried herbs and spices, including such favorites as sumac berries, nigella seeds, dried limes, turmeric, ginger and garlic, are meticulously displayed by a herbalist in the village market of Khwaja Bahauddin, in northern Afghanistan.

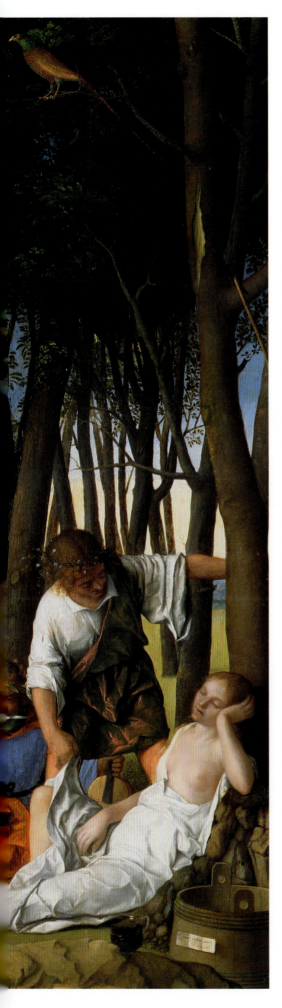

Italian revelers disport themselves among objects—and foods—from the east in Giovanni Bellini's painting of 1514, *The Feast of the Gods*. This is the first Western image of the much admired and imitated Ming blue and white porcelain, newly arrived from China via the Middle East. Earlier imports include grapes and wine, originally from the region between Black and the Caspian Seas; pears from the Caucasus; and peaches from China.

During the 1,200 years when Silk Road trade flourished, its culinary treasures entered Europe in the same ways as they moved between China, Mesopotamia and the Levant: with armies, emigrants and merchants. By the ninth century, for instance, the Vikings of Scandinavia were traveling south via the Volga River and the Caspian Sea to Baghdad, where they exchanged furs, walrus ivory and amber for the spices and silks that Baghdad imported from the east.

This was fairly small-scale commerce, however, compared to that which rose around the Mediterranean. On the one hand, there was Spain. From the eighth to the tenth centuries CE, Silk Road trade was almost completely in the hands of Arabic dynasties, who established a cosmopolitan civilization that glittered in contrast to that of rural Europe. The Arabs brought not only scholars, artists, and builders, but also such new ingredients for cookery as rice, sugar cane, oranges, and almonds.

Arab influences wrought great changes in Italy, as well. Growing rich on trade, the ports and city states of Venice, Genoa and Naples helped give birth to the European Renaissance—a revival nourished in part by the Greek philosophical texts preserved by Arabic scholars, as well as by the architecture, painting and craftsmanship of the Islamic world. Along with these, as always, came that most pleasant art of civilization, cookery. Through Venice and Genoa flowed the vegetables, fruits and cooking techniques of the Islamic world, such as bringing out the flavor of individual ingredients by careful seasoning and moderate cooking rather than making purees and porridges that disguised the ingredients. New, as well, were preparations of rice and pasta, vegetables such as eggplants and spinach, and various uses of rose water, orange peel, preserved fruits, sugar, pepper, cinnamon and saffron.

Thus it was that the culinary heritage of Persia and China, India and central Asia, woven together by Silk Road trade, passed into Italy—first into the courts that grew as its city states became principalities, then to its middle classes and peasantry. Although the new cuisine would spread north, I have chosen to stop on the shores of the Mediterranean. Italy's imaginative use of vegetables, along with that of India, Persia, Turkey and central Asia, seem to me to embody the tasty, inexpensive and cheerful food that is a lasting legacy of the ancient Silk Road.

Introduction / 51

TOWARD A SILK ROAD CUISINE

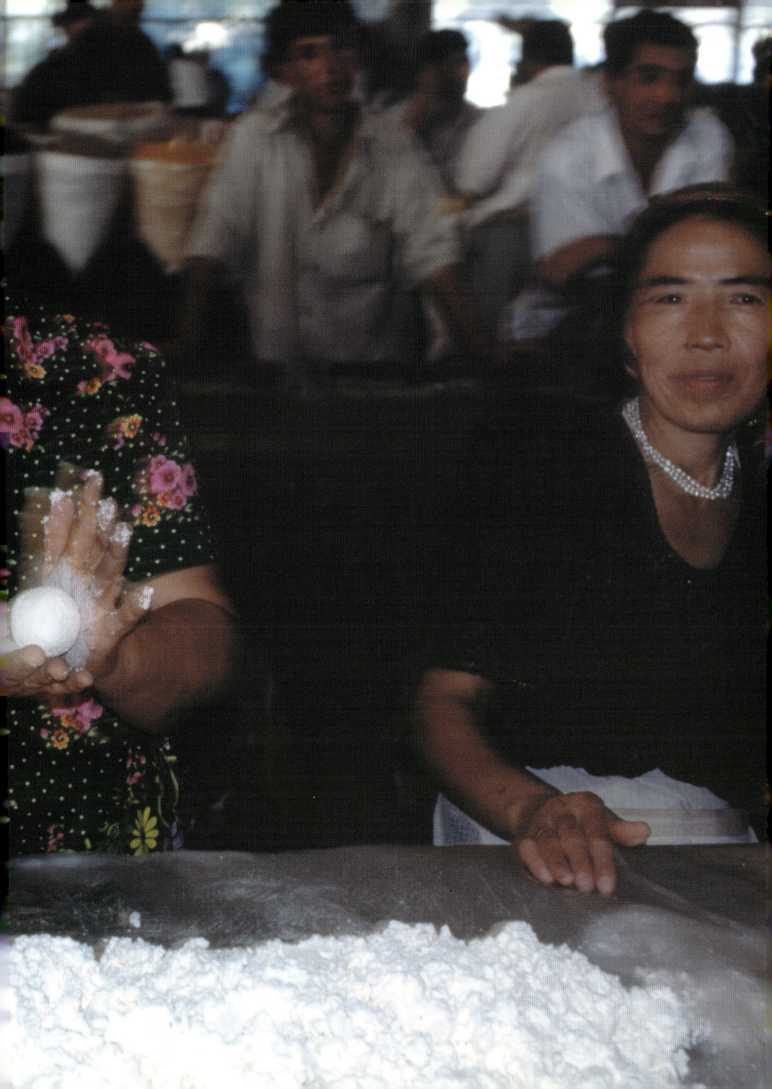

This book is a collection of 150 vegetarian recipes from countries touched by Silk Road trade. Among the recipes are dishes from China and Persia, from India and Turkey, Italy, Egypt, the Levant, and from western and central Asia. While the dishes reflect the diversity of regional tastes, they are unified by many shared characteristics, such as the love of flat breads, use of rice, and cooking of noodles and dumplings Because cooks along the Silk Road delighted in new ingredients, I have not hesitated to use New World foods like tomatoes, potatoes, green beans, corn, and wild and brown rice, introduced long after the overland trade had vanished, but now some of the favorite ingredients in the region.

I've designed the book for both vegetarians and non-vegetarians. The recipes include the proper balance of proteins and carbohydrates.

I've also harmonized ingredients in accord with the ancient philosophy—prevalent in all Silk Road regions to some degree—of balancing hot and cold foods. The practice has many schools: It is known as yin-yang philosophy in China, ayurveda in India, and hot and cold in Iran, and was called the Salerno Regimen in medieval Europe. All subscribe to the idea that the body's humors, which reflect the elements of the earth, must be kept in balance by proper diet. Briefly, it classifies the energy in foods as hot and cold, wet and dry: Hot foods are high in energy, cold foods low. While classifications vary, the general rule is that wheat, nuts, a few fresh vegetables and fruits, and all dried vegetables and fruits are hot; rice and most fresh vegetables and fruits are cold. If you have a hot nature or the weather is hot, you should be eating cold foods; if you have a cold nature or the weather is cold, you should be eating hot ones. Gender and age are also factors to be considered. Balanced dishes, though, are the ideal. They include just the right proportions of hot and cold ingredients—the combination of walnuts and pomegranates is, as my mother used to say, a marriage made in heaven—which seems to also make them delicious.

Timeless nomad traditions at the far reaches of the Silk Road: In the piedmont wintering grounds of the Shahsavan tribe, in western Iran (above), women use a tandoor—a buried stone oven—to cook flat bread. At right, smoke from a hearth fire streams from a Mongolian tent (yurt or ger), near Ürümqi in present day China.

Above all, I've tried to create the most inviting dishes from once-exotic foods that are now widely available. These are foods meant for sharing: Cooking and eating should be happy activities, and nothing can be happier than family and friends dining together.

In truth, the legendary hospitality of the Silk Road—hospitality that I encountered on every journey I made—was one of the inspirations for this book. Again and again, my hosts not only welcomed me, but also shared what they had with wonderful personal warmth and generosity—often beyond their means. To understand just how deep this welcoming spirit runs, consider the recent experience of the environmentalist John Hare. While traveling in Mongolia, he and his guide Dasha stopped near three gers—round nomad tents also known as yurts. The tents were deserted, but the door to one stood open:

"'Go on in,' said Dasha. 'I expect the owner has moved off for a few weeks to settle his flocks in another grazing area.'

"On the little cast-iron stove in the centre of the circular tent stood a pot of fermented milk (kumis) and some rock hard cheese. Pinned to the solid wooden pole which kept the tent erect was a picture of Genghis Khan.

"'They've left a meal for you,' Dasha explained. 'It's the custom in these parts to leave doors unlocked so that passing strangers can help themselves to food and drink.'"

Introduction / 55

This book is meant for browsing as well as for cooking. You'll see that I have organized the recipes into sections on salads; soups; eggs; rice; fruit and vegetable braises; pasta, pizza and bread; pastries, desserts and candies. In addition, you will find chapters on teas, coffee and drinks, and on preserves, pickles and spice mixes.

None of these recipes is particularly difficult or time consuming. As a guide, I've listed preparation and cooking times for each dish, and noted whether it can be made in advance and how many people it will serve.

Almost all the ingredients in the recipes are available at your local supermarket or farmers' market. During the last couple of decades—with an increase in ethnic awareness and health concerns, and a trend toward simpler, more rustic ingredients such as flour with bran, brown rice, and fresh and seasonal food—America has become a kind of modern Silk Road entrepôt, where wonderful ingredients from all over the world are available to everyone. Ingredients that might be less commonly known or that require preliminary preparation are marked with an asterisk, which indicates that they are discussed in the "Silk Road Glossary" on pages 306 to 324. In the glossary entries you will find the history of each ingredient, its use, and explanations of how to shop for it and prepare it. The glossary also offers perfectly good substitutes for many ingredients that may seem exotic.

Other elements in the book are there to welcome you to the Silk Road and give you a feel for its landscape and people. In many a recipe you will find a headnote, describing the region that is home to the dish or telling you something of my own memories of it. There are photographs, as well, to give a sense of the land, the people and their food. As you enjoy the book, I hope the exotic will become familiar.

At right, a nosegay of autumn-flowering saffron crocuses reveal their golden stamens, the most precious of spices (page 122). Flanking them are some of the dishes you will find in this book. *(On this page, top to bottom):* Samarkand Mung Bean Salad (page 86); Madras Red Lentil Soup (page 108); Kermani Polow with Saffron and Pistachios (page 150); Sicilian Fava Bean, Garlic & Dill Crostata (206). *(Opposite, top to bottom):* 1001 Nights Chewy Saffron Ice Cream (page 270); Indian Cauliflower and Potato Curry (page 192); Gujarati Pan Mung Bean Bread (page 234); Armenian Spiced Rose Petal Tea (page 277).

Introduction / 56

Introduction / 57

Salads

Caspian Olives with Pomegranate & Angelica

Servings: 4
Preparation time: 15 minutes
Cooking time: none

- 1 cup walnuts, toasted
- 5 cloves garlic, peeled
- 1 cup fresh mint or 1 tablespoon dried mint
- 1 cup chopped fresh cilantro
- 1 tablespoon chopped fresh oregano or 1/8 teaspoon dried oregano
- 1 tablespoon angelica powder*
- 1/2 teaspoon salt
- 1/4 teaspoon freshly ground pepper
- 1 teaspoon sugar (optional, if pomegranate is too sour)
- 2 tablespoons olive oil
- 1 cup fresh pomegranate juice or 4 tablespoons pomegranate paste diluted in 1 cup water*
- 1 pound green pitted olives

GARNISH
- 1 tablespoon walnuts, toasted and chopped
- 3 sprigs cilantro

Separated from the Iranian plateau by the great green wall of the Alborz Mountains, the Caspian Sea is a huge inland salt lake, convenient, during the Silk Road era, for transporting to the west spices from India and silk from China. The high mountains, the sea, and the frequent rainfall make this region rich in many kinds of agriculture: Its paddies produce most of Iran's rice; its high valleys are quilted with wheat fields and pastures; and among the mountains are walnut and chestnut groves. There are also fine olive and pomegranate farms at the foot of the Alborz—hence this recipe.

1. Mix all the ingredients except the olives in a food processor until you have a grainy paste. Transfer to a serving bowl, add the olives, mix well and adjust seasoning to taste. Cover and refrigerate for 15 minutes (can be kept in the refrigerator for 3 days).

2. Garnish with walnuts and cilantro.

3. Serve with toasted bread cut into 4-inch pieces. This mix is also excellent as a sauce for rice, pasta or egg dishes according to your fancy.

Salads / 60

Sicilian Roasted Pepper & Eggplant Salad

Throughout the Silk Road era, Sicily, a Mediterranean island separated from the tip of Italy by only a few miles and from Tunis by 100 miles of sea, played an important role as a gateway for spices, ingredients and cooking styles from the East traveling to Europe and back. Few civilizations have not touched it. The Phoenicians settled in Panormous, now Palermo; the Carthaginians founded Tripani; and the Greeks established Syracuse and Messina. The Romans considered it their breadbasket and completely depleted its resources. It was subsequently invaded by Vandals, Goths, Byzantines, Arabs and Normans. It's no wonder that Sicilian cuisine is so cosmopolitan.

1. Preheat the oven to 500°F. Place the peppers on a baking sheet and roast for 20 minutes.

2. Remove peppers from the oven and place in a plastic bag. Seal the bag and let stand for 30 minutes (the steam loosens the outer silky skin of the peppers).

3. Meanwhile, wash the eggplants and dice into 1-inch cubes, rinse with cold water and pat dry.

4. Place the eggplant cubes on an oiled baking sheet, and shake the sheet well so that the oil adheres to the eggplant. Bake in the 500°F preheated oven for 30 minutes or until tender. Transfer to a serving bowl.

5. Remove the peppers from the plastic bag and peel off the silky skins using paper towels.

6. Seed the peppers, slice into 1/2-inch strips and transfer to the bowl.

7. To make the dressing, mix all the salad dressing ingredients (except the goat cheese or mozzarella) thoroughly. Pour the dressing over the eggplant cubes and pepper strips, toss well, and adjust seasoning to taste. Cover and refrigerate (up to 48 hours).

8. Just before serving, top with goat cheese or mozzarella. Serve with focaccia bread or crostini (slices of toasted Italian bread rubbed with a garlic clove).

VARIATION

In Syria, 1 tablespoon pomegranate paste is added to the dressing in this recipe.

Servings: 4
Preparation time: 15 minutes
Cooking time: 50 minutes

- 3 large bell peppers (your choice of colors)
- 6 Chinese eggplants*
- 2 tablespoons vegetable oil

SALAD DRESSING

- 2 cloves garlic, peeled and crushed
- 2 tablespoons fresh lime juice
- 1/2 teaspoon salt
- 1/4 teaspoon freshly ground black pepper
- 1/4 teaspoon cayenne
- 1/2 teaspoon ground cumin
- 1/4 teaspoon paprika
- 1/4 teaspoon sugar
- 1/2 cup chopped fresh flat-leaf parsley or cilantro
- 1/4 cup olive oil
- 4 ounces fresh goat cheese or mozzarella, sliced

Rayy Eggplant & Sun-Dried Yogurt in Lavash Rolls

Makes 20 pieces
Preparation time: 20 minutes
Cooking time: 25 minutes

FILLING
3 tablespoons vegetable oil
2 large onions, peeled and thinly sliced
10 cloves of garlic, peeled and sliced
1 cup shelled walnuts
1 1/2 cups fresh mint leaves
1 cup sun-dried yogurt (kashk in Persian, whey in English)*
1/2 teaspoon salt
1/2 teaspoon freshly ground pepper

EGGPLANT WRAP
4 Chinese eggplants, thinly sliced lengthwise
2 tablespoons vegetable oil
20 long strands of garlic chives
3 lavash bread loaves, cut into twenty 2-by-3-inch strips (store the bread in a plastic bag to keep it soft for wrapping)

DIP
1/2 cup plain yogurt

Rayy is now little more than a village a few miles southeast of Tehran, but it once was a great city, with a history going back to the third millennium BCE. During the 8th century CE it was a major entrepot on the Silk Road, its splendors rivaled only by those of Baghdad and Damascus. It was the birthplace of Haroun al-Rashid, the eighth-century caliph of Baghdad, whose wild (and fictional) adventures enliven the 1001 Nights. In the thirteenth century the Mongols almost entirely destroyed the city. All those who could fled to the nearby mountain village of Tehran, where the villagers are said to have hidden from the Mongol horde in dwellings dug out under their gardens of fruit trees.

1. In a wok or deep skillet, heat the oil over medium heat, add the onion and garlic, and stir-fry for 10 minutes or until the onions are translucent.

2. Puree the fried onion and garlic with the remaining filling ingredients in a food processor, adjust the seasoning to taste and set aside.

3. Preheat the oven to 500°F.

4. Arrange the eggplant slices on an oiled baking sheet. Brush the eggplant with oil. Bake for 10 to 15 minutes until golden brown. Remove from the baking sheet and place on paper towels to absorb excess oil.

5. Rinse the chives in warm water to soften them and make them flexible for wrapping. Pat dry.

6. Spread one tablespoon of filling in the center of a piece of lavash bread. Place a piece of eggplant on top, roll up the bread and eggplant, and tie with a piece of chive. Repeat until you have 20 rolls.

7. To prepare the dip, blend the remaining filling with 1/2 cup yogurt and transfer to a serving bowl.

8. Place the dip in a tray and arrange the rolls around it.

Georgian Tomatoes Stuffed with Walnuts & Pomegranates

Servings: 6
Preparation time: 20 minutes
Cooking time: 26 minutes

- 6 large, firm tomatoes
- 1/2 cup olive oil
- 1 teaspoon coriander seeds
- 1 teaspoon cumin seeds
- 1 large onion, peeled and thinly sliced
- 6 cloves garlic, peeled and crushed
- 1 1/2 cups walnuts, finely ground
- 2 teaspoons salt
- 1/2 teaspoon freshly ground black pepper
- 1/2 teaspoon chili paste or 1/4 teaspoon cayenne
- 1/4 teaspoon ground cinnamon
- 1/2 teaspoon ground marigold*
- 1 cup chopped fresh parsley or cilantro
- 1/4 cup pomegranate paste
- 1 tablespoon sugar
- 1 teaspoon coarse salt

1. Remove the stems from the tomatoes. Cut a slice off the tops and set aside. Scoop out some of the tomato pulp using a spoon or melon baller and reserve for later use.

2. In a wok or large skillet, heat 2 tablespoons oil over medium heat. Add the coriander and cumin seeds, and cook for 10 seconds. Add the onion and stir-fry for 10 minutes. Add the garlic and stir-fry for 1 minute longer. Reduce heat to low. Add the reserved tomato pulp, walnuts, salt, pepper, chili paste, cinnamon, marigold, parsley, pomegranate and sugar, and cook for another 5 minutes.

3. Adjust seasoning to taste.

4. Stuff the tomatoes with the filling and replace their tops.

5. Place the stuffed tomatoes side by side in an ovenproof, oiled dish. Drizzle with the remaining olive oil and sprinkle a little coarse salt over each tomato. Place the dish under the broiler for 5 to 10 minutes until the tomatoes are tender and their tops are slightly burnt, yet still hold their shape.

6. Serve, hot or cold, with bread, yogurt, rice, pasta or couscous.

Alexandrian Spicy Dried Fava Bean Spread

Servings: 4
Preparation time: 30 minutes
Cooking time: 45 minutes

- 2 cups dried, split and skinned yellow fava beans, picked over and rinsed*
- 1/4 cup oil
- 1/4 teaspoon crushed asafetida
- 1 large onion, peeled and thinly sliced
- 4 garlic cloves, peeled and crushed
- 1 1/2 teaspoons salt
- 1/2 teaspoon freshly ground black pepper
- 1/8 teaspoon ground paprika
- 1/2 teaspoon ground coriander
- 1/2 teaspoon ground cumin
- 1/4 teaspoon ground cinnamon
- 1/4 teaspoon ground turmeric
- 1/2 teaspoon chili paste
- 2 tablespoons lime juice
- 1/2 cup chopped fresh cilantro

GARNISH
- 1 tablespoon cilantro leaves

Alexandria lies on the western edge of the Nile, with its back to Egypt and its face to the Mediterranean. Founded by Alexander the Great, who was buried there in a golden tomb, it was long famed for luxury, scholarship, and trade, and it remains among the most cosmopolitan of cities. Fava beans cooked in this way are so popular in Egypt they might be called a national food; in the age of the pharaohs, however, they were taboo, probably because Egyptians, like many other ancient cultures, believed them to be the food of the dead.

1. Place the skinned beans in a medium-sized saucepan and add 6 cups of water. Discard any beans that float. Bring to a boil, partially cover and cook over medium heat for 45 minutes until beans are tender. Drain and set aside.

2. Heat the oil in a wok or deep skillet and add asafetida. Add the onion and stir-fry for 10 minutes. Add the garlic and stir-fry for 2 minutes. Add the cooked beans and the remaining ingredients, and stir-fry for 3 minutes. Remove from heat. Use a masher to mash the mixture until you have a grainy, soft paste. Adjust seasoning to taste.

3. Transfer to a serving platter, garnish with cilantro, and serve with rice or warm flat bread.

NOTE

If you soak the yellow fava beans in water overnight and then drain, you can eliminate step 1 and begin with step 2.

In the photograph, this recipe is made without mashing the fava beans in step 2, which is also an option.

Grocery Shopping from 1001 Nights

The text is an extract from "The Story of the Porter and the Three Ladies," from *The Arabian Nights* translated by Husain Haddawy.

The paintings are details from a sixteenth-century Persian miniature by Mir Seyyed Ali depicting various grocery shopping scenes.

I heard, O happy King, that once there lived in the city of Baghdad a bachelor who worked as a porter. One day he was standing in the market, leaning on his basket, when a woman approached him. She wore a Mosul cloak, a silk veil, a fine kerchief embroidered with gold, and a pair of leggings tied with fluttering laces. When she lifted her veil, she revealed a pair of beautiful dark eyes graced with long lashes and a tender expression, like those celebrated by the poets. Then with a soft voice and a sweet tone, she said to him, "Porter, take your basket and follow me." Hardly believing his ears, the porter took his basket and hurried behind her, saying, "O lucky day, O happy day." She walked before him until she stopped at the door of a house, and when she knocked, an old Christian came down, received a dinar from her and handed her an olive green jug of wine. She placed the jug in the basket and said, "Porter, take your basket and follow me." ... the porter lifted the basket and followed her until she stopped at the fruit vendor's, where she bought yellow and red apples, Hebron peaches and Turkish quinces, and seacoast lemons and royal oranges, as well as baby cucumbers. She also bought Aleppo jasmine and Damascus lilies, myrtle berries and mignonettes, daisies and gillyflowers, lilies of the valley and irises, narcissus and daffodils, violets and anemones, as well as pomegranate blossoms. She placed everything in the porter's basket and asked him to follow her.

...The porter, followed her until she came to the grocer's, where she bought whatever she needed of condiments, such as olives of all kinds, pitted, salted, and pickled, tarragon, cream cheese, Syrian cheese, and sweet as well as sour pickles. She placed the container in the basket and said, "Porter, take your basket and follow me." The porter carried his basket and followed her until she came to the dry grocer's, where she bought all sorts of dry fruits and nuts: Aleppo raisins, Iraqi sugar canes, pressed Ba'albak figs, roasted chick-peas, as well as shelled pistachios, almonds, and hazelnuts. She placed everything in the porter's basket, turned to him, and said, "Porter take your basket and follow me."

The porter carried the basket and followed her until she came to the confectioner's, where she bought a whole tray full of every kind of pastry and sweet in the shop, such as sour barley rolls, sweet rolls, date rolls, Cairo rolls, Turkish rolls, and open-worked Balkan rolls, as well as cookies, stuffed and musk-scented kataifs, amber combs, ladyfingers, widows' bread, Kadi's tidbits, eat-and-thanks, and almond pudding. She walked ahead until she came to the druggist's, where she bought ten bottles of scented waters, lilywater, rosewater scented with musk, and the like as well as ambergris, musk, aloewood, and rosemary. She also bought two loaves of sugar and candles and torches. When she placed the tray in the basket, the porter said to her, "Mistress, if you had let me know, I would have brought with me a nag or a camel to carry all these purchases."

Kurdish Chickpea, Cilantro, & Cumin Salad

Servings: 4
Preparation time: 15 minutes
Cooking time: 10 minutes

- 1/4 cup olive oil
- 1/4 teaspoon crushed asafetida
- 1 tablespoon toasted cumin seeds
- 1 small red onion, peeled and finely chopped
- 1 clove garlic, peeled and crushed
- 1/2-inch ginger root, peeled and grated, or 1/4 teaspoon dried ginger
- 1/2 teaspoon salt
- 1/2 teaspoon freshly ground pepper
- 1 hot green chili (serrano), chopped or 1/8 teaspoon cayenne
- 2 tablespoons fresh lime juice
- 1 large tomato, peeled and sliced
- 2 cups canned chickpeas (garbanzo beans) already cooked, drained and rinsed or 1 cup dried chickpeas (see note below)
- 1/2 cup chopped fresh cilantro

BED OF GREENS
4 cups shredded greens, romaine lettuce or arugula (optional)

NOTE
If using dried chickpeas, pick over and rinse. Soak for two hours and drain. Place in a medium-sized heavy-bottom saucepan, cover with 6 cups of water, 1/2 teaspoon salt, and bring to a boil. Reduce heat, partially cover, and simmer over medium heat for 1 1/2 hours or until the chickpeas are tender.

Legend has it that vegetarian Persia was first introduced to meat when the devil, disguised as a cook tricked the king into eating meat. It resulted in two snakes growing on the king's shoulders that had to be fed the brains of two young men each day. The two sisters in charge of the king's kitchen saved Persia's youth by substituting sheep's brains and helping the young men escape into the mountains. These men are said to be the ancestors of the Kurds. This salad is very popular in India, Armenia, Turkey and throughout Iran.

1. Heat the oil in a wok or large skillet over medium heat until very hot. Add the asafetida. Add the cumin and cook for 20 seconds. Add the onion and garlic, and stir-fry for 5 minutes or until the onions are translucent.

2. Add the remaining ingredients except for the cilantro and stir-fry for 20 seconds. Reduce heat to low, cover and simmer for 5 minutes.

3. Adjust seasoning to taste and just before serving add the cilantro. Serve on the bed of greens with couscous, bread, rice, pasta or bulgur according to your fancy.

VARIATION

You can also make this salad by replacing the chickpeas with 2 cups cooked black beans, 1 cup kidney beans or 1 cup white beans, or a mixture of all three.

Salads / 68

Bekaa Valley Bulgur Salad with Tomato & Parsley (Tabbouleh)

The Bekaa Valley, also called Al Biqa, where this salad is very popular, is a broad, fertile valley in central Lebanon covered with vineyards and wheat fields. I have also eaten this salad in Turkey, where it is called Kisir and usually made with half the quantity of parsley and a sauce sharpened by pomegranate rather than lime juice.

1. Place the bulgur in a medium-sized bowl, add 1 cup tomato juice, cover and refrigerate for at least 1 1/2 hours, until the bulgur is tender (can also be left overnight in the refrigerator).

2. Place the bulgur, parsley, mint, green pepper, jalapeno, cucumber, scallions, and tomatoes in a large salad bowl, and set aside.

3. To make the salad dressing, thoroughly mix all the salad dressing ingredients and adjust seasoning to taste. Pour the dressing over the salad and toss well.

4. Create a bed of greens on individual plates and place the bulgur salad in the center.

5. Serve with toasted bread, rice or pasta according to your fancy. A good way to serve tabbouleh is to have small hearts of romaine lettuce available for scooping it up.

Servings: 4
Preparation time: 45 minutes plus 1 1/2 hours soaking
Cooking time: none

1 cup fine grain bulgur (cracked wheat), rinsed in a fine mesh colander and set aside
1 cup fresh tomato juice (1 large tomato)*
4 cups flat-leaf parsley, finely chopped
1/2 cup chopped fresh mint or 1 teaspoon dried mint
1/2 green bell pepper, seeded and diced
1/2 jalapeno pepper, seeded and diced (optional)
2 pickling cucumbers cut into 1/2-inch cubes or 1 seedless cucumber
4 scallions, finely chopped
4 medium tomatoes, peeled and diced into 1/4-inch cubes

SALAD DRESSING
1 clove garlic, peeled and crushed
1/2 cup fresh lime juice
1 1/2 teaspoons salt
1 teaspoon freshly ground black pepper
1/2 teaspoon sugar
1/2 cup olive oil

BED OF GREENS
4 hearts of romaine lettuce or 4 endives

Sichuan Toasted Sesame & Cabbage Salad

Servings: 6
Preparation time: 20 minutes
Cooking time: none

- 1 head Chinese cabbage (napa, about 2 pounds), washed, pat dried, and shredded
- 1 long seedless cucumber or 4 pickling cucumbers, peeled and thinly sliced
- 1 large carrot (about 1/4 pound), peeled and shredded
- 1/2 cup chopped fresh parsley or scallions

SALAD DRESSING
- 2 cloves garlic, peeled and crushed
- 1 teaspoon salt
- 1 teaspoon toasted ground Sichuan pepper
- 1 tablespoon sugar
- 4 tablespoons rice vinegar
- 1 tablespoon olive oil
- 2 tablespoons toasted sesame oil

GARNISH
- 1/2 cup toasted sesame seeds*

NOTE
You can also use this salad dressing for 1 1/2 pounds blanched asparagus, broccoli or French green beans.

1. Place the cabbage, cucumber, carrots and parsley in a salad bowl and set aside.

2. To make the salad dressing, thoroughly mix all the salad dressing ingredients and adjust seasoning to taste.

3. Pour the dressing and toasted sesame seeds over the salad and toss well.

4. Serve with plain rice, pasta, bulgur or bread.

Salads / 70

Chinese Noodle Salad

1. Bring 2 quarts of water to a boil and add the noodles. Cook for 1 to 8 minutes (depending on your noodles and instructions on the packet) until tender, drain, rinse and transfer to a serving dish. Add the carrots, sweet pea pods and scallions, and set aside.

2. To make the dressing, thoroughly mix all the dressing ingredients and adjust seasoning to taste.

3. Pour the dressing over the salad. Toss well and adjust seasoning to taste.

Servings: 4
Preparation time: 15 minutes
Cooking time: 8 minutes

- 1 pound Chinese egg noodles (or rice noodles or mung bean vermicelli)
- 2 large carrots, peeled and shredded
- 1/2 cup sweet pea pods, sliced
- 2 fresh scallions, shredded

SALAD DRESSING

- 2 cloves garlic, peeled and crushed
- 4 tablespoons toasted sesame oil or 1/3 cup sesame paste
- 4 tablespoons olive oil
- 4 tablespoons light soy sauce
- 1 tablespoon rice vinegar
- 1/2 teaspoon chili paste (optional)
- 1 teaspoon salt
- 1 teaspoon freshly ground white pepper
- 1 tablespoon sugar

GARNISH
- 1/2 cup coarsely chopped peanuts

NOTE

If you use rice noodles, soak them for 15 to 20 minutes in warm water, until tender. Drain and rinse with cold water.

If you use mung bean vermicelli, soak in water for 15 minutes, drain, parboil for 1 minute and drain again.

Georgian Rice Salad with Eggplant & Tart Cherries

Servings: 4
Preparation time: 30 minutes
Cooking time: 45 minutes

- 2 cups basmati rice
- 4 cups water
- 1 tablespoon vegetable oil, butter, or ghee
- 3 teaspoons salt
- 4 Chinese eggplants, about 2 pounds
- 4 cloves garlic, peeled and chopped
- 1/2 teaspoon cayenne
- 1 teaspoon ground cumin
- 2 teaspoons ground paprika
- 1/4 cup olive oil
- 1 cup pitted, dried tart cherries*

SALAD DRESSING
- 1/2 cup sour cherry syrup*
- 2 tablespoons lime juice
- 1/4 cup olive oil
- 1/2 teaspoon salt
- 1 cup chopped fresh flat-leaf parsley
- 1 cup chopped fresh scallions

BED OF GREENS
- 4 cups shredded greens, arugula or romaine lettuce

GARNISH
- 1/2 cup chopped, pistachios or toasted walnuts

NOTE
If you do not use Chinese eggplants, you will need 2 large eggplants—peeled, seeded and bitterness removed.

Known in Greek mythology as Colchis, the land of the Golden Fleece, Georgia lies along the eastern shore of the Black Sea. The land—the Greater and Lesser Caucasus Mountains and a broad central plain—is influenced by varied climates and offers myriad produce, from the vineyards of the dry interior to the tea and lemon plantations of the subtropical coast. Georgia's position between the Caucasus Mountains and the Black Sea made it an important part of the Silk Road routes; this and its rich land also drew the attention of a number of conquerors, including Arabs, Mongols, Turks, and Persians, during its long history. Georgian cuisine often combines walnuts (for its nutty taste) with fruit (to counteract the oiliness of the nuts). I have adapted this wonderful rice salad from a Georgian pilaf.

1. Pick over and wash the rice by placing it in a large container and covering it with lukewarm water. Agitate gently with your hand, then pour off the water. Repeat five times until the rice is completely clean.

2. Combine the rice with 3 cups of water, 1 tablespoon oil and 2 teaspoons salt, and bring to a boil over medium heat. Gently stir once with a wooden spoon. Cover and cook over medium heat for 20 minutes, until all the water has evaporated. Remove from heat and set aside.

3. Wash the eggplants, dice into 1/2-inch cubes and thoroughly blot dry.

4. In a large bowl, mix the garlic, cayenne, cumin, paprika and remaining salt. Add the eggplant cubes and mix well so that the spices adhere to the raw eggplants.

5. Heat 1/4 cup of olive oil in a wok or deep skillet over medium heat until very hot and fry the eggplant cubes for 10 minutes, until golden brown. Add 1 cup of water, cover and cook over low heat for another 15 minutes until tender. Remove from heat and allow to cool.

6. Combine the eggplant, cooked warm rice and tart cherries in a salad bowl and set aside.

7. To make the dressing, thoroughly mix all the salad dressing ingredients and adjust seasoning to taste. Pour over the salad, toss well, serve on a bed of greens and garnish with pistachios or walnuts.

Amoli Rice Salad with Barberries & Orange Peel

Servings: 6
Preparation time: 40 minutes
Cooking time: 40 minutes

- 2 cups basmati rice
- 4 cups water
- 1 tablespoon vegetable oil, butter or ghee
- 2 teaspoons salt
- 1 cup finely slivered orange peel*
- 2 large carrots, peeled and shredded
- 1 cup sugar
- 2 tablespoons olive oil
- 1/2 cup almonds or pine nuts
- 1 cup dried barberries, cleaned, washed with cold water and drained*
- 1/2 cup raisins

SALAD DRESSING
- 1 clove garlic, peeled and crushed
- 2 tablespoons fresh lime juice
- 1/2 teaspoon salt
- 1/2 teaspoon freshly ground black pepper
- 1/4 cup olive oil
- 1 cup chopped fresh parsley
- 1 cup chopped fresh scallions

BED OF GREENS
- 4 cups shredded greens, arugula or romaine lettuce

NOTE
This salad is also delicious when made with wild rice (page 145)

Amol, on the Mazanderan plain, along the south coast of the Caspian Sea, was an important ancient city along one of the branches of the Silk Road. Today it is a pretty town of mosques, shrines and houses whose walls are painted with birds and flowers; its chief business is rice, which grows all around. I have adapted this salad from a rice dish popular there.

1. Pick over and wash the rice by placing it in a large container and covering it with lukewarm water. Agitate gently with your hand, then pour off the water. Repeat five times until the rice is completely clean.

2. Combine the rice with 3 cups of water, 1 tablespoon oil and 2 teaspoons salt, and bring to a boil over medium heat. Gently stir once with a wooden spoon. Cover and cook over medium heat for 20 minutes, until all the water has evaporated. Remove from heat and set aside.

3. In a saucepan, cover the orange peel with water, boil for 10 minutes over medium heat, then drain and rinse (this is done to remove the bitterness from the orange peel).

4. Place the orange peel, shredded carrots, sugar, and 1 cup water in the same saucepan, bring to a boil and simmer for 10 minutes over medium heat. Remove from heat and set aside.

5. Heat 2 tablespoons olive oil in a wok or deep skillet over medium heat. Add the almonds, barberries and raisins and stir-fry for just 20 seconds. Remove from heat. Be careful! The barberries are delicate and burn very easily.

6. Add the orange peel-carrot mixture and cooked rice to the wok.

7. To make the salad dressing, thoroughly mix all the ingredients and adjust seasoning to taste. Pour over the rice mixture, toss well and serve on a bed of greens.

Mesopotamian Rice Salad with Green Lentils, Dates, & Raisins

Servings: 4
Preparation time: 30 minutes
Cooking time: 40 minutes

- 2 cups basmati rice
- 6 cups water
- 2 1/2 teaspoons salt
- 1 tablespoon vegetable oil, butter, or ghee
- 1 cup dried brown lentils
- 1/2 cup raisins
- 1 cup medjool dates (about 6), pitted and sliced
- 1 cup chopped fresh scallions
- 1 green bell pepper, seeded and chopped into 1/4-inch cubes
- 1 jalapeno pepper, seeded and chopped
- 1 cup chopped fresh flat-leaf parsley

SALAD DRESSING
- 2 cloves garlic, peeled and chopped
- 1/2 cup fresh lime juice
- 2 teaspoons salt
- 1 teaspoon freshly ground black pepper
- 1/4 teaspoon chili paste or cayenne (optional)
- 1/2 teaspoon ground cinnamon
- 2 teaspoons ground cumin
- 1/2 cup olive oil

BED OF GREENS
- 4 cups shredded greens, arugula or romaine lettuce

I have combined long-grain Basmati rice—popular throughout Iran and the Fertile Crescent—lentils, dates and raisins to create a salad with truly wonderful flavors.

1. Pick over and wash the rice by placing it in a large container and covering it with lukewarm water. Agitate gently with your hand, then pour off the water. Repeat five times until the rice is completely clean.

2. Combine the rice with 3 cups water, 1 tablespoon oil and 2 teaspoons salt, and bring to a boil over medium heat. Gently stir once with a wooden spoon. Cover and cook over medium heat for 20 minutes, until all the water has evaporated. Remove from heat and set aside.

3. Pick over and wash the lentils and place in a medium-sized saucepan. Cover with 3 cups of water and 1/2 teaspoon salt and bring to a boil. Simmer for 15 to 20 minutes over medium heat, until tender. Drain and set aside to cool.

4. Combine the raisins, dates, scallions, bell pepper, jalapeno pepper, parsley, cooked rice and cooked lentils in a large mixing bowl.

5. To make the salad dressing, thoroughly mix all the salad dressing ingredients and adjust seasoning to taste. Pour the dressing over the salad, toss well and serve on a bed of greens.

Tunisian Couscous Salad with Pine Nuts & Barberries

Tunisia was once part of the ancient city state of Carthage, which fell to the Romans in 146 BCE. The Romans valued it for its mines, quarries and fisheries; for its long Mediterranean shoreline; and especially for its rich agriculture: The land still produces wheat, olives, dates and citrus. The Romans called the region Africa; the Arabs, who conquered it in the seventh century, called it (with Algeria and Morocco) Jazirat al-Maghrib, meaning "islands of the west." In 777 a Persian, Ibn Rostam, born and raised in Tunisia, was proclaimed imam by the Berber tribes of Algeria and soon thereafter formed the Rostamid Kingdom, which ruled the western part of north Africa for over 100 years. There is little documentation of the exchange of foods and cooking styles between Tunisia and other regions, but the similarities in the use of fruit, berries and nuts in Persian, Georgian and North African cooking indicates that there must have been a healthy trade. Couscous is the semolina grains of durum wheat, very popular in North African cuisine.

1. In a large saucepan (you will need plenty of room for the couscous to expand) bring 2 1/2 cups of water and 1 teaspoon salt to a boil. Add the couscous, 2 tablespoons oil and the saffron, and bring back to a boil. Remove from heat, cover tightly with plastic wrap and let stand for 15 minutes. Uncover and fluff the couscous grains with a fork and set aside.

2. In a medium-sized saucepan, cover the orange peel with water, boil for 10 minutes over medium heat, drain and rinse to remove bitterness. Place the orange peel, carrot strips, sugar and orange juice in the same saucepan, and bring to a boil. Reduce heat and cook for 10 minutes over medium heat. Remove from the heat and set aside.

3. Heat 2 tablespoons oil in a wok or deep skillet over medium heat. Add the onions and fry for 15 minutes until golden brown. Add the pine nuts, barberries and raisins, and stir-fry for 20 seconds. Be careful, barberries burn very easily. Remove from the heat.

4. Stir in the orange and carrot mixture and couscous.

5. To prepare the dressing, thoroughly mix all the salad dressing ingredients. Pour the dressing over the salad, toss well and adjust seasonings to taste.

6. Serve on a bed of greens.

Servings: 4
Preparation time: 20 minutes
Cooking time: 35 minutes

COUSCOUS
2 1/2 cups water
1 teaspoon salt
2 cups medium-grain, instant couscous
2 tablespoons vegetable oil
1/8 teaspoon saffron dissolved in 1 tablespoon hot water

SALAD MIX
1 cup chopped orange peel*
2 large carrots, peeled & Julienned
1/2 cup sugar
1 cup orange juice
2 tablespoons oil
1 medium-sized onion, peeled and finely sliced
1/2 cup pine nuts
1/2 cup barberries*
1/2 cup raisins

SALAD DRESSING
2 tablespoons fresh lime juice
1/2 teaspoon cayenne
2 teaspoons ground cumin
1 teaspoon ground coriander
1/2 teaspoon freshly ground black pepper
1 teaspoon salt
1/2 cup olive oil
1/2 cup chopped fresh parsley, cilantro or chives

BED OF GREENS
4 cups shredded greens, arugula or romaine lettuce

Uzbek Potato Salad

Servings: 6
Preparation time: 30 minutes
Cooking time: 20 minutes

2 large potatoes (1 pound)
1 large carrot, peeled and chopped
1 cup fresh shelled or frozen green peas
2 apples, firm and sweet
2 tablespoons fresh lime juice
2 hard-boiled eggs, peeled and chopped (optional)
1 cup fresh chopped scallions
1 chopped celery stalk
1/2 cup raisins

SALAD DRESSING
1/2 cup sour cream or 1/3 cup mayonnaise
1 1/2 tablespoons Dijon mustard
2 tablespoons red wine vinegar
2 tablespoons fresh lime juice
1 1/2 teaspoons salt
1 teaspoon freshly ground black pepper
1 tablespoon curry powder
2 tablespoons olive oil

GARNISH
1 cup coarsely chopped toasted walnuts

Lying in Central Asia and watered by the Amu Darya and the Syr Darya, Uzbekistan has had a long and glittering history, particularly during the days of the Silk Road, when such cities as Samarkand, Khiva and Bokhara were staging posts on the trade routes. Their warehouses were crammed with silks, carpets, gold, and silver; and their palaces and libraries were famous. Internationally inclined by history (today, the population of Uzbekistan is the most representative of the cultural diversity that represented the Silk Road region), the Uzbeks took readily to New World foods such as the potato, which arrived in Spain from the Andes in the sixteenth century and probably reached Central Asia in the next century. The Uzbeks were delighted to incorporate the new vegetable into their traditional recipes, as in this salad.

1. Cover the potatoes with water, bring to a boil, cover and cook over medium heat for 20 minutes until the potatoes are cooked. Peel and dice the potatoes.

2. Steam the chopped carrots and peas for 5 minutes and set aside.

3. Peel, core, and cut the apples into 1/2-inch cubes, place them in a large serving bowl, and sprinkle with 2 tablespoons lime juice (this prevents discoloring).

4. Add the potatoes, carrots, peas, eggs, scallions, celery, and raisins to the bowl.

5. To make the dressing, thoroughly mix all the salad dressing ingredients. Pour the dressing over the salad, toss well and adjust seasoning to taste.

6. Sprinkle the walnuts over the salad and serve with rice, couscous or bread according to your fancy.

Baalbek Chickpea & Sesame Spread (Hummus)

An oasis town in eastern Lebanon, Baalbek seems to have been the chief religious center of the Phoenician fertility god, Baal, frequently denounced by Old Testament prophets. The Greeks, who occupied Baalbek in the fourth century BCE, identified Baal with the sun god, Helios, and named the city Heliopolis; it fell to the Romans in 16 BCE and to the Arabs in CE 637. An eighteenth-century earthquake destroyed much of the city, but ruins of temples to Jupiter, Venus, and Bacchus, god of wine, remain.

1. Place the chickpeas, garlic, 1 1/2 teaspoons salt, lime juice, sesame, cumin, cayenne, olive oil and parsley in a food processor. Add 1/4 cup of the drained chickpea liquid and mix in the food processor until you have a thick puree.

2. Adjust seasoning to taste and transfer to a serving dish. Sprinkle with chopped parsley and serve with toasted pita, lavash bread or crostini.

Servings: 4
Preparation time: 5 minutes
Cooking time: none

- 2 cups canned chickpeas (garbanzo beans) already cooked, drain and save liquid or 1 cup dried chickpeas, cooked (see note below)
- 6 cups water
- 2 cloves garlic, peeled and crushed
- 1 1/2 teaspoons salt
- 4 tablespoons fresh lime juice
- 3 tablespoons sesame or tahini paste
- 1 teaspoon ground cumin
- 1/4 teaspoon cayenne
- 1 tablespoon olive oil
- 1 tablespoon chopped fresh flat-leaf parsley, cilantro or basil

NOTE

If using dried chickpeas, pick over and rinse. Soak for two hours and drain. Place in a medium-sized heavy-bottom saucepan, cover with 6 cups of water, 1/2 teaspoon salt, and bring to a boil. Reduce heat, partially cover, and simmer over medium heat for 1 1/2 hours or until the chickpeas are tender.

Salads / 79

Shirazi Cucumber & Pomegranate Salad

Servings: 4
Preparation time: 25 minutes
Cooking time: none

- 1 medium red onion, peeled and thinly sliced
- 2 long seedless cucumbers, or 6 pickling cucumbers, peeled and thinly sliced
- 2 medium pomegranates, seeded (2 cups)*

SALAD DRESSING
- 1 clove garlic, peeled and crushed
- 1 tablespoon lime juice
- 1 tablespoon pomegranate paste*
- 1/4 teaspoon red hot pepper flakes or 1/4 teaspoon chili paste
- 1 teaspoon sugar or honey
- 1 teaspoon toasted sesame oil
- 1 teaspoon salt
- 1/2 teaspoon freshly ground black pepper
- 1/2 cup olive oil

BED OF GREENS
- 4 cups shredded greens, arugula or lettuce

GARNISH
- 1/2 cup walnuts, toasted and coarsely chopped

Shiraz is the Persian city of poets and the closest to the tribal regions of Iran, where my inspiration for this salad originated. It is a favorite throughout the Silk Road region and can be found, with slight variations, in almost every country there.

1. Place the onion slices in a sieve, sprinkle with 1 tablespoon salt and leave for 10 minutes (to remove any tang from the onion). Rinse with cold water, blot dry and set aside.

2. Combine the onion, cucumber and pomegranate seeds in a serving bowl and set aside.

3. To make the salad dressing, thoroughly mix all the salad dressing ingredients.

4. Pour the dressing over the salad, toss well and adjust seasoning to taste. Serve on a bed of greens and garnish with walnuts. This salad goes particularly well with rice or pasta.

Bengali Chickpea Vegetable Fritters

Servings: 4
Preparation time: 15 minutes
Cooking time: 10 minutes

DIPPING SAUCE
1/2 cup rice vinegar
1 tablespoon chopped fresh cilantro

VEGETABLES
1 seedless cucumber or 4 pickling cucumbers, washed and quartered lengthwise
1/2 pound firm tofu, sliced into 1-by-3-inch slices
1 Chinese eggplant, sliced lengthwise into 1/4-by-3-inch strips
4 stalks asparagus, trimmed
1 large carrot, peeled and cut into 1/4-inch-thick sticks
1 small zucchini, cut into 1-inch-thick sticks
2 mushrooms, cut into quarters
1/4 cauliflower, cut into florets
8 green beans, trimmed
1/2 bell pepper, seeded and cut lengthwise into 1/8-inch-wide strips
6 sage leaves

BATTER
2 cups chickpea flour
2 tablespoons rice flour
1 1/3 cups warm water
1 teaspoon baking powder
2 teaspoons salt
1 hot green chili chopped or 1 teaspoon chili paste
2 teaspoons cumin seeds
2 teaspoons nigella seeds
1 teaspoon garam masala*
1 tablespoon olive oil
2 cups corn oil for frying

NOTE
You can substitute 2 cups cake flour and 1 cup sparkling water for the chickpea flour and warm water.

1. Combine the vinegar and cilantro for the dipping sauce in a bowl and set aside.

2. Prepare the vegetables as specified, wash, pat dry and set aside.

3. In a mixer, combine all the batter ingredients except the corn oil and mix until you have a smooth, thick batter. Transfer the batter to a bowl and let sit for 20 minutes.

4. Heat the oil in a wok or a large, deep skillet over medium to high heat (the temperature is important here, should be 375°F).

5. Dust the vegetable pieces with flour, (keeping them separated), then dip in the batter. Remove the vegetables from the batter, allowing any extra batter to drip back in the bowl.

6. Deep-fry for 4 to 5 minutes, until golden brown. Using a slotted spatula, remove the vegetables and allow to drain on paper towels.

7. Transfer to a serving dish and serve immediately with the dipping sauce on the side.

Salads / 82

Alexandrian Stir-Fried Celery Roots

Servings: 4
Preparation time: 10 minutes
Cooking time: 8 minutes

- 2 tablespoons vegetable oil, butter or ghee
- 2 teaspoons cumin or caraway seeds
- 2 large celery roots, peeled and sliced into 1/4-by-4-inch sticks
- 2 tablespoons fresh lime juice
- 1 teaspoon sugar
- 1 teaspoon salt
- 1/2 teaspoon freshly ground pepper
- 1/4 teaspoon ground turmeric
- 1/3 cup water
- 1/4 cup chopped fresh parsley

1. Heat the oil in a wok or deep skillet over medium-high heat. When the oil is hot, add the cumin and cook for 10 seconds until it becomes aromatic. Add the celery roots and stir-fry for 2 minutes. Add the lime juice, sugar, salt, pepper and turmeric, and stir-fry for 1 minute longer.

2. Add 1/3 cup water, reduce heat, cover and cook for 5 minutes longer or until the celery is cooked yet crisp. Remove from the heat and sprinkle with parsley.

3. Transfer to a serving dish and serve hot or cold on rice, couscous or bulgur according to your fancy.

Armenian Bulgur & Pomegranate Stuffed Grapevine Leaves

Servings: 6
Preparation time: 1 hour
Cooking time: 2 1/2 hours

WRAPPERS
50 canned leaves or fresh grapevine leaves*

FILLING
1 cup brown lentils
1/2 cup oil, butter or ghee
1 onion, peeled and thinly sliced
1/2 cup bulgur
1/2 cup dried pitted prunes, chopped
2 tablespoons raisins
1 1/2 teaspoons salt
1/2 teaspoon pepper
1/4 teaspoon nutmeg
1/2 teaspoon ground cumin
1 cup fresh mint or 1 tablespoon dried mint flakes
1/4 cups chopped fresh parsley
1 tablespoon pomegranate paste

SAUCE
4 tablespoons olive oil
2 cups vegetable stock or water
1/2 cup sugar
1/4 cup vinegar
1/4 cup fresh lime juice
1/2 teaspoon chili flakes
1 teaspoon salt

1. Bring 3 cups water, 1/2 teaspoon salt and the lentils to a boil in a small saucepan. Reduce heat, cover and simmer for 15 minutes, drain (save the liquid) and set aside.

2. Heat 3 tablespoons oil in a wok or deep skillet over medium heat until very hot. Add the onion and stir-fry for 10 minutes. Add the bulgur and stir-fry for 5 minutes longer. Add the prunes, raisins, salt, pepper, nutmeg, cumin, mint, parsley, pomegranate paste and saved drained liquid. Bring to a boil, reduce heat, cover and cook for 15 minutes, until the bulgur is tender and all the water has been absorbed. Add the cooked lentils and stir well. Adjust seasoning to taste. Remove from heat and allow to cool.

3. Preheat oven to 350°F. Place three layers of grapevine leaves on the bottom of a large non-reactive ovenproof dish oiled with the remaining oil.

4. To stuff the grapevines leaves, place a leaf on top of a flat board with the vein side up and nip off the little stem. Top with 1 tablespoon filling. Roll up the leaf, folding in the ends to prevent the filling from leaking out while cooking. Arrange the stuffed grapevine leaves side by side in the pan.

5. Pour stock and 4 tablespoons oil into the pan. Place a small ovenproof plate on top of the stuffed grapevine leaves to pack them down. Cover and bake in the oven for 1 hour.

6. Mix the sugar, vinegar, lime juice and chili flakes. Remove the baking dish from oven, uncover the grapevine leaves and baste with this syrup. Cover and return to oven. Bake for 30 to 45 minutes longer.

7. When the grapevine leaves are tender, taste sauce and adjust seasoning. The sauce should be quite reduced. Serve in the same baking dish or on a platter, while hot or warm, with bread and yogurt.

VARIATION

Substitute 1 cup rice and 1/2 cup pine nuts for the lentils and bulgur.

You can also make an Uzbek variation by stuffing 6 large parboiled onions (or quinces) and 6 large peeled turnips instead of the grapevine leaves.

Beijing-Style Bok Choy with Mushrooms

1. In a small bowl, dissolve the cornstarch in 1/4 cup water. Add the soy sauce, vinegar, sesame oil, chili paste, sugar, salt and pepper. Stir well and set aside.

2. Heat the oil in a wok. Add the garlic, ginger and mushrooms, and stir-fry for 2 minutes over high heat.

3. Add the bok choy and the sauce, cover and simmer over low heat for 5 to 10 minutes until the bok choy are tender.

4. Adjust seasoning to taste and transfer to a serving dish. Serve with rice.

Servings: 4
Preparation time: 10 minutes
Cooking time: 12 minutes

- 1 teaspoon corn starch
- 2 tablespoons light soy sauce
- 1 teaspoon rice vinegar
- 1 tablespoon toasted sesame oil
- 1/4 teaspoon chili paste
- 1/2 teaspoon sugar
- 1/2 teaspoon salt
- 1/2 teaspoon freshly ground pepper
- 1/4 cup vegetable, peanut, or walnut oil
- 2 cloves garlic, peeled and crushed
- 1/2-inch ginger, peeled and grated
- 1 pound shitake mushrooms, washed and sliced (discard stems)
- 6 baby bok choy, trimmed, washed and quartered lengthwise*

NOTE

This recipe uses baby bok choy, which are delicate and cook easily. If you use large bok choy, then the white stalks, which are very hard and need cooking, should be cut off and diced into 2-inch pieces, and cooked with the garlic in step 2. The green parts are then added in step 3.

Samarkand Mung Bean Salad

Servings: 4
Preparation time: 15 minutes
Cooking time: 35 minutes

- 1 cup green mung beans, picked over and washed
- 4 cups water
- 1 teaspoon salt
- 1 small onion, peeled and thinly sliced
- 2 cloves garlic, peeled and crushed
- 1 hot green chili, seeded and finely chopped
- 2 tablespoons toasted cumin seeds
- 1/2-inch fresh ginger, peeled and grated, or 1/4 teaspoon powdered ginger
- 1 teaspoon salt
- 1/2 teaspoon freshly ground black pepper
- 1/2 teaspoon curry powder
- 1 teaspoon sugar
- 2 tablespoons fresh lime juice
- 1/4 cup vegetable oil
- 1 large fresh tomato, peeled and diced
- 1/3 cup chopped fresh cilantro (or substitute parsley, basil or tarragon)
- 2 cups shredded greens, arugula or romaine lettuce

GARNISH
A few sprigs of cilantro

Throughout its long history, Samarkand was an important trading center, importing goods from both the east and west. Mung beans, native to India where they are called green or golden gram, were among the culinary imports, much enjoyed along the entire Silk Road. They are high in protein: If you serve this salad with rice, it becomes a complete meal.

1. Place the mung beans in a medium-sized heavy-bottom saucepan, add 4 cups water and 1 teaspoon salt, and bring to a boil. Cover and cook over medium heat for 25 to 30 minutes until the mung beans are tender. Remove from heat, drain in a fine-mesh colander and transfer to a large mixing bowl.

2. Combine all the remaining ingredients and add to the mung beans. Toss well and adjust seasoning to taste. Transfer to a serving dish and garnish with a few sprigs of cilantro. Serve with rice, couscous or pasta. This salad can be covered and kept in the refrigerator for up to 3 days.

Salads / 86

Fertile Crescent Young White Turnips with Dates

1. Heat the oil in a wok or deep skillet over medium-high heat. When the oil is hot, add the cumin and cook for 10 seconds until it becomes aromatic. Add the turnips and dates, and stir-fry for 2 minutes. Reduce heat to low, add the salt, pepper and 1 cup water, cover and cook for 10 to 15 minutes until the turnip is tender.

2. Transfer to a serving dish and serve with rice or bulgur.

Servings: 4
Preparation time: 10 minutes
Cooking time: 17 minutes

- 2 tablespoons vegetable oil or butter
- 1 teaspoon cumin or caraway seeds
- 2 pounds young white turnips, peeled and shredded
- 1/2 cup pitted medjool dates, sliced
- 1 teaspoon salt
- 1/2 teaspoon freshly ground pepper
- 1 cup water

Tashkent Daikon & Pomegranate Salad

Servings: 4
Preparation time: 15 minutes
Cooking time: none

- 1 daikon (2 pounds, white radish), peeled and grated (use large holes to grate)
- 1 carrot, peeled and julienned
- 1 cup pomegranate seeds (2 pomegranates)
- 1/2 cup blanched almonds

SALAD DRESSING
- 2 tablespoons rice vinegar
- 1 tablespoon toasted sesame oil
- 1 teaspoon salt
- 1/2 teaspoon fresh ground pepper
- 1 teaspoon sugar

1. Allow the grated daikon to soak in ice water for 15 minutes, rinse, drain and pat dry.

2. Place the daikon, carrots, pomegranate seeds and almonds in a serving bowl.

3. For the dressing, thoroughly mix all the ingredients and adjust seasoning to taste. Pour over the salad, toss well, cover and chill for 30 minutes.

Uzbek Carrot Salad

1. Blanch carrots, drain, allow to cool and place in a serving dish.

2. For the dressing, thoroughly mix all the ingredients and adjust seasoning to taste. Pour over the carrot, toss well, cover and chill for 30 minutes.

Servings: 4
Preparation time: 15 minutes
Cooking time: none

1 pound carrots, peeled and julienned

SALAD DRESSING
1 clove garlic, peeled and crushed
2 tablespoons light soy sauce
2 tablespoons rice vinegar
2 tablespoons toasted sesame oil
1 tablespoon sugar
1/4 teaspoon chili paste
2 tablespoons toasted sesame seeds
2 tablespoons chopped fresh chives

NOTE
This salad is made by Korean Uzbeks who were relocated from Korea to Uzbekistan in the 1900s by the Russians in an agreement with the Japanese.

Levantine Roasted Eggplant & Sesame Dip (Baba Ghanoush)

Servings: 4
Preparation time: 15 minutes
Cooking time: 40 minutes

- 2 large eggplants (about 3 pounds)
- 2 tablespoons freshly squeezed lime juice
- 1/4 cup sesame paste
- 4 cloves garlic, peeled and crushed
- 1 1/2 teaspoons salt
- 1 teaspoon ground cumin
- 1/4 teaspoon cayenne (optional)

GARNISH
- 1/2 cup chopped fresh cilantro or parsley
- 2 tablespoons olive oil
- 1/4 pomegranate, seeded* (optional)
- Lavash or pita bread, or tortillas, toasted and cut into 4-inch pieces

NOTE

The traditionally the eggplants are grilled, turning them frequently, for about 40 minutes over a charcoal or wood fire that has burned down to embers. It is much simpler to just bake them in the oven.

The Levant (from the French lever, *"to rise," or "point of sunrise" or the "East" as a noun) generally includes all the countries along the eastern shore of the Mediterranean but more specifically refers to what is now Lebanon, the Phoenicia of Biblical times. Its fabled trading ports, Sidon, Tyre and Byblos—now small Lebanese towns—once linked the western cities of the Silk Road with Europe. Baba Ghanoush is sometimes called "poor man's caviar."*

1. Rinse the eggplants and prick them in several places with a fork to prevent bursting.

2. Preheat oven to 450°F. Bake the eggplants in the center rack for about 40 minutes, turning occasionally. Be sure to place a tray underneath to catch the drippings.

3. Remove the eggplants from the oven and place them on a cutting board. Allow them to stand until they are cool enough to handle. Remove the skins and seeds, and chop the eggplants. Transfer them into a mixing bowl and blend with the lime juice.

4. Gradually add the sesame paste, garlic, salt, cumin and cayenne, and blend thoroughly. Adjust seasoning to taste.

5. Transfer to a shallow dish and garnish with cilantro, olive oil and pomegranate seeds. Serve with lavash bread, salads or rice according to your fancy.

VARIATION

Persian Eggplant Borani

In Iran a very similar recipe is made with 1 cup drained yogurt instead of the sesame paste.

Fruits on Sticks

In which we learn that Chinese street vendors have enjoyed selling fruits on sticks for centuries

Haw fruit skewers for sale, haw fruit skewers for sale! I've just left the pleasure precincts, come out of the tea houses. In the snap of a finger, I've passed by the realm of kingfisher green and red as quickly as a turn of the head I am at the fortress of orioles and flowers. I must convey that I am of the tradition of an old native of the capital.

These fruits are raised in the finest gardens, just picked from their local sites. There are sweet-sweet-luscious, full-spouting-fragrant, aromatic-and-perfumed, red fresh-peeled-and-juicy round-eyed lichees from Fuzhou. And from Lanqi District there are sour-sour-tart, shady-shady-cool, soft-limp-green, nurtured-to-the-full, springtime cymbidia with the leaves still on. From Songyang District are supple-supple-soft, quite-quite-white, frost-frozen persimmon cakes soaked in honey and covered with sugar powder. From Wuzhou Prefecture comes juicy-juicy-tender, glitter-glitter-bright dragon-twined jujube balls kneaded in sugar; there are sweet and sour golden tangerines, dried on the tree and simmered in honey; I have fragrant-crispy almonds simmered in sugar. I'm not bragging on the number and kind, but my profession sends me from trading in Xuancheng to gathering in Wei for these fixed-with-sugar, mixed-with honey, minced-into-strips, soft little skewered pears. O you fine and handsome gents and dandies in your high halls and grand lofts! O you sing-song girls and beautiful women of embroidered galleries and perfumed chambers—would I dare open my mouth as big as an ocean? Is it all just an empty boast? Try them, taste them, you'll desire no other. Once you eat them, I'll sell you more!

Text from the Chinese drama *Pai-hua t'ing* from about 1250. Translated by Stephen H. West.

Above: A street vendor in Chengdu sells jujubes on sticks.

Xian Eggplant & Pomegranate Salad

Servings: 4
Preparation time: 15 minutes
Cooking time: 30 minutes

- 6 Chinese eggplants, about 2 pounds
- 3 tablespoons olive oil
- 2 medium onions, peeled and thinly sliced
- 2 cloves garlic, peeled and crushed
- 1 large tomato, peeled and sliced
- 3 tablespoons pomegranate paste
- 2 teaspoons salt
- 1 teaspoon sugar
- 1 tablespoon toasted sesame oil
- 1/2 teaspoon freshly ground black pepper
- 1/2 cup chopped fresh mint or 1 teaspoon dried

NOTE

If you do not use Chinese eggplants, you will need 2 large eggplants, peeled, seeded and bitterness removed.*

Great cities have risen and fallen at Xian since the 11th century bce (called Changan in ancient times). During the great Silk Road trading days of the Han and Tang dynasties it was one of the most splendid cities in the world. Today this salad is a popular Xian dish. It is similar to the traditional Persian salad Naz Khatun ("lady flirt") and is perhaps an example of the cultural exchange along the Silk Road.

1. Cut the eggplant into 1-inch cubes, rinse and thoroughly pat dry.

2. In a wok or deep skillet, heat the oil over medium heat and stir-fry the onion and garlic for 5 minutes or until translucent.

3. Add the eggplant cubes and stir-fry for 10 minutes. Add the tomato, pomegranate paste, salt, sugar, pepper and mint. Reduce heat, cover and simmer for 10 to 15 minutes until the eggplant cubes are tender.

4. Add the sesame oil, stir well and adjust seasoning to taste. Transfer to a serving dish and serve, hot or cold, with rice.

VARIATION

Indian Five Spice Eggplant & Yogurt Salad

Substitute 1/2 teaspoon cumin seeds, 1/2 teaspoon fennel seeds, teaspoon nigella seeds and 1/2 teaspoon mustard seeds for the o garlic and tomato in step 2 and 3. In step 4 add 1/4 cup yogurt.

Konya Eggplants with Onion & Garlic (Imam Bayaldi)

Servings: 6
Preparation time: 30 minutes
Cooking time: 1 hour 6 minutes

6 Italian eggplants, peeled (leave the stems in tact)*

FILLING
1 cup olive oil
2 large onions, peeled and thinly sliced
6 cloves garlic, crushed and peeled
1/2 cup fresh chopped mint
1 teaspoon salt
1 teaspoon sugar
1 teaspoon ground cumin
2 large tomatoes, peeled and sliced

1. Make a slit, lengthwise, in each eggplant without opening the ends. Soak the eggplants in a container of cold water with 2 tablespoons coarse salt for 20 minutes. Drain, rinse, pat dry and set aside.

2. In a large skillet, heat 1/4 cup oil over medium heat and slightly brown the eggplants on all sides.

3. Preheat the oven to 350°F.

4. Arrange the eggplants side by side on an oiled baking dish.

5. In the same skillet, heat 2 tablespoons oil over medium heat and add the onion and garlic. Stir-fry 5 minutes. Add the remaining ingredients for the filling and stir-fry for 1 minute longer. Remove from the heat.

6. Open up the slits in the eggplants with your hands and stuff each eggplant with the onion mixture. Drizzle the remaining oil and 1/4 cup water over them. Cover with aluminum foil and bake for about 1 hour, until soft.

Chinese Tofu Wonton Soup

Servings: 6
Preparation time: 30 minutes
Cooking time: 15 minutes

FILLING
- 2 cups shredded napa cabbage
- 1 pound firm tofu, drained and wrapped in several paper towels (press down and let stand for 15 minutes to extract the liquid)
- 4 Chinese black mushrooms (soaked in warm water for 15 minutes), drained, stemmed and shredded, or 4 fresh shitake, sliced
- 1 carrot, peeled and shredded
- 1/2-inch fresh peeled ginger, grated
- 2 tablespoons chopped fresh cilantro
- 5 fresh scallions, shredded
- 1 egg
- 1 teaspoon salt
- 1/4 teaspoon freshly ground white pepper
- 2 bird chilies, chopped, or 1 teaspoon garlic-chili paste*
- 2 teaspoons toasted sesame oil*
- 1 teaspoon dark soy sauce
- 2 teaspoons cornstarch

WRAPPERS
- A 1-pound package thin wonton wrappers (24) or gyoza skin

SOUP
- 8 cups vegetable stock* or water
- 1 tablespoon dark soy sauce
- 1 teaspoon salt
- 1/2 teaspoon white pepper
- 2 tablespoons rice vinegar
- 1 teaspoon toasted sesame oil
- 1/4 cup fresh basil or cilantro leaves
- 1/4 cup pea shoots

Wonton soup is well known as a specialty of Chinese cooking; however, with slight variations, a very similar soup is popular from China to Turkey. This Chinese version uses soy and sesame oil in the stock and is very close to the Azerbaijani version called dushbarreh and the Uzbek chuchvara, both of which use vinegar and cilantro instead of soy and sesame oil and are served with yogurt, or sour cream.

1. To make the filling, sprinkle 1 teaspoon salt on the shredded Napa cabbage and let stand for 5 minutes. Then cover with 3 layers of paper towel and squeeze down with your hands to remove any excess juices.

2. Combine all the ingredients for the filling in a food processor and pulse to coarsely chop (do not puree).

3. Open the wrapper packaging and cover the wrappers with a towel to prevent drying.

4. To make the wonton, place 1 teaspoon of the filling in the center of each wrapper and brush the edges with water. Fold over to form a triangle and pinch edges to seal. Place in a baking sheet and sprinkle with cornstarch to prevent them from sticking together. Cover with a towel to prevent drying.

5. To make the soup, bring the vegetable stock to a boil in a medium-sized pot. Add the soy sauce, salt, pepper, vinegar, and sesame oil. Adjust seasoning to taste. Simmer over low heat for 10 minutes. Keep warm.

6. To cook the wontons: In another medium size pot bring 8 cups of water and 1 tablespoon oil to a boil over high heat. Add 5 wontons at a time, cover and bring the water back to a boil. Gently stir to prevent the wontons from sticking together. Boil uncovered, for 3 to 4 minutes, until the wontons float to the top. Remove the wontons using a slotted spoon and set aside. Continue this procedure for the remaining wontons.

7. Just before serving, divide the cooked wontons among the individual bowls. Place some basil leaves and pea shoots in the bowls, and pour the hot stock into the bowls. Serve hot.

Beijing Hot & Sour Noodle Soup

Keep in mind that Asian noodles, as opposed to Italian ones, are always cooked in boiling water until they are tender, never al dente. Furthermore, the water used for cooking the noodles is never salted.

For this recipe I recommend the early harvest, small and tender baby bok choy. Bok choy, which means "white vegetable" in Cantonese, is now available in many groceries in the U.S.

1. Bring 3 quarts water to a boil in a large pot. Add the noodles and boil for 1 to 8 minutes, until the noodles are tender (according to the package directions). Drain, rinse and set aside.

2. Bring the vegetable stock to a boil in a medium-sized pot over medium heat. Add the ginger root, lemon grass, mushrooms and corn. Bring back to a boil, reduce heat, partially cover and simmer over medium heat for 15 minutes.

3. Add the tofu, carrot, soy sauce, salt, pepper, sugar, chilies and sesame oil, and simmer for 15 minutes longer.

4. Mix 1 cup of the hot soup with the diluted corn starch, then add it to the soup, stirring constantly for about 2 minutes over medium heat, until the soup has thickened.

5. Add the lime juice and bok choy, and continue to cook for 5 minutes longer. Adjust seasoning to taste. Keep warm.

6. Just before serving, divide the cooked noodles among 4 individual bowls and gently pour the hot soup over them.

Servings: 4
Preparation time: 15 minutes
Cooking time: 45 minutes

- 3 quarts water
- 1/2 package Chinese noodles, fresh or dried, about 4 ounces
- 6 cups vegetable stock* or water
- 1/2-inch ginger root, peeled and grated
- 1 stalk lemon grass (remove hard outer layers and use bulb only), finely chopped*
- 5 dried wood ear mushrooms (5 ounces), soaked in warm water for 15 minutes, stems removed and shredded; or 1/2 pound fresh shitake mushrooms, shredded*
- 1 cup sweet corn kernels
- 1 pound chopped, firm tofu, sliced into 1/2-inch cubes
- 1 carrot, peeled and shredded
- 3 teaspoons soy sauce
- 1 teaspoon salt
- 1/4 teaspoon pepper
- 1 teaspoon sugar
- 2 Thai bird or serrano chilies, chopped, or 1 teaspoon chili paste
- 2 teaspoons sesame oil
- 3 teaspoons cornstarch, diluted with 1/4 cup cold water
- 2 tablespoons fresh lime juice or 3 tablespoons rice vinegar
- 3 baby bok choy, trimmed and quartered lengthwise, or 1 cup white cabbage, shredded

Caspian Butternut Squash, Bulgur & Wild Orange Soup

Servings: 6
Preparation time: 15 minutes
Cooking time: 1 hour

- 2 tablespoons vegetable oil, butter or ghee
- 1 onion, peeled and thinly sliced
- 1 fresh hot green chili, chopped or 1/4 teaspoon cayenne
- 2 pounds butternut squash, peeled and cut into 1-inch cubes (4 cups)
- 1 cup walnuts, ground
- 4 cups vegetable stock or water
- 1/2 cup rice flour* diluted in 2 cups water
- 1 cup bulgur rinsed in a fine-mesh colander and soaked in 1 cup milk for 40 minutes
- 2 teaspoons salt
- 1 teaspoon freshly ground black pepper
- 1 teaspoon sugar
- 1/2 teaspoon cinnamon
- 1/2 teaspoon ground cumin
- 1/2 teaspoon cooking rose water (optional)
- 1 cup parsley leaves or 6 sage leaves
- 1 cup Seville orange juice* or 1 cup orange juice mixed with 1/4 cup lime juice

This soup, very popular in the Caspian Sea region, is also popular in Italy, where sage is used to replace the parsley, and Parmesan cheese is used in lieu of bulgur. It is also found throughout Uzbekistan.

1. Heat the oil in a medium-sized pot, over medium heat. Add the onion and stir-fry for 10 minutes until translucent. Add the chili, butternut squash and walnuts and stir-fry for 1 minute.

2. Add 4 cups vegetable stock. Bring to a boil. Partially cover and simmer over medium heat for 30 minutes until the squash is tender.

3. Add the diluted rice flour, bulgur soaked in milk, salt, pepper, sugar, cinnamon, cumin and rose water, and bring back to a boil, stirring constantly. Cover and simmer over low heat for another 20 minutes. If the soup is too thick, add some warm water and bring back to a boil. Add the parsley and Seville orange juice, and adjust seasoning to taste. Just before serving, pour into a tureen.

Balkh Brown Lentil Soup

Besides being a delicious and versatile legume, lentils have the highest protein content, after soybeans, of any vegetable at almost 25%. This may be one of the reasons they are so popular in the valley between the Hindu Kush and the Amu Darya (Oxus River) in what is present-day Afghanistan, Uzbekistan and Tajikistan. This soup is also popular in India, Iran and North Africa. Balkh was an important Sogdian trading center. These ancient Central Asian people established an empire in the region that controlled most Silk Road commerce during the sixth and seventh centuries.

1. Heat the oil in a medium-sized heavy pot over medium heat. Add the cumin seeds and stir-fry for 20 seconds until aromatic (keep a lid handy to stop any seeds from flying out). Add the onions, garlic and butternut squash and stir-fry for 10 minutes.

2. Add 8 cups water, salt, pepper and lentils, and bring to a boil. Partially cover and simmer over medium heat for about 50 minutes until the lentils are tender, stirring occasionally.

3. Add the diluted rice flour, chili, angelica powder and Seville orange juice, and bring to a boil. Reduce heat, cover partially and simmer over medium heat for 40 minutes longer, stirring occasionally. If the soup is too thick, add some warm water and bring back to a boil.

4. Adjust seasoning to taste. Just before serving, sprinkle with parsley and serve hot with lavash bread. This recipe may be made up to 24 hours in advance and stored in the refrigerator. Reheat before serving.

Servings: 6
Preparation time: 15 minutes
Cooking time: 1 hour 40 minutes

- 3 tablespoons vegetable oil, butter or ghee*
- 1 teaspoon cumin seeds
- 2 large onions, peeled and thinly sliced
- 4 cloves garlic, crushed and peeled
- 1/2 pound butternut squash or pumpkin, peeled and cut into 1-inch cubes
- 8 cups water
- 1 tablespoon salt
- 1/2 teaspoon freshly ground black pepper
- 2 cups brown lentils, picked over and washed
- 2 tablespoons rice flour* diluted in 2 cups of water
- 1 whole serrano chili or 1/4 teaspoon cayenne
- 1 tablespoon angelica powder*
- 2/3 cup Seville orange juice* or 1/2 cup fresh orange juice mixed with 4 tablespoons fresh lime juice
- 1 cup chopped fresh parsley

NOTE
EGYPTIAN FAVA BEAN SOUP
Substitute 2 cups of dried, skinned fava beans for the butternut squash and reduce the lentils to 1/2 cup.

Damavand Yogurt & Cucumber Cold Soup with Walnuts & Rose Petals

Servings: 4
Preparation time: 15 minutes
Cooking time: none

- 1 long seedless cucumber or 4 pickling cucumbers, peeled and diced
- 3 cups plain whole or low-fat yogurt
- 1/4 cup chopped scallions
- 2 tablespoons chopped fresh mint
- 2 tablespoons chopped fresh dill
- 2 tablespoons chopped fresh oregano or 1/2 teaspoon dried oregano
- 1 tablespoon chopped fresh thyme or 1/2 teaspoon dried thyme
- 4 tablespoons chopped fresh tarragon or 1/2 teaspoon dried tarragon
- 2 cloves garlic, crushed, peeled and finely chopped
- 1/4 cup shelled walnuts, coarsely chopped
- 2 teaspoons salt
- 1 teaspoon freshly ground black pepper
- 1 cup water
- 1/2 cup raisins, washed and drained

GARNISH
- 1 tablespoon dried mint flakes
- 3 tablespoons dried rose petals
- 1 pita bread, toasted and cut into 1/2-inch cubes

NOTE
You can eliminate the water and use this recipe as a delicious sauce.

You can also replace the 3 cups of yogurt with 4 cups plain soy milk and 1 tablespoon fresh lime juice, and eliminate the water.

I always loved the use of rose petals in this wonderful cold yogurt soup. thirty years ago, I even found it used in a small café on the foothills of the magnificent Damavand Mountain in northern Iran, where rose petal wine has been made for 2,000 years.

1. Combine the cucumber, yogurt, scallions, mint, dill, oregano, thyme, tarragon, garlic, walnuts, salt and pepper in a serving bowl. Mix thoroughly with 1 cup water and adjust seasoning to taste.

2. Add a few ice cubes and mix well.

3. Just before serving, add the raisins, stir well and pour the soup into a tureen or individual serving bowls. Garnish with mint, rose petals and pita bread croutons.

Susa Noodles Soup with Fresh Herbs

Servings: 6
Preparation time: 20 minutes
Cooking time: 2 hours

- 1/2 cup vegetable oil, butter or ghee
- 4 large onions, peeled and thinly sliced
- 10 cloves garlic, crushed and peeled
- 2 teaspoons salt
- 1 teaspoon freshly ground black pepper
- 1 teaspoon turmeric
- 1/4 cup dried chickpeas
- 1/2 cup kidney beans or black beans
- 10-12 cups water
- 1/2 cup lentils
- 1 fresh beet, peeled and diced in 1/2-inch pieces (optional)
- 1/2 pound Persian noodles or linguine noodles, broken in half
- 1 tablespoon unbleached flour, diluted in 2 cups water
- 1/2 cup coarsely chopped fresh chives or scallions
- 1/2 cup chopped fresh dill
- 1 cup coarsely chopped fresh parsley
- 6 cups washed and chopped fresh spinach or 3 pounds thawed frozen spinach, chopped
- 1 cup sun-dried yogurt (whey) or sesame paste, or 1/4 cup rice vinegar

NANA DAQ
(GARNISH)

- 2 tablespoons vegetable oil
- 2 cloves garlic, crushed, peeled and chopped
- 2 tablespoons dried mint flakes, crushed
- 1/2 teaspoon turmeric

See photograph on page 11

1. Heat the oil in a large pot over medium heat. Add the onions and stir-fry for 10 minutes until translucent. Add the garlic, salt, pepper, turmeric, chickpeas and kidney beans and stir-fry for another 1 minute. Pour in 10 cups of water and bring to boil. Reduce heat, partially cover and simmer for 45 minutes over medium heat.

2. Add the lentils and beet pieces and cook for 20 minutes longer.

3. Add the noodles and flour, and cook for 10 minutes, stirring occasionally.

4. Add the chives, dill, parsley and spinach, and continue to cook, stirring from time to time, for 30 minutes longer or until the beans are tender. If the soup is too thick, add some warm water and bring back to a boil. Reduce heat to low, cover and keep warm.

5. To make the nana daq garnish, heat a small skillet over medium heat, add the garlic and stir-fry for 1 minute until golden brown. Remove from heat, add the mint and turmeric, and stir well. Set aside.

6. Just before serving, remove for heat, add the sun dried yogurt and stir for 5 minutes using a wooden spoon. Adjust seasoning to taste.

7. Pour the soup into a tureen and garnish with the nana daq.

Soups / 102

Genoese Minestrone with Pesto Sauce

The uncooked pesto sauce added to this classic Italian soup just before serving, makes it a Genoese specialty with a unique flavor.

1. Heat the oil in a heavy-base, medium-sized pot over medium heat. Add the cumin seeds and cook for 10 seconds, until aromatic (keep a lid handy to catch any seeds that might fly out). Add the carrot, fennel, celery, potato and beans, and stir-fry for 5 minutes. Add 8 cups stock and salt. Bring to a boil, reduce heat, partially cover and simmer over medium heat for 1 1/2 hours or until the beans are tender. Add more stock if necessary.

2. Add the tomatoes, pepper, lime juice and bring to a boil. Add the pasta and continue to cook for 10 to 15 minutes until the pasta is al dente, stirring occasionally to prevent sticking.

3. To make the pesto sauce, place the basil, garlic and pine nuts in the food processor, and pulse, gradually adding the olive oil and cheese, a little at a time, until you have a creamy, soft sauce.

4. Just before serving, remove the soup from heat, add the pesto and stir with a wooden spoon. Adjust seasoning to taste.

Servings: 6
Preparation time: 20 minutes plus 2 hours for soaking beans
Cooking time: 1 hour 50 minutes

- 1 cup white beans (lima, butter or cannellini), picked over, rinsed, soaked in 6 cups of water for 2 hours, rinsed and drained.
- 4 tablespoons olive oil
- 2 tablespoons cumin seeds (optional)
- 1 carrot, peeled and thinly sliced
- 1/2 fennel bulb, trimmed and thinly sliced
- 1 stalk celery, thinly sliced
- 1 large potato, peeled and diced
- 8-10 cups vegetable stock* or water
- 2 teaspoons salt
- 2 medium tomatoes, peeled and sliced
- 1/2 teaspoon freshly ground black pepper
- 2 tablespoons fresh lime juice
- 5 ounces pasta (tagliatelle, spaghetti or shells), optional

PESTO SAUCE
- 2 cup fresh basil leaves
- 3 tablespoons pine nuts
- 2 cloves garlic
- 1 tablespoon grated Parmesan cheese
- 1 tablespoon grated sharp pecorino cheese
- 1 cup extra virgin olive oil

NOTE
If you use canned beans, drain them and reduce the stock to 6 cups. Reduce cooking time in step 1 to 20 minutes.

Azerbaijani Pomegranate & Spinach Soup

Servings: 4
Preparation time: 10 minutes
Cooking time: 45 minutes

- 4 tablespoons vegetable oil
- 2 teaspoons cumin seeds
- 4 cloves garlic, crushed and peeled
- 1-inch fresh ginger, peeled and grated
- 1/4 cup rice flour*
- 2 cups vegetable stock* or water
- 4 cups pomegranate juice (8 medium pomegranates) or 1/2 cup pomegranate paste diluted in 2 cups of water
- 2 teaspoons salt
- 1 teaspoon freshly ground black pepper
- 1/4 teaspoon cinnamon
- 1/4 cup sugar
- 1 tablespoon angelica powder
- 1 cup baby spinach, washed and drained
- 1 cup fresh mint leaves, shredded, or 2 teaspoons dried mint

GARNISH
- 1 teaspoon dried mint flakes
- 1 cup pomegranate seeds (1 large pomegranate)
- 1 cup toasted, coarsely chopped walnuts or pine nuts

This soup is popular all the way from Tabriz in Iran to Samarkand in Uzbekistan. Ruy Gonzalez de Clavijo, a Spanish diplomat who visited Tamerlane in Samarkand in 1403, wrote, "When it came time for them to partake of the rice and soup, they all three gathered round one bowl using one spoon amongst them, which when one had done with, another would take up, and so sharing together." Perhaps more diplomats and politicians should eat their soup this way.

1. Heat 4 tablespoons oil in a medium, heavy pot over medium heat. Add the cumin, and stir-fry for 20 seconds until aromatic. Add the garlic and ginger, and stir-fry for 1 minute. Add rice flour and stir-fry for 3 minutes longer. Add the stock and bring to a boil. Reduce heat, partially cover and simmer over medium heat for 20 minutes.

2. Stir in the pomegranate juice, salt, pepper, cinnamon, sugar, angelica powder, spinach and mint. Bring back to a boil, reduce heat and simmer over low heat for 15 minutes.

3. Adjust seasoning to taste; the soup should be sweet and sour.

4. Pour the soup into a tureen and garnish with the mint flakes, pomegranate seeds and walnuts.

Kermani Pistachio & Barberry Soup

The tastiest and meatiest pistachios in the world come from the Kerman region of central Iran. Although Kerman was not, strictly speaking, on the Silk Road, it was very much on the Spice Route that formed a network of tributaries with the Silk Road. This is one of many Kermani recipes that incorporates pistachios.

1. Grind the pistachios in a food processor or grinder. Add 2 cups of the stock and continue to grind until you have a smooth, creamy pistachio puree. Set aside.

2. To prepare the garnish, heat 1 tablespoon oil in a heavy-base, medium-sized pot over medium heat. Add 1/2 cup shelled whole pistachios, 1/2 cup barberries and 1 teaspoon sugar, and stir-fry for 20 seconds (the barberries can burn easily; be careful). Use a slotted spoon to transfer the mixture from the pot to a small bowl. Set aside.

3. In the same pot, heat 1 tablespoon oil until very hot. Add the cumin and coriander, and cook for 10 seconds until the seeds stop crackling (keep a lid handy to avoid losing the seeds that fly out). Add the ginger, chili, onion, leeks and garlic. Cover and allow to gently stew for 5 minutes. Add the rice flour, pistachio puree, remaining stock, salt, turmeric and pepper, stir gently with a wooden spoon and bring to a boil.

4. Reduce heat, partially cover and simmer over very low heat for 30 minutes, stirring occasionally.

5. Add the Seville orange juice and adjust seasoning to taste.

6. Pour the soup into a tureen, garnish with the pistachio and barberry mixture, and serve hot or cold.

Variations

Catalan Almond Soup
Substitute 1 cup blanched almonds and 1 cup white bread cubes soaked in 2/3 cup water for the pistachios and rice flour.

Nomad Walnut Soup
Substitute walnuts for the pistachios. In step 4, in the last 10 minutes of cooking, add 1 teaspoon dried mint, 1 teaspoon dried fenugreek and 3 egg yolks. Stir until egg is firm.

Servings: 4
Preparation time: 10 minutes
Cooking time: 55 minutes

1 cup unsalted pistachios, shelled
6 cups vegetable stock or water

GARNISH
1 tablespoon vegetable oil
1 cup shelled pistachios
1/2 cup barberries, rinsed*
1 teaspoon sugar

1 tablespoon vegetable oil, butter or ghee
2 tablespoons cumin seeds
1 teaspoon coriander seeds
1/2 teaspoon fresh ginger, grated
1 Thai bird chili, chopped, or 1/4 teaspoon cayenne
1 small onion, thinly sliced
2 leeks (white and green parts), chopped
2 cloves garlic, peeled and chopped
1 cup rice flour
1 teaspoon salt
1/4 teaspoon turmeric
1 teaspoon freshly ground back pepper
1 cup Seville orange juice or 3/4 cup fresh orange juice mixed with 1/4 tablespoon fresh lime juice, or 1 1/2 tablespoons sherry vinegar

Tusy Mung Bean, Tarragon & Kohlrabi Soup

Servings: 6
Preparation time: 20 minutes
Cooking time: 1 1/4 hour

- 4 tablespoons vegetable oil, butter or ghee
- 2 large onions, peeled and thinly sliced
- 6 cloves garlic, crushed and peeled
- 1 cup dried mung beans (picked over and washed thoroughly)
- 2 teaspoons salt
- 1 teaspoon freshly ground black pepper
- 1 teaspoon turmeric
- 8 cups vegetable stock* or water
- 1/2 cup rice
- 3 cups peeled and diced fresh kohlrabi (about 3 medium-sized)
- 1 cup chopped fresh cilantro
- 1 cup chopped fresh parsley
- 1 cup chopped fresh tarragon
- 1 cup chopped fresh chives or scallions
- 1/2 cup chopped fresh summer savory or 2 tablespoons dry savory
- 1 teaspoon dry mint flakes
- 1/2 cup liquid whey (or sour cream, lime juice or rice vinegar)

GARNISH
- 1 tablespoon mint flakes

NOTE

For best results, make this soup a day in advance to give the flavors a chance to meld; reheat it just before serving. Add the garnish at the last minute, after pouring the soup into a tureen or individual serving bowls.

Tus, on the northern plain of Iran not far from Mashhad, was a Silk Road center until it was destroyed by the Mongols in the 13th century. It is the birthplace and burial site of Ferdowsi, author of the Iranian national epic, The Shahnameh, *or Book of Kings. I have named this dish in honor of his birthplace, although the recipe was actually inspired by summers spent in Mashhad, a city of pilgrimage shrines and beautiful gardens.*

1. Heat the oil in a large, heavy-base pot over medium heat. Add the onion and stir-fry for 10 minutes. Add the garlic, mung beans, salt, pepper and turmeric and stir-fry for 1 minute longer. Pour in the vegetable stock and bring to a boil. Reduce heat, partially cover and simmer for 30 minutes over medium heat, stirring occasionally with a wooden spoon.

2. Add the rice, kohlrabi, cilantro, parsley, tarragon, chives, savory and mint flakes. Cover partially and simmer for another 30 minutes over medium heat, stirring occasionally.

3. Check to see if the beans and vegetables are done. Stir in the whey and adjust seasoning to taste. Use a hand-held mixer to puree the ingredients in the pot.

4. Pour the soup into a tureen or individual bowls and garnish with mint flakes.

Soups / 106

Gujarati Carrot & Yogurt Soup

Gujarat, a state on the west coast of India, bound by the Arabian Sea to the south and west, Pakistan to the northwest and Rajasthan to the north, is the gourmet center of Indian vegetarian cooking. This soup is popular throughout the Spice Route region that linked India to the Silk Road.

1. Heat 1 tablespoon of the oil in a large, heavy-base pot until very hot. Add the mustard seeds and cook for 20 seconds or until the seeds stop crackling (keep a lid handy to stop the seeds from jumping out of the pot). Add the curry leaves, onion, garlic, ginger, chili, bell pepper, carrots, sugar and salt, and stir-fry for 10 minutes. Add the vegetable stock and bring to a boil. Reduce heat and simmer over low heat for 30 minutes, until the carrots are tender. Remove from heat and discard the curry leaves.

2. In a food processor, beat the yogurt with the dissolved rice flour for 5 minutes (this will prevent curdling).

3. Add the yogurt to the pot over low heat, stirring constantly clockwise with a wooden spoon for 5 minutes, until the soup begins to simmer gently. Cover and allow to simmer over very low heat for another 15 minutes, stirring occasionally. If the soup is too thick, add some warm water and bring back to a boil. Adjust seasoning to taste.

4. Pour the soup into a tureen or individual bowls just before serving and garnish with chives.

Servings: 4
Preparation time: 20 minutes
Cooking time: 1 hour

- 1/4 cup vegetable oil, butter or ghee
- 1 tablespoon black mustard seeds
- 10 curry leaves* (fresh or dry)
- 1 small onion, peeled and chopped
- 2 cloves garlic, peeled and chopped
- 1/2-inch fresh ginger, peeled and grated, or 1/4 teaspoon ginger powder
- 2 Thai bird or serrano chilies, chopped
- 1 red bell pepper, seeded and chopped
- 1 pound carrots (about 6 large carrots), peeled and grated
- 1/2 teaspoon sugar
- 2 teaspoons salt
- 3 cups vegetable stock* or water
- 2 cups plain yogurt
- 1/4 cup rice flour, dissolved in 1 cup water

GARNISH
- 1/4 cup chopped fresh chives or 1/2 cup chopped fresh cilantro

NOTE
This soup can be served over rice—a delicious combination.

Madras Red Lentil Soup

Servings: 6
Preparation time: 20 minutes
Cooking time: 1 hour

2 1/2 cups red lentils (dal masoor), picked over
4 tablespoons vegetable oil, butter or ghee
1 teaspoon fenugreek seeds
1 teaspoon mustard seeds
1 tablespoon cumin seeds
1 teaspoon coriander seeds
4 curry leaves*
1 onion, peeled and thinly sliced
2 cloves garlic, crushed and peeled
1-inch fresh ginger, peeled and grated
1 Thai bird or serrano chili, chopped, or 1/2 teaspoon cayenne
1/2 teaspoon turmeric
1 teaspoon sugar
2 teaspoons salt
6 cups water
2 tablespoons rice flour, dissolved in 2 cups cold water*
2 cups chopped fresh tomatoes, peeled and seeded (canned tomatoes can be substituted)
2 tablespoons fresh lime juice

GARNISH
1 cup chopped fresh cilantro

1. Place the red lentils in a container, cover with water, agitate with your hands and drain. Repeat 5 times (or until the water is clear), and set aside.

2. Heat 4 tablespoons oil in a heavy-base, medium-sized pot over medium heat. Add the fenugreek, mustard, cumin and coriander seeds, and cook for 10 seconds or until the seeds stop crackling (keep a lid handy to avoid losing the seeds which may jump out). Add the curry leaves and onion, and stir-fry for 10 minutes until the onions are translucent. Add the garlic, ginger, chili, turmeric, sugar and salt, and stir-fry for 1 minute longer.

3. Add the red lentils and 6 cups water, and bring to a boil. Reduce heat, cover partially, and simmer over medium heat for 30 minutes or until the lentils are tender. Discard the curry leaves. Mash the lentils with a hand-held mixer (or the back of a large spoon) until you have a diluted lentil puree.

4. Add the diluted rice flour, tomatoes and lime juice and bring back to a boil. Reduce heat, cover partially and simmer over low heat for another 15 minutes.

5. Just before serving, season to taste, pour into a tureen or individual serving dishes and garnish with fresh cilantro.

Mesopotamian Barley, Lentil & Tahini Soup

Servings: 6
Preparation time: 20 minutes
cooking time: 2 hours

- 2 tablespoons vegetable oil, butter or ghee
- 1 large onion, peeled and thinly sliced
- 2 leeks, finely chopped (use both white and green parts)
- 1 bird chili, chopped, or 1/4 teaspoon cayenne
- 2 cloves garlic, crushed and peeled
- 1/2 cup dried chickpeas
- 12 cups vegetable stock or water
- 1 cup barley
- 1/2 cup dried green lentils, picked over
- 3 teaspoons salt
- 1 teaspoon freshly ground black pepper
- 2 large tomatoes, peeled and chopped
- 1/2 teaspoon ground turmeric
- 2 cups chopped fresh Swiss chard
- 1/2 cup chopped fresh dill
- 1/2 cup chopped fresh parsley
- 1/2 cup chopped fresh cilantro
- 1/2 cup sesame paste, sour cream or whey
- 2 tablespoons fresh lime juice

GARNISH
- 1/2 teaspoon freshly ground black pepper
- 2 tablespoons chopped fresh parsley

1. Heat the oil in a large pot over medium heat. Add the onion, leeks, chili and garlic, and stir-fry for 10 minutes.

2. Add the chickpeas and vegetable stock, and bring to a boil. Reduce heat to medium-low, partially cover and simmer for 40 minutes. Add the barley, lentils, salt and pepper and bring back to a boil. Reduce heat to simmer, partially cover and cook for 30 minutes until the barley and lentils are tender, stirring occasionally.

3. Add the tomatoes and herbs, cover and simmer over low heat for 40 minutes longer. Add the sesame paste and lime juice. Using a hand-held mixer, plunge it into the pot and puree some of the ingredients.

4. If the soup is too thick, add some warm water and bring back to a boil. Adjust seasoning to taste, adding salt, pepper or lime juice as needed.

5. Just before serving, pour the soup into a tureen or individual serving bowls. Garnish with black pepper and parsley or a sprig of your favorite herb.

The Poet of Journeys

I have put duality away, I have seen that the two worlds are one;
One I seek, One I know, One I see, One I call

Among the most beloved of Persian poets is Jalal al-Din Rumi, who might almost be called a son of the Silk Road. He was born in a small town near Balkh, in what is now Afghanistan, in 1207. When Mongol tribes threatened the region, his jurist father took the family to Samarkand and then to Damascus, where the young Rumi studied with eminent Arab scholars. Eventually the family settled in what is now central Anatolia in Turkey but was then the small kingdom of Laranda, part of the Seljuk empire. They lived in its capital, Konya.

Laranda's sultan welcomed refugee artists and scholars. Rumi's father was appointed teacher of theology in a Konya seminary and, upon his death, was succeeded by Rumi himself. Then in 1244, Rumi met a Sufi missionary, Shams-e Tabrizi, who changed his life.

Shams was part of a visionary society that arose from Islam in the seventh and eighth centuries. Sufism was (and is) the faith of mystics and Gnostics who loved God for his own sake and strove for union with him. Rumi would become the exemplar of this mystic faith. Loveable in himself, he sought divine love everywhere and explored it in 40,000 lyric verses. It was he who founded the Mevlevi order of Sufis, more widely known, because of their ritual dancing, as the Whirling Dervishes.

Indeed, music and dance permeate Rumi's verse, along with a wealth of allusions from his vast store of classical and religious scholarship and—what endears him to his readers—images from every aspect of daily life. For Rumi, everything—birds, flowers, animals humble and grand, crafts, and especially food and cookery—was a manifestation of divine love. Every living thing strove toward union with it.

Thus one of his most famous anecdotes concerns the lowly chickpea, which one day cries from the pot where it is boiling, "Why are you burning me? Since you bought me and approved of me, why are you turning me upside down?"

The cook replies that he is not boiling the chickpea because he hates it but to temper and soften it so that it may be eaten by humans, mingle with their vital spirit, and rise on the ladder of creation toward God. "You when green and fresh were drinking in the garden," he says. "That water drinking was for the sake of this fire." Everything in creation, including humanity, must be "cooked": It must mature in the fire of experience if it is to approach union with God.

So this ascetic visionary, much given to fasting—Rumi once said, "The best recipe is hunger"—taught his lessons through metaphors of sensual experience. In Rumi's stories, peaches and pomegranates, pickles and cider, salt and sweet, wine and bread, all play major parts as manifestations of the love of God.

And the end of life, in his vision, was "a time of joyful meeting" at last. He bade his friends not weep as he lay dying in the autumn of 1273:

> *If wheat springs from my dust when I am dead*
> *And from the grain that grows there you bake bread,*
> *What drunkenness will rise and overthrow*
> *With frenzied love the baker and his dough—*
> *It is a tipsy song his ovens sing!*

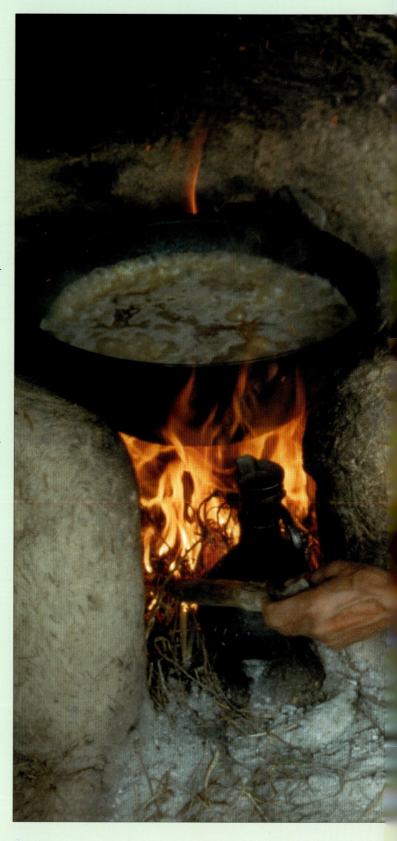

A Rumi Tale of Sufi Hospitality

In which we learn that he who imitates is lost

A Sufi traveler broke a long journey at a monastery; he took his ass to the stable, fed and watered it, and joined the Sufis and other travelers in the house.

The Sufis in the monastery were poor and hungry, but felt obliged by the laws of hospitality to entertain the traveler. Without a word to him, they sold his ass to buy all kinds of food and drink, and in the evening threw a big party to honor him, feed themselves, and drown their sorrows.

The traveler, all unknowing, was delighted with the banquet and with the riotous dancing and clapping that followed. He soon joined the ring of the sama—a Sufi dance—stamping his feet and clapping with the best of them. When the singing began, he shouted happily along with the rhythmic refrain: "The ass is gone, the ass is gone, the ass is gone."

In the cold light of morning, when the revelers had said their goodbyes and gone on their way, the traveler went to the stable to retrieve his mount. The ass was not there. He assumed the stable boy had taken it to a spring for water and sat down to wait.

The stable boy returned, but without the beast.

"Where is my ass?" said the traveler.

"What ass?"

"The same ass I left with you last night."

The stable boy gave the traveler a knowing look. "Honest to God," he said. "I came to tell you that your hosts had sold your ass, but you were singing, 'The ass is gone' with more gusto than anyone else. So I thought, 'It's your doing. Why should I be responsible?'"

And all the traveler could reply was, "A thousand curses on imitation!"

Kurdish Bulgur & Yogurt Soup (Tarkhineh)

Tarkhineh (also called tarkhanah and kishk) was a perfect cereal combination for nomads and travelers along the Silk Road. It is made by mixing bulgur with yogurt or milk and allowing it to ferment. It is then salted, sun dried and formed into sheets or pellets. These can then be crumbled in water to make soups, eaten on their own, or eaten with honey or jam as a breakfast cereal. There are also many variations flavored with aromatic herbs and spices. Tarkhineh is possibly a Parthian invention and has traveled throughout the Silk Road as far as Hungary in the West and Mongolia in the East.

Servings: 4
Preparation time: 15 minutes
Cooking time: 1 hour

- 4 tablespoons butter, vegetable oil or ghee
- 3 medium onions, peeled and sliced
- 1 clove garlic, crushed and peeled
- 1 teaspoon fennel seeds or 1/2 cup fresh fennel, chopped
- 2 teaspoons salt
- 1 teaspoon fresh ground pepper
- 1 Thai bird or serrano chili, seeded and chopped, or 1/4 teaspoon cayenne
- 4 cups vegetable stock* or water
- 1 cup tarkhineh* or homemade tarkhineh (see directions below)
- 1 cup chopped fresh cilantro
- 1/2 cup fresh dill or 2 tablespoons dried dill
- 1 tablespoon dried mint
- 1/2 teaspoon dried thyme
- 1/2 cup yogurt, beaten for 5 minutes with 1 teaspoon cornstarch

1. Heat the oil in a medium pot over medium heat. Add the onions and fry for 15 minutes, stirring occasionally, until golden brown.

2. Add the garlic and fennel seeds, and stir-fry for 1 minute. Add the salt, pepper, chili and stock, and bring to a boil.

3. Add the tarkhineh, bring back to a boil, reduce heat, partially cover, and simmer over medium-low heat for 30 minutes, stirring occasionally, until the tarkhineh is soft. Add the cilantro, dill, mint, and thyme and bring back to a boil. Reduce heat to low and simmer for another 5 minutes.

4. Just before serving, remove from heat and gradually add the yogurt, stirring constantly for 5 minutes with a wooden spoon to prevent curdling. Transfer to a tureen or individual dishes just before serving.

HOMEMADE TARKHINEH

Ready-made tarkhineh can be found in Afghan and Middle Eastern groceries, but you can also make it at home. Place 1 cup warm water in a mixing bowl and sprinkle with 1 tablespoon yeast. Allow to stand for 10 minutes, undisturbed. Gradually add 1 cup all-purpose unbleached flour, sifted with 1/2 teaspoon salt, 2 cups bulgur, and 1 cup yogurt, and stir well until you have a sticky dough. Transfer to a bowl. Cover and allow to ferment, at room temperature, for 8 hours (traditionally this was made without yeast and was left for a week or so to ferment). Add more flour if the dough is too sticky. Form the dough into hazel-nut-sized balls and place on a baking sheet lined with parchment paper. Dry in the sun or overnight in a 140°F convection oven. Keep in plastic wrap and use as needed.

Oxus Tamarind & Coconut Soup

Servings: 4
Preparation time: 20 minutes
Cooking time: 1 hour 10 minutes

- 4 tablespoons vegetable oil, butter or ghee
- 2 teaspoons black mustard seeds
- 1 teaspoon fenugreek seeds
- 1 onion, peeled and thinly sliced
- 8 curry leaves*
- 1 tablespoon curry powder
- 2 teaspoons sambar masala*
- 2 hot green chilies, seeded and chopped
- 1 pound kohlrabi or butternut squash, peeled and diced (into 1-inch cubes)
- 1 cup red lentils (dal masoor)
- 6 cups vegetable stock* or water
- 2 tablespoons salt
- 1/2 teaspoon freshly ground black pepper
- 2 cups coconut milk, light cream or soybean milk*
- 1/2 cup rice flour, diluted in 2 cups water
- 2 tablespoons tamarind paste
- 2 tablespoons sugar
- 2 cups chopped fresh cilantro

The Oxus is the ancient Western name for the river Amu Darya (called Jayhun by the Arabs), one of the longest rivers in central Asia, running sixteen hundred miles from the Panj River in the Pamirs to the Aral Sea. In its upper course it borders Afghanistan, Tajikistan, Uzbekistan and Turkmenistan.

1. Heat the oil in a heavy base, medium-sized, pot over medium heat until very hot. Add the mustard seeds and fenugreek seeds, and cook for 10 seconds until aromatic or the seeds stop crackling (keep a lid handy to stop seeds from flying out). Add the onion and stir-fry for 5 minutes. Add the curry leaves, curry powder, masala, chili, kohlrabi, and red lentils, and stir-fry for another minute. Add 6 cups stock, salt and pepper, and bring to a boil. Cover and simmer for 40 minutes until the kohlrabi is tender. Add more stock if necessary. Remove the curry leaves.

2. Use a hand-held mixer and partially puree the soup. Add the coconut milk, rice flour, tamarind and sugar and stir gently. Bring back to a boil. Reduce heat, cover, and simmer over low heat for 15 minutes, stirring occasionally.

3. Adjust seasoning to taste. Just before serving, add the cilantro and serve in a tureen or individual bowls.

Soups / 116

Eggs

Simply Silk Road Eggs

> **SILK ROAD YOGURT SAUCE**
> *This is a favorite sauce for fried eggs along the Silk Road region.*
>
> *1. In a bowl, mix one cup plain yogurt with 1/2 teaspoon salt, 1/2 teaspoon fresh ground pepper, 1/2 teaspoon paprika and 1/2 teaspoon ground cumin. Spoon over the hot fried eggs. Serve with flat bread.*

People who don't cook sometimes say, "I can cook an egg and that's about it." Actually, to cook a perfect egg takes some practice. The following are a few techniques I have found to be helpful, but to get it just right for your taste, you will have to experiment.

Boiled Eggs

1. Place the eggs in a heavy-bottom, medium-sized saucepan, cover with cold water and bring to a boil over medium heat.

2. Turn off heat.

3. Cover and let stand 3 minutes for soft boiled eggs, 4 minutes for medium boiled eggs and 7 minutes for hard boiled eggs (these times are for sea level; in the mountains the times need to be considerably increased depending on the altitude).

4. Plunge into cold water to stop the eggs from cooking any further.

5. Peel and serve with salt and pepper, your favorite bread, and butter.

Poached Eggs

1. Fill a deep skillet with 3 cups water. Add a drop of vinegar and a pinch of salt and bring to a boil over medium heat.

2. Carefully break each egg, into a bowl (one egg at a time) and slip into the boiling water. Cover and cook for 1 minute, then uncover and cook for 5 minutes or until the eggs turn opaque and are set. Sprinkle with salt and pepper to taste.

3. Remove each egg with a slotted spatula (shake gently to ensure all the water drips off) and serve on top of your favorite toasted bread, rice or pasta.

Fried Eggs

1. Choose an 8-inch skillet pan for 2 eggs.

2. Heat the skillet over medium-low and add 2 tablespoons butter, ghee or oil. When the butter starts to sizzle, it is hot enough.

3. Gently break each egg (one at a time) into the skillet.

4. Cook the eggs for about 1 minute until the whites begin to set. Then cover and cook over medium-low heat for about 4 minutes to have a gentle whites and creamy yolks.

5. Serve with the Silk Road yogurt sauce and flat bread.

Persian Omelet with Saffron & Rose water

The word omelet comes from sixteenth-century France, but omelets were around long before then. One of the earliest references to what might be considered an omelet was first mentioned in a tenth-century Arab cookbook: This was the Persian kuku. From it descended the Arab eggah, the Italian frittata and the Spanish tortilla (which unlike the Mexican pancake also known as a tortilla, is an omelet).

There are two kinds of omelets: open and rolled. For an open omelet, the vegetables and other fillings are cooked first, then with beaten eggs, and the whole allowed to cook. For rolled omelet, the filling is cooked and set aside. The eggs are cooked until they begin to set, then the filling is added, the omelet rolled around it and allowed to cook a little more until golden brown. You can prepare the filling up to a day in advance.

1. To make the batter, break the eggs in a mixing bowl. Add the milk, salt, saffron water and rose water, and whisk for 20 seconds (about 20 strokes).

2. To make individual omelets, heat the oil in an 8-inch nonstick omelet pan over medium heat until very hot. Pour a thin layer of egg mixture (about 2 tablespoons) into pan, and lift and tilt the pan to evenly coat it with the egg. Once it has set, sprinkle on a few rose petals and a little confectioners' sugar.

3. Tilt the pan and roll the omelet out onto a platter. Continue until you have made all 4 omelets. Serve hot with flat bread and fresh basil.

Servings: 4 individual omelets
Preparation time: 15 minutes
Cooking time: 20 minutes

EGG MIXTURE
- 4 eggs
- 2 tablespoons milk
- 1/8 teaspoon salt
- 1/8 teaspoon ground saffron dissolved in 1 tablespoon hot water
- 1 teaspoon cooking rose water
- 4 teaspoons vegetable oil, butter or ghee

FILLING
- A few fresh or dried organic rose petals
- 1/2 cup confectioners' sugar

GARNISH
- 1/2 cup fresh basil leaves

- 2 loaves of flat bread, sliced Italian bread, or tortillas, toasted

Saffron

Long treasured as a medicine, perfume, dye, and seasoning, saffron consists of the golden stigmas of the autumn-flowering purple crocus, *Crocus sativus*. It takes the stigmas of 75,000 blossoms—an acre of flowers—to make one pound of the spice. These must be picked from the crocus by hand, making saffron, currently selling for about $55 an ounce, the most expensive spice in the world.

The beautiful little saffron crocus is native to western Asia and Iran: The name comes from the Persian *safra*, meaning "yellow." It has been cultivated throughout the region since ancient times. The Persians' Sumerian predecessors, from the third millennium BCE, called saffron "the perfume of the gods"; in fact, there exists a Sumerian recipe for beer, intended no doubt for the most exalted of drinkers, that includes toasted pomegranate seeds, myrtle, oak, sumac, cumin and, most importantly, saffron.

Like the Sumerians before them, the Persians valued the spice as a medicine. It still is made into a tea that is said to suppress coughs and induce sleep; on the other hand, saffron may be used as an antidepressant, and too much is said to induce madness. As crocus cultivation spread north and east into the Mediterranean and India, so did medicinal claims for the spice. It was, it seems, almost a universal panacea. Thus the medieval physicians of Salerno, who created the medical regimen named after that city, wrote:

> *Saffron arouses joy in every breast,*
> *Settles the stomach, gives the liver rest.*

In the classical world and later, saffron was considered an aphrodisiac, which is perhaps why it was used to perfume Greek halls and baths, not to mention the villas of the famous courtesans known as hetaerae. It was also said to have been sprinkled on the streets of Rome to welcome Emperor Nero in the first century—less as an aphrodisiac, perhaps, than as an extravagant compliment to that most extravagant of rulers.

This rare spice's reputation followed it as cultivation spread along the trade routes into Kashmir and farther east. Golden yellow became a royal color—and a sacred one. Shortly after the Buddha died in the fifth century BCE, his priests chose saffron dye to color their robes. (The distinctive golden color remains, although the dye is now usually made from cheaper turmeric.) Perhaps in token of its erotic associations, saffron was also used to dye the veils of brides in ancient Tyre as well as the breasts and arms of newly married Indian women.

All of these virtues aside, saffron remains a wonderful seasoning and coloring for food, especially grain. This is a fact long appreciated in the traditions of countries along the routes of the old Silk Road and beyond, for the cultivation of saffron spread not only to India but also to Italy, Spain, France and even England. As you will see in this book, the spice enhances the rice dishes of Iran, Uzbekistan, and Afghanistan; it is essential for the paellas of Spain and the couscouses of Morocco. And fortunately for the modern cook's pocketbook, only the tiniest amount will produce a remarkable fragrance, flavor and color.

Opposite: A woman picks the stigmas of the saffron crocus (in a bunch below) to make the spice that is worth more than its weight in gold.

This page: A young worker near Srinagar, India, displays her harvest (below). The stigmas from her crocuses should be ground with sugar (below top left) and diluted with water (below, bottom left) for the finest flavor.

Silk Road Onion & Tomato Omelet

I am calling this a Silk Road omelet because it is popular throughout much of the region from Uzbekistan and Iran to Turkey and Spain. Even though tomatoes are a New World food, they have been adopted by these countries as their own.

Servings: 4 individual omelets
Preparation time: 15 minutes
Cooking time: 20 minutes

4 eggs
2 tablespoons milk
1/8 teaspoon salt
4 teaspoons vegetable oil, butter or ghee

FILLING
2 tablespoons vegetable oil, butter or ghee
1 small onion, peeled and sliced
1/4 fresh bell pepper, seeded and chopped
2 cloves garlic, peeled and crushed
2 medium tomatoes, peeled and sliced
1/2 teaspoon salt
1 teaspoon freshly ground black pepper
1/4 cup chopped fresh basil or parsley
fresh basil leaves for garnish

1. To make the batter, break the eggs in a mixing bowl. Add the milk, and salt, and whisk for 20 seconds (about 20 strokes).

2. To make the filling, heat 2 tablespoon oil in a medium skillet over medium heat and stir-fry the onion and bell pepper for 5 minutes or until they become translucent. Add the garlic and stir-fry for 1 minute longer.

3. Add the tomatoes, salt, pepper and basil, and stir-fry for another minute. Remove from heat and set aside.

4. To make an individual omelet, heat 1 teaspoon oil in a small non-stick 8-inch omelet pan or a flat skillet over medium heat until very hot. Pour a thin layer of the egg mixture into the pan (about 2 tablespoons). Lift and tilt the pan, and then jerk it toward you with a wrist motion so that the whole pan is coated with the batter. Once the egg has set, place 2 tablespoons of filling in the center. Tilt the pan and roll the omelet out onto a platter. Continue until you have made all the omelets. Serve hot with lavash bread and garnish with fresh basil.

Bokhara Pancake

BOKHARA PANCAKE

Servings: 4
Preparation time: 10 minutes, plus 2 hours refrigeration
Cooking time: 5 minutes

1 cup unbleached all-purpose flour
1/2 teaspoon salt
4 eggs
3/4 cup milk
2/3 cup cold water
2 tablespoons unsalted butter

GARNISH
2 tablespoons confectioners' sugar
1 tablespoon rose water
2 tablespoons fresh lime juice

1. Mix the flour and salt, and set aside.

2. In a mixing bowl, beat the eggs while gradually adding the milk, water and butter. Slowly add the flour while beating continually and rapidly. Once all the flour has been added, beat for another minute.

3. Strain the mixture through a sieve, cover and refrigerate for 2 hours.

4. Paint a non stick skillet or crêpe pan with oil over medium heat. When it starts to smoke, remove the skillet from the heat.

5. Whisk the batter before pouring and then pour about 1/4 cup onto the skillet.

6. Tilt the skillet until the batter entirely coats the bottom. Put the skillet back over the heat and with a rubber spatula loosen the edges. Flip over and cook the second side until it is a light golden brown. Transfer to a plate and repeat. Sprinkle with confectioners' sugar, a drop of rose water and lime juice.

Eggs

Solomon's Apple Omelet

*As an apple tree among the trees of the wood,
so is my beloved among young men.
With great delight I sat in his shadow,
and his fruit was sweet to my taste.
He brought me to the banqueting house,
and his intention toward me was love.
Sustain me with raisins,
refresh me with apples;
or I am faint with love.*
—*Song of Solomon*

1. Heat the oil in a large skillet over medium heat, and stir-fry the apples and lime juice for 2 minutes. Add the cinnamon and cayenne, cover, and cook for 5 to10 minutes over medium heat until the apples are tender.

2. Spread out the apple mixture in the skillet evenly and continue to cook until the juices have evaporated. Reduce heat. Add the egg mixture, cover and cook over low heat for 3 to 5 minutes or until the eggs have set.

3. Transfer to a serving platter and serve immediately with bread, rice, couscous or pasta according to your fancy.

Sumerian Quince Omelet

The "apple" in the biblical song above was probably a quince, hence this recipe. Some believe that the song comes from an ancient Sumerian marriage ceremony.

1. Heat the oil in a large skillet over medium heat, add the quince, lime juice and onion and cook for 10 to 15 minutes, stirring occasionally, until the quince is tender. Add the carrot, raisins, dates, almonds and pistachios, and stir-fry for 1 minute.

2. Spread out the quince mixture in the skillet evenly and continue to cook until the juices have evaporated. Reduce heat. Add the egg mixture, cover and cook over low heat for 3 to 5 minutes or until the eggs have set.

3. Transfer to a serving platter and serve immediately with bread, rice, couscous or pasta according to your fancy.

Servings: 4
Preparation time: 15 minutes
Cooking time: 20 minutes

- 2 tablespoons vegetable oil, butter or ghee
- 3 medium-sized apples (1 pound), cored, peeled and sliced
- 1 tablespoon fresh lime juice
- 1/8 teaspoon cinnamon
- 1/8 teaspoon cayenne
- 4 eggs lightly beaten with 1/2 teaspoon salt and 1/2 teaspoon freshly ground black pepper

SUMERIAN QUINCE OMELET

Servings: 4
Preparation time: 15 minutes
Cooking time: 20 minutes

- 2 tablespoons vegetable oil, butter or ghee
- 2 small quinces (1 pound), cored and thinly sliced
- 1 tablespoon fresh lime juice
- 1 small onion, peeled and thinly sliced
- 1 carrot, peeled and grated
- 1/4 cup raisins
- 4 dates, pitted
- 1 tablespoon blanched almonds
- 1 tablespoon unsalted pistachios, shelled and chopped
- 4 eggs lightly beaten with 1/2 teaspoon salt and 1/2 teaspoon freshly ground black pepper

Sicilian Eggplant with Saffron Soufflé

Makes 4 soufflés
Preparation time: 35 minutes
Cooking time: 55 minutes

- 2 tablespoons olive oil
- 2 Chinese eggplants, about 1 pounds, peeled and cut into 1/2-inch cubes*
- 1 large onion, peeled and thinly sliced
- 2 cloves garlic, peeled and crushed
- 1 large tomato, peeled and chopped
- 2 tablespoons chopped parsley
- 2 tablespoons fresh chopped basil
- 1/4 teaspoon ground saffron, dissolved in 1 tablespoon hot water
- 1 teaspoon salt
- 1 teaspoon freshly ground black pepper
- 1 tablespoon lime juice
- 4 soufflé dishes, 8 ounces each
- 1/2 cup grated Parmesan or cheddar cheese
- 2 tablespoons unsalted butter
- 2 tablespoons all-purpose flour
- 1 cup warm milk (do not boil)
- 3 large egg yolks
- 6 large egg whites

NOTE
This soufflé can also be made in a 9-inch-diameter ceramic soufflé dish using the same recipe. It can also be cooked using 2 cups of chopped vegetables such as carrots, cauliflower, spinach, zucchini or mushrooms.

1. Heat 2 tablespoons oil in a large skillet, add the eggplant and onion, and stir-fry for 10 minutes. Add the garlic and tomato, and stir-fry for 5 minutes longer. Add parsley, basil, saffron water, salt, pepper and lime juice. Remove from heat and transfer to a large mixing bowl. Set aside.

2. Preheat oven to 400°F. Generously butter 4 8-ounce soufflé dishes, sprinkle the bread crumbs into the dishes and shake to coat all sides. Shake out any excess bread crumbs.

3. Melt the butter in a medium-sized saucepan over medium heat. When the butter is foamy, whisk in the flour and stir for 1 minute. Remove from heat and add 3 tablespoons warm milk, and whisk vigorously until all the milk has been absorbed by the flour. Replace over low heat and gradually add the remaining milk. Mix for 5 to 10 minutes until the mixture has thickened. Remove from heat.

4. Add the sauce to the eggplant, stir in the Parmesan cheese and beat in the egg yolks, one at a time. Stir for about 3 minutes until the mixture is smooth.

5. Whip the egg white until stiff but not dry. Fold the egg white gently and gradually through the eggplant mixture using a rubber spatula.

6. Pour the mixture into the prepared soufflé dishes until 2/3 full. Place the soufflé dishes in a warm baking dish. Bake for 25 to 35 minutes in the preheated oven until the soufflé has puffed up, is golden brown and a tester comes out clean. Remove from the oven, and serve at once with bread and salad.

Eggs / 126

Delhi Curried Potato & Egg Patties

1. In a saucepan, cover the potatoes with water and cook over medium heat for 30 minutes. Peel and mash them in a food processor.

2. Add the remaining ingredients (except the oil) to the food processor and pulse until you have a thick batter (do not over mix the batter). Cover and refrigerate for 30 minutes.

3. Heat 1/2 cup oil in a large flat skillet over medium heat until the oil begins to smoke. Scoop up 1/4 cup of batter, roll in flour, flatten slightly into a patty and fry in the hot oil for about 3 minutes on each side or until golden brown. Remove and drain on a paper towel. Repeat until you have used all the batter.

4. Serve the patties on a serving platter with bread, yogurt and fresh herbs, or sprinkle with confectioners' sugar.

Makes: 8 patties
Preparation time: 45 minutes
Cooking time: 35 minutes plus 30 minutes refrigeration

- 2 large potatoes (about 1 pound)
- 4 eggs
- 2 cloves of garlic, peeled and crushed
- 1 teaspoon salt
- 1/4 teaspoon freshly ground black pepper
- 1 teaspoon curry powder or 1/4 teaspoon saffron, dissolved in 1 tablespoon hot water
- 1/2 teaspoon baking soda
- 1/4 cup chopped fresh flat-leaf parsley
- 1/2 cup vegetable oil, butter or ghee for frying

VARIATIONS

BUTTERNUT SQUASH PATTIES
Substitute butternut squash for the potatoes. In step 1, peel the butternut squash first, chop, parboil for 1 minute, then proceed as indicated in the remaining steps.

LEEK & WALNUT PATTIES
Substitute 2 large, fresh, finely chopped leeks and 1/2 cup ground walnuts for the potatoes in step 1 and stir-fry for 5 minutes before combining with other ingredients.

Persian Cauliflower Kuku

Servings: 6
Preparation time: 5 minutes
Cooking time: 25 minutes

- 6 eggs
- 1/2 teaspoon baking powder
- 1 tablespoon flour or bread crumbs
- 1/2 cup milk or soy milk
- 1/2 cup Parmesan cheese, grated, or fresh mozzarella, shredded
- 1/4 cup vegetable oil, butter or ghee
- 1 small red onion, peeled and thinly sliced
- 2 cloves garlic, peeled and crushed
- 1 small head cauliflower or 1 pound frozen florets, coarsely chopped
- 2 teaspoons salt
- 1/2 teaspoon freshly ground black pepper
- 1 teaspoon ground cumin
- 1/4 teaspoon ground paprika
- 1/4 teaspoon turmeric
- 1 green bird chili, chopped, or 1/8 teaspoon cayenne
- 1/4 cup chopped fresh parsley or basil

NOTE

You may replace the cauliflower with a combination of 1 pound mushrooms and 1 pound spinach. Or use 1 pound leeks (thinly sliced, white part only), asparagus, zucchini, or eggplant.

Because the cauliflower was called chou de Chypre *(Cyprus cabbage) in French, some have thought it came from Cyprus. It is more likely, however, that it came from India or southern Iran and was introduced into Europe by the Arabs.*

1. Break the eggs into a mixing bowl, add the baking powder, flour, milk and cheese, and whisk lightly.

2. Heat the oil in a medium-sized nonstick skillet over low heat. Add the onion and stir-fry for 5 minutes until translucent. Add the garlic, cauliflower, salt, pepper, cumin, paprika, turmeric, chili and parsley, and stir-fry for 5 to 10 minutes until the cauliflower is soft.

3. Pour the egg mixture over the cauliflower in the skillet. Cook over low heat for 6 to 10 minutes until set.

4. Place the skillet under a preheated broiler for 1 minute to brown the top.

5. Serve warm or cold with yogurt and flat bread. Garnish with herbs.

VARIATION

The above is the simplest and most earthy way to make a kuku.

You can, however, if you have the time or the inclination, cook it in the oven using four 6-inch oiled muffin pans or one 9-inch baking dish. Mix all the ingredients in a mixing bowl and pour into the muffin pans or baking dish. Bake in a 400°F preheated oven for 45 minutes. Remove from the oven. Allow to cool for 10 minutes. To unmold the kuku from the muffin pans, loosen the edges with a rubber spatula, cover the pan with a baking sheet and, holding the baking sheet and muffin pan together, turn them upside down. The kuku muffins should fall onto the baking sheet.

Caspian Fresh Herb Kuku Rolled in Lavash Bread

Makes 50 bite-sized rolls
Preparation time: 20 minutes
Cooking time: 40 minutes

12 eggs
1 teaspoon baking powder
2 teaspoons advieh* (Persian spice mix)*
2 teaspoons salt
1 teaspoon freshly ground black pepper
4 cloves garlic, peeled and crushed
2 cups finely chopped fresh garlic chives or scallions
2 cups finely chopped fresh parsley
2 cups finely chopped fresh, coriander leaves
2 cups chopped fresh dill
1 tablespoon dried fenugreek leaves
2 teaspoons dried barberries (optional)
2 tablespoons all-purpose flour
1/2 cup olive oil for baking
Parchment or baking paper
3 lavash bread rolls cut into 2-by-3-inch strips (store the bread in plastic bags to keep it soft for wrapping)
50 long strands of chives, soaked in warm water, drained and patted dry to make more flexible.

DIP
2 cups labneh* or plain yogurt
2 cloves garlic, crushed and peeled
1 teaspoon dried mint
1/2 teaspoon salt
1/2 teaspoon freshly ground pepper
1 teaspoon dried organic rose petals

This fresh herb kuku is traditionally Iranian but popular from Erzurum in Turkey to Samarkand in Uzbekistan. In Iran it is eaten on New Year's Day (the festival of Nowruz, at the spring equinox): The green of the herbs symbolizes rebirth, while the eggs represent fertility and happiness for the year to come. Here, I have cut the kuku and rolled individual pieces in lavash bread tied with a long strand of chive to make it a finger food. You can, however, serve it as you please.

1. Preheat oven to 400°F.

2. Break the eggs into a large bowl. Add the baking powder, advieh, salt, and pepper. Lightly beat with a fork. Add the garlic, chopped herbs, fenugreek, barberries (optional) and flour. Mix thoroughly but do not over mix.

3. Oil a baking sheet and line it with baking paper. Oil the baking paper with 1/2 cup oil. Pour in the egg mixture and bake uncovered for 30 to 40 minutes.

4. Remove the baking sheet from the oven, allow to cool and cut the kuku into 2-by-3-inch strips. Place each kuku strip on a lavash strip and roll it up. Tie up each roll with a long strand of chive.

5. To make the dip, combine all the ingredients in a small bowl.

6. Arrange the rolls on a serving platter and serve with the dip on the side.

Alexandrian Chickpea Patties (Falafel, Tameya)

Servings: 4
Preparation time: 10 minutes plus 30 minutes refrigeration
Cooking time: 30 minutes

- 2 cups canned chickpeas, drained and rinsed
- 1 cup roasted chickpea flour
- 1 clove garlic, peeled
- 1 tablespoon tahini paste
- 1/2 teaspoon baking soda
- 1 teaspoon salt
- 1/4 teaspoon freshly ground black pepper
- 1/2 teaspoon chili paste or cayenne
- 1/2 teaspoon sugar
- 1/2 teaspoon turmeric
- 1/2 teaspoon ground coriander
- 1 teaspoon ground cumin
- 2 eggs, lightly beaten
- 1/3 cup chopped fresh dill or cilantro
- 2 cups oil for frying
- 1/2 cup sesame seeds

GARNISH
- Parsley, basil and mint sprigs
- Yogurt
- Pita bread

NOTE
If using dried chickpeas (use 1 cup) or fava beans (use 2 cups), place them in a medium saucepan, cover with water and bring to a boil. Reduce heat, cover partially and simmer over medium heat for 1 1/2 hours. Drain and set aside. Or you can soak them overnight, drain, rinse and set aside.

The ancient Egyptians cultivated fava beans, but according to the Greek historian Herodotus, their priests considered them to be unclean and would not even look at them, let alone eat them. The Chinese referred to fava beans as Iranian beans. Today, falafel made with fava beans is considered an Egyptian national dish. In Iran, and Syria, falafel is made using chickpeas; but in Lebanon it is also made with equal portions of dried fava beans and chickpeas.

1. In a food processor, combine the chickpeas, chickpea flour, garlic, tahini paste, baking soda, salt, pepper, chili paste, sugar, turmeric, coriander, cumin, eggs and dill, and pulse until you have a soft dough (do not over mix).

2. Cover and refrigerate for at least 30 minutes or up to 24 hours.

3. In a deep skillet, heat 2 cups oil over medium heat until very hot.

4. Remove the dough from the refrigerator, and if the dough is too sticky to handle, add more chickpea flour. Spread the sesame seeds on a plate. Place a bowl of warm water next to your cooking pan. Repeatedly dampening your hands, separate the dough into lumps the size of walnuts. Flatten each lump between your palms into an oval shape and roll in the sesame seeds. Fry the patties for about 3 minutes on each side, until golden brown, adding more oil if necessary. There should be enough oil so that the patties are completely immersed in it. When done, remove the patties using a slotted spoon and drain on paper towels.

5. Arrange the patties on a platter, garnish with parsley, basil and mint sprigs, and serve with warm pita bread and yogurt.

VARIATION

Fava Bean Patties (Falafel)

In step 1, replace the chickpeas and the chickpea flour with 2 cups dried (second skin removed), cooked or soaked fava beans.* For fresh fava beans, use 4 cups with the second skin removed.

Eggs / 132

Rice

Gilani Smothered Rice (Kateh) Master Recipe

Servings: 4
Preparation time: 5 minutes
Cooking time: 35 minutes

- 2 cups long-grain white basmati rice (Indian)
- 3 1/2 cups cold water
- 2 teaspoons salt
- 2 tablespoons vegetable oil, butter or ghee

NOTE

You can use any kind of pot to make this rice, though with non-stick pots the rice will not stick to the bottom.

If using American long-grain rice, wash the rice once only and use only 2 cups of water in step 3.

For brown rice, use 4 cups water and cook for 40 minutes.

For wild rice, use 4 cups water and cook for 1 hour.

Most rice in Iran is grown in the Gilan region, near the shores of the Caspian Sea. This recipe is the favored method of cooking rice in Gilan, where rice is a part of the meal at breakfast, lunch and dinner.

1. Pick over the rice carefully to remove its many small solid particles of grit.

2. Wash the rice by placing it in a large container and covering it with lukewarm water. Agitate gently with your hand, then pour off the water. Repeat five times until the rice is completely clean.

3. In a medium nonstick pot, combine the rice, water, salt and oil. Bring to a boil over high heat. Gently stir twice with a wooden spoon to loosen any grains that stick to the bottom. Reduce heat to medium, cover firmly with the lid to prevent steam from escaping and cook for 30 minutes. Remove from heat and allow to cool for 5 minutes on a damp surface without uncovering pot.

4. Transfer to a serving platter and serve hot with a topping of your choice.

VARIATION

Damascus Sweet Rice

In step 3 add 3 tablespoons cooking rose water, 4 cardamom pods, 1 cup pitted medjool dates, 1/2 cup raisins, 1/2 cup blanched almonds, and 1/2 teaspoon ground saffron that is dissolved in 2 tablespoons hot water.

Punjabi Pilaf

In step 3 add 1 teaspoon toasted cumin seeds, one 3-inch cinnamon stick, 2 bay leaves, 2 black cardamom pods and 2 whole cloves.

Persian Rice (Dami) Rice Cooker Method

Servings: 4
Preparation time: 10 minutes
Cooking time: 1 1/4 hours

3 cups long-grain white basmati rice
4 cups cold water
1 tablespoon salt
1/2 cup vegetable oil, butter or ghee
1/4 teaspoon ground saffron threads, dissolved in 1 tablespoon hot water (optional)

1. Pick over and wash the rice per the Gilani Smothered Rice master recipe on page 136.

2. In the rice cooker, combine the rice, water, salt and oil. Gently stir with a wooden spoon until the salt has dissolved. Start the rice cooker.

3. The rice will be ready after 30 minutes; however, if you want a golden crust, leave it to cook for another 45 minutes.

4. Pour saffron water over the rice. Unplug the rice cooker.

5. Keep the cooker covered and allow the rice to cool for 5 minutes.

Variation

Steamed Brown Basmati Polow
(Rice Cooker Method)

For 3 cups brown basmati rice, use 6 cups water in step 2. The amount of salt, oil and saffron water remain the same. Increase the cooking time from 30 minutes to 40 minutes.

NOTE
If using American long-grain rice, wash the rice once only and use only 3 cups of water in step 2.

Persian Saffron Rice with Golden Crust (Chelow)

Servings: 4
Preparation time: 5 minutes
Cooking time: 1 hour 10 minutes

- 3 cups long-grain white basmati rice
- 8 cups cold water
- 2 tablespoons salt
- 1 cup vegetable oil, butter or ghee
- 1 cup whole milk or plain yougurt
- 1/2 teaspoon ground saffron threads, dissolved in 2 tablespoons hot water
- 2 eggs (optional), beaten

REHEATING RICE

Place the rice in a saucepan with 1/2 cup water and cook over low heat for 15 to 20 minutes.

NOTE

You can use any kind of pot to make this rice, but nonstick pots make unmolding the rice much easier.

If using American long-grain rice, wash the rice once only.

1. Pick over and wash the rice per the Gilani Smothered Rice master recipe on page 136.

2. In a large nonstick pot, bring 8 cups water and 2 tablespoons salt to a boil. Add the rice to the pot and boil briskly for 6 to 10 minutes, gently stirring twice with a wooden spoon to loosen any grains that stick to the bottom. Once the rice rises to the top of the pot, it is done.

3. Drain the rice in a large, fine-mesh strainer and rinse with 3 cups lukewarm water.

4. In a bowl, whisk together 3/4 cup oil, the milk, 1 tablespoon saffron water, eggs and 2 spatulas full of the rice. Spread this mixture over the bottom of the rice pot. This will form the golden crust, or tah dig.

5. One spatula full at a time, gently mound the remaining rice onto the tah dig layer. Shape it into a pyramid to leave room for the rice to expand.

6. Cover the pot and cook the rice for 10 minutes over medium-high heat.

7. Mix 1/2 cup cold water with 4 tablespoons oil and pour over rice. Sprinkle on the remaining saffron water. Place a clean dishtowel or 2 layers of paper towel over the pot to absorb condensation and cover with the lid to prevent steam from escaping. Reduce the heat to low and cook 50 minutes longer.

8. Remove the pot from the heat and cool it, still covered, on a damp surface for 5 minutes to loosen the crust.

9. There are two ways to serve the rice. The first is to hold the serving platter tightly over the uncovered pot and invert the two together, unmolding the entire mound onto the platter. The rice will emerge as a golden-crusted cake, to be garnished with edible flowers and herbs, then served in wedges. The second serving style is to spoon the rice into a pyramid on the serving platter, taking care not to disturb the bottom crust as you do so. After the pyramid is shaped, detach the crust with a wooden spatula and arrange it in pieces around the pyramid or serve it on a small side platter.

Rice Crust Variations

Rice with Potato Crust

Replace step 4 in the golden crust rice recipe on the left with step 4a below.

4a. In a bowl, whisk together oil, water, 1 tablespoon saffron water, salt, pepper and 1 cup parboiled rice, and spread this mixture over the bottom of a heavy-base, nonstick pot. Arrange the potatoes, close together, in one layer over the mixture. Continue with step 5 of the main recipe above.

Rice with Eggplant & Garlic Crust

You may substitute 3 Chinese eggplants cut into 1/2-inch-thick and 4-inch-long slices and 6 cloves of garlic, peeled and thinly sliced, for the potatoes in step 4a above.

Rice with Lettuce Crust

Substitute 4 layers of washed Boston lettuce fitted into the bottom of the pot for the potatoes in step 4a above.

Rice with Bread Crust

Replace step 4a. above with the following:

In a bowl, whisk together oil, water, 1 tablespoon saffron water, salt, pepper and spread over the bottom of the pot. Place lavash bread, cut to fit the bottom and sides of the pot over the mixture. Continue with step 5.

RICE WITH POTATO CRUST

- 1 cup vegetable oil, butter or ghee
- 2 tablespoons water
- 1 tablespoon saffron water (from the main ingredients)
- 1/4 teaspoon salt
- 1/4 teaspoon freshly ground black pepper
- 1 cup parboiled rice (from step 2)
- 2 large potatoes, peeled and thinly sliced (1/8 inch)

Vietnamese Sticky Rice

Servings: 4
Preparation time: 10 minutes plus 8 hours to soak rice
Cooking time: 45 minutes

- 2 cups long-grain Thai sticky rice (long-grain, sweet glutinous rice)
- 2 tablespoons toasted sesame seeds or poppy seeds
- 2 tablespoons rice vinegar or fresh lime juice

NOTE

This rice can also be cooked in a rice cooker. Combine soaked and drained rice with 2 1/2 cups water and cook in the rice cooker for 20 minutes. Unplug and allow to sit, uncovered, for 5 minutes.

Glutinous rice is misnamed: The rice contains no gluten. It is a variety that is high in amylopectin, a starch that makes the grains stick together when cooked in water. So the best way to cook this rice is by steaming it.

1. Wash the rice by placing it in a large container and covering it with water, then pour off the water. Continue until the water being poured off is clear. Drain in a fine-mesh colander.

2. Cover rice with 6 cups cold water and soak for 8 hours or overnight, until the rice is soft. Drain and rinse with water, and set aside.

3. Line a steamer with two layers of dampened cheese cloth, spread the rice on top and cover tightly (if using bamboo steamers, use a wok). Fill the steamer or wok to about 3/4 inch below the level of the rice in the steamer (refill with hot water if necessary). Bring the water to a boil and steam the rice for 45 minutes over high heat, sprinkling with cold water twice while it cooks (refill steamer with more water if necessary).

4. Remove from the heat and sprinkle with sesame seeds and vinegar. Fluff with a fork or chopstick.

5. Transfer it to a serving platter and serve with your favorite topping.

Japanese Rice

JAPANESE RICE

Servings: 4
Preparation time: 5 minutes
Cooking time: 30 minutes

- 2 cups Japanese short-grain rice
- 2 1/2 cups water

NOTE

You may cook this rice in a rice cooker. Combine rice and water, cover and cook in the rice cooker for 30 minutes. Unplug and allow to sit for 10 minutes without uncovering.

1. Wash the rice by placing it in a large container and covering it with water, then pour off the water. Continue until the water being poured off is clear. Drain in a fine-mesh colander.

2. Place the rice in a medium-sized nonstick pot and add the water. Cover and bring to a boil over medium heat. Reduce heat to low and cook for 30 minutes.

3. Remove from heat and allow to sit, still covered, for 10 minutes.

Thai Soft Sweet Sticky Rice in Banana Leaf

It is said that this rice was used by a traveler to sustain him on his journey to visit Buddha, and that when he got there, all he had to offer Buddha was the leftover rice. Since then, it has been traditionally used as an offering at religious festivals. It is somewhat similar in this respect to the Kanu Festival rice in India (page 143) that is made with coconut flakes. In China this rice is made with peanuts, shitake mushrooms and lily blossoms. I like to make this rice using cardamom and rose water.

1. Wash the rice by placing it in a large container and covering it with water, then pour off the water. Continue until the water being poured off is clear.

2. Bring 4 cups water to a boil in a medium-sized pot over high heat. Remove from heat, add the rice and allow to soak for 30 to 40 minutes until the rice is soft. Drain in a fine-mesh colander, and rinse with cold water and set aside.

3. Bring the salt, sugar, coconut milk, cardamom pods and rose water to a boil in a medium saucepan over high heat. Reduce heat to medium, add the drained rice, stirring constantly with a wooden spoon until the rice grains are shiny and sticky (about 5 minutes). Remove from heat and allow to cool.

4. Unwrap the banana leaves, remove the hard stems, cut into 9-inch strips and soak in a container of warm water for 5 minutes. Rinse each leaf thoroughly and carefully. Drain and pat dry. Fan over a gas flame for 1 second to soften.

5. Place 1/4 cup cooked rice in the center of a banana leaf (dull side up). Top with a few slices of bananas. Fold and form into a bundle, and tie with a piece of twine. Line a steamer with two layers of dampened cheese cloth, arrange the rice bundles on top and cover tightly (if using bamboo steamers, use a wok). Fill the pot or wok to about 3/4 inch below the level of the rice in the steamer (refill with hot water if necessary). Bring the water to a boil and steam the rice for 30 minutes over high heat.

6. Unwrap the bundle and serve with a curry braise, pages 183 and 192.

Makes: 8 bundles
Preparation time: 40 minutes
Cooking time: 30 minutes

2 cups long-grain Thai sticky rice (long-grain, sweet glutinous rice)
4 cups water
1/2 teaspoon salt
1/3 cup sugar
3 cups unsweetened fresh or canned coconut milk*
2 green cardamom pods
1 tablespoon rose water (optional)
2 ripe bananas, peeled and sliced
1 package frozen banana leaves, thawed*
kitchen twine

NOTE
Traditionally this rice is combined with beans, wrapped in banana leaf and steamed. You can cook 1/2 cup split mung beans or toasted black beans in 2 cups water for 30 minutes over medium heat, until soft. Drain, combine with the rice, wrap in the banana leaf and steam.

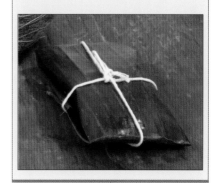

A Rumi Tale of Dreams

In Which We Learn to Take the Cash and Let the Credit Go

A Jew, a Christian and a Muslim stopped at a Silk Road caravanserai, whose keeper honored them with a gift of halva. The Muslim, who had been fasting, wanted to eat the sweet right away. His friends, however, had already eaten. They preferred to save the treat for the morning. After some argument, all agreed that the halva should be saved and that whoever had the best dream during the night should have it all.

In the morning, the Jew said that in his dream, Moses had taken him to a mountain and revealed to him wonders; therefore, he should have the halva. The Christian replied that in his dream, Jesus had taken him to the fourth sphere of heaven and showed him great secrets. Therefore he should have the halva, he said, because heavenly dreams were clearly better than earthly ones.

Raising his eyebrows at these obvious inventions, and picking crumbs of halva from his beard, the Muslim told his story: "Mohammed came to me and said, 'Now that one of your friends has gone with Moses to the mountain and seen wonders, and the other has gone with Jesus to heaven and learned secrets, what are you waiting for? You had better get up quickly and eat the halva,'" he said. "How could I refuse to obey the Prophet?"

Kanu Festival Tamarind & Coconut Pullao

This sweet and sour rice is offered for thanksgiving at the Kanu Festival in January. On the fourth day, called Kanu Pongal, women prepare small balls of this rice from the new harvest, color them in different hues, place them on a plantain leaf and offer them along with sugarcane to Surya, the Hindu sun god, in gratitude.

1. Cook the rice per the Gilani Smothered Rice recipe on page 136 and set aside.

2. In a wok or medium-sized nonstick pot, heat 1 tablespoon oil over medium heat, add the cashews and raisins, and stir-fry for 20 seconds. Remove the nuts and raisins with a slotted spoon and set aside.

3. In the same wok, heat the remaining oil over medium-high heat until very hot and add the asafetida, mustard seeds, coriander seeds, cumin seeds, peppercorns, fenugreek seeds and sesame seeds, and cook for 10 seconds until aromatic (keep a cover handy to catch any seeds that try to pop out). Add the chilies and stir-fry for 20 seconds.

4. Add the tamarind, sugar and salt, and bring to a boil. Reduce heat, add the cooked rice and coconut flakes, and stir gently with a wooden spoon until the sauce blends thoroughly with the rice. Adjust seasoning to taste, adding more sugar or tamarind paste as necessary. This rice should have a distinct sweet and sour flavor.

5. Remove from heat, uncover, and add the nut mixture and chopped cilantro. Fluff the rice gently with a fork. Transfer to a serving dish and serve with a green salad.

> **Servings:** 4
> **Preparation time:** 20 minutes
> **Cooking time:** 45 minutes
>
> 2 cups long-grain white basmati rice
> 4 tablespoons peanut oil
> 1/2 cup raw cashew nuts
> 1/2 cup raisins
> 1/2 teaspoon ground asafetida*
> 1 teaspoon mustard seeds
> 1 teaspoon coriander seeds
> 2 teaspoons cumin seeds
> 1/2 teaspoon black peppercorns
> 1/2 teaspoon fenugreek seeds
> 1/4 cup raw sesame seeds
> 2 hot green chilies, seeded and sliced
> 1/4 cup tamarind paste*
> 1/4 cup sugar
> 2 teaspoons salt
> 1 packed cup unsweetened coconut flakes
> 2 cups chopped fresh cilantro

California Brown Rice Pilaf

Servings: 4
Preparation time: 15 minutes
Cooking time: 50 minutes

- 2 cups long-grain brown basmati rice
- 4 tablespoons vegetable oil, butter or ghee
- 1 medium-sized onion, peeled and thinly sliced
- 2 cloves garlic, peeled and crushed
- 1 cup peas, frozen or fresh
- 1/4 teaspoon turmeric or 1 teaspoon curry powder
- 2 teaspoons salt
- 1/2 teaspoon freshly ground black pepper
- 4 cups warm vegetable stock or water
- 1 cup chopped fresh parsley, cilantro or basil

NOTE

You can also make plain brown rice (without the onions and garlic) in a medium-sized pot or rice cooker by combining 4 tablespoons oil, 2 cups long-grain brown basmati rice, 2 teaspoons salt and 4 cups water. Stir well with a wooden spoon, bring to a boil, reduce heat, cover and cook over medium heat for 40 minutes.

Brown rice (unpolished, so that it retains its husk and bran) was rarely eaten in the countries along the old Silk Road. There, rice was considered a luxury, and milled white rice was its best form. Personally, I have grown to like, and sometimes favor, the earthy taste and texture of brown rice. It is, of course, healthier to eat, but with the variety of food we have these days that need not be too much of a concern. Make this rice for its good taste and wholesome texture.

1. Wash the rice in a large container, rinse until the water is clear and drain off the water.

2. Heat 4 tablespoons oil over medium heat in a medium nonstick pot. Add the onion and stir-fry for 10 minutes or until translucent. Add the garlic, peas, turmeric, salt, pepper and rice, and stir-fry for 1 minute longer.

3. Add 4 cups stock and stir once (gently with a wooden spoon) to keep rice from sticking to the bottom of the pot.

4. Bring to a boil. Reduce the heat to low and cover firmly with the lid to prevent steam from escaping. Cook for 40 minutes over medium-low heat.

5. Remove from heat and let stand for 10 minutes before removing the lid. Sprinkle parsley on top of the rice, fluff with a fork and transfer to a serving platter.

Turkish White Basmati Rice Pilaf

This Turkish specialty can be cooked similarly to the California Brown Rice recipe above except that you should reduce the vegetable stock to 2 1/2 cups and the cooking time to 20 minutes.

Minnesota Wild Rice

Servings: 4
Preparation time: 10 minutes
Cooking time: 1 hour

2 cups uncooked wild rice (black sweet rice)
4 cups water
2 teaspoons salt
2 tablespoons vegetable oil, butter or ghee

Wild rice is actually the seed of an aquatic grass and is not a member of the rice family. In China it is harvested more for its shoots than its grain. But it's a delectable grass and deserves to be included in a modern Silk Road cookbook.

1. Wash the rice by placing it in a large fine-mesh sieve and rinsing under running water. Agitate gently with your hands and drain off the rice water.

2. Bring 4 cups water to a boil in a medium nonstick pot. Pour in the rice, gently stir once with a wooden spoon and bring back to a boil.

3. Reduce heat to medium, cover and cook for 35 minutes. Reduce heat to very low. Add the salt and oil, stir gently, cover tightly to prevent steam from escaping and steam over very low heat for 25 minutes.

4. Transfer to a serving platter and serve with salad.

NOTE

Use this recipe to make wild rice. Then blend it with various ingredients by following the instructions for Amoli Rice Salad with Barberries & Orange Peel on page 74 (photograph here on the left).

I find a combination of cooked wild rice and regular white or brown rice very tasty. You can cook them separately and combine them just before serving according to your fancy.

The Rose

All along the paths of the Silk Road, wherever irrigation permits, roses grow, and May is the month of roses. In Hotan (once Khotan) at the edge of the Taklimakan desert, for instance, all the people of the town still get together to harvest their roses; the petals are turned into wine. To the west there is Ashkhabad, about 30 miles from the Iranian border in what is now Turkmenistan. It was the western meeting place along a number of caravan routes, and although it lay beside the Kara Kum desert, intelligent irrigation had made it fertile. It grew crops from wheat to melons. And the people of Ashkhabad loved roses, as an English traveler named Stephen Graham discovered in May 1914.

We reached Ashkhabad, the first great city of Turkestan, about eleven o'clock at night, and its platform presented an extraordinary scene. The whole forty-five minutes of our stay it was crowded with all the peoples of central Asia—Persians, Russians, Afghans, Tekkes, Bokharans, Khivites, Turcomans—and every one had in his hand, or on his dress, or in his turban roses. The whole long pavement was fragrant with rose odours. Gay Russian girls, all in white and in summer hats, were chattering to young officers, with whom they paraded up and down, and they had roses in their hands. Persian hawkers, with capacious baskets of pink and white roses, moved hither and thither; immense and magnificent Turcomans lounged against pillars or walked about...they too had roses in their fingers.

It might almost have been an Iranian scene, because Iranians love roses and consider the flowers peculiarly their own. As Western poets would, they saw the delicate, evanescent blossom as the symbol of the brevity of life's joys. So the eleventh-century poet Omar Khayyam wrote (in Edward FitzGerald's English translation):

Look to the rose that blows about us—"Lo,
Laughing," she says, "into the world I blow:
At once the silken tassel of my purse
Tear, and its treasure on the garden throw."

These wonderful plants began their slow journey to the West in the third century BCE, when they appeared in the botanical garden of Aristotle, in Athens. They had been sent from Persia, along with other specimen plants that might prove useful to medicine, by Alexander the Great. The conqueror, once a pupil of Aristotle, was always interested in the flora and fauna of the countries that fell to him.

During the centuries that followed, as roses spread north into Europe, Westerners began to use the beautiful flowers in the same way as Persians . Roses were (and still are) given as gifts, scattered on fountains or walkways during festivities—perhaps this is the parent of the red carpet—and fashioned into decorations for dining tables.

The culinary delights of the rose, however, never assumed the central importance that they have in Persian cooking. I hope they will: The flower's delicate fragrance and taste is something worth exploring.

Fresh rose petals, for instance, may be used in salads, used to make a strong wine, steeped to produce rose tea (and the fruit, or hip, may be turned into rose-hip tea), and cooked into jam or used to scent honey. The fresh petals may also be mixed with stored sugar to make rose petal sugar, infused with the subtle taste and memorable aroma of the flower.

Dried rose petals, more intense in flavor, can be put to any of these uses. Most important, dried petals, with cinnamon, cardamom and cumin, form the delicate Persian spice mix called advieh, which gives many dishes their distinctive flavor.

In other forms—as rose water and oil or attar of roses—the flowers have given savor at least since 500 BCE. At around that time, if not earlier, Persians began to extract both water and essential oil from the petals of that same damask rose that Omar Khayyam loved.

In Iran, rose water and oil still are produced by ancient methods, primarily at Qamsar and Naisar, two small towns near Kashan in the center of the country.

Workers pick the roses in the early morning, when the scent is at its peak.

The flowers are transferred to a rose water factory, where they are spread over the floor of a cool room and sorted. Then the fresh petals are steamed in a clay-sealed cauldron; the perfumed vapor rises through a bamboo pipe into a second pot set in cold running water.

Cooling condenses the vapors into liquid rose water and more intense oil. The first is bottled for cooking; the second is used for perfume (*"atr"* in Persian, which is the source of the English "attar"); and the leftover petals are fed to animals.

Few scents are more characteristic of Iran than that of rose water. Even thousands of years ago, Zoroastrians used it in their purification rites. Today it is still found everywhere: One offers it to guests to dip their fingers in before and after meals, for instance. It serves as an air freshener both at home and in public places. It is part of every woman's makeup, and men use it to clean their mustaches and beards.

And, of course, it is essential to Persian cooking. It is used to flavor rice pudding, baklava, and the wonderful Persian and Turkish chewy ice cream, for instance. And it makes a very good sharbat (page 287).

Its name in Persian, golab—literally, "rose water"—has its own history. In the seventh century, Arabs borrowed the word as a term for a drink with water and honey or syrup. In English, golab became julep, originally used for any sweet drink that helped medicines go down, then for any comforting drink. Golab's latest incarnation was in Kentucky, in the mint and whiskey mixture known as the mint julep.

With rose water and attar of roses, you might say, the practical cook answers the poet's lament for the brevity of beauty. Another Persian poet, the mystic Jalal al-Din Rumi, put the case neatly. In Dick Davis's translation, his verse says,

When the rose is withered and the garden is gone
You will hear no more the nightingale's song;
When the rose is withered and the garden laid bare
In attar of roses the scent is still there.

Previous page: Rose pickers gather petals for weighing. Workers are paid by the kilo.

Opposite: A boy sacks rose petals in Qamsar, Iran. This page: They will be distilled into rose water (right) and perfume.

Kermani Polow with Saffron & Pistachios

Servings: 4
Preparation time: 15 minutes
Cooking time: 45 minutes

- 2 cups white basmati rice
- 4 tablespoon vegetable oil, butter or ghee
- 1 medium onion, peeled and thinly sliced
- 1 cup pistachios, shelled and rinsed
- 4 cardamom pods, crushed
- 1/4 teaspoon ground saffron threads dissolved in 2 tablespoons hot water (optional)
- 2 teaspoon salt
- 4 cups warm vegetable stock or water
- 2 tablespoons butter
- 1 cup chopped fresh dill
- 1 tablespoon organic rose petals

VARIATION

You can substitute almonds, cashews, or hazelnuts for the pistachios.

In season, you can also garnish with fresh pomegranate seeds.

1. Pick over and wash the rice per the Gilani Smothered Rice master recipe on page 136.

2. Heat 4 tablespoons oil in a wok over medium heat. Add the onion slices and fry for 15 minutes until golden brown. Add the rice, pistachios, cardamom and saffron water, and stir-fry for 1 minute. Add the salt and warm vegetable stock, and bring to a boil; stir gently once. Reduce heat to medium-low, cover tightly and cook for 30 minutes.

3. Remove from heat, add the butter, sprinkle the dill and rose petals over the top, and fluff with a fork. Cover and let stand for 10 minutes before serving.

4. Transfer to a serving dish and serve with your favorite fruit and vegetable braise (pages 174–195).

Xian Stir-Fried Rice

Servings: 4
Preparation time: 30 minutes
Cooking time: 45 minutes

5 tablespoons peanut oil
1 Thai bird or serrano chili, sliced
2 cloves garlic, crushed and peeled
5 fresh shitake mushrooms, stems removed and shredded
1 large carrot, peeled and shredded
1 celery stalk, shredded
1 cup fresh or frozen peas
2 cups napa cabbage, shredded
4 cups cooked rice (you can use the rice recipe on page 136)
2 fresh scallions, shredded
1/4 cup fresh basil, shredded
2 tablespoons toasted sesame oil
4 eggs
1 teaspoon salt
1 teaspoon freshly ground pepper

1. Heat the oil in a wok or deep skillet over high heat. Add the chili, garlic, mushrooms, carrot, celery, peas and cabbage, and stir-fry for 2 minutes.

2. Add the cooked rice, scallions, basil and sesame oil and stir-fry for 2 minutes longer.

3. Make a trough in the center of the rice. Add 1 tablespoon peanut oil, the eggs, salt and pepper, reduce heat to low, cover and cook for 1 minute, until the eggs firm up. Stir gently, mixing the eggs through the rice.

4. Transfer the rice onto a serving dish.

VARIATION

Stir-Fried Rice Noodles

You can substitute 1/2 pound thin rice noodles (rice sticks) for the cooked rice. To prepare the rice noodles, snip the noodles in half, soak in warm water for 20 minutes, drain, rinse and shake off any excess water. Proceed with step 2.

Delhi Mustard Seed & Yogurt Pullao

Servings: 4
Preparation time: 15 minutes
Cooking time: 35 minutes

- 1/2 cup oil, butter or ghee
- 2 teaspoons black mustard seeds
- 2-inch fresh ginger, peeled and crushed
- 4 cloves garlic, peeled and crushed
- 2 Thai bird or serrano chilies, seeded and chopped
- 2 teaspoons salt
- 2 cups long-grain white basmati rice, picked over and washed per master recipe (on page 136)
- 2 cups plain yogurt, beaten
- 2 cups chopped fresh cilantro or parsley

1. In a wok or medium-sized nonstick pot, heat 4 tablespoons oil, add the mustard seeds, and cook for 10 seconds until the seeds stop crackling and become aromatic (keep a lid handy to catch any seeds that might fly out).

2. Add the ginger, garlic, chili, salt and rice, and stir-fry for 1 minute.

3. Add 3 cups boiling water, gently stir, and bring to a boil. Reduce heat, cover and cook over medium heat for 20 minutes.

4. Remove from the heat, uncover and gently swirl the yogurt over the rice. Sprinkle the cilantro over the rice, cover and allow to steep for 15 minutes. Uncover and fluff the rice with a fork. Transfer to a serving dish and serve with a salad.

Variation

Traditionally this rice is made by cooking the rice separately (per master recipe on page 136) and then adding spices, garlic, ginger, yogurt and cilantro to 5 cups of the cooked rice in step 4.

Uzbek Carrot Palov with Cumin

The original version of this festive dish comes from Uzbekistan. There it is made with short-grain rice and large amounts of fat from the fat-tailed sheep of the region—a welcome addition to the diet of people whose daily food is mostly flat bread and tea. Although women generally have done most of the cooking in Uzbekistan, palovs were generally made by men (this is also the case for paella in Spain). Today women make it as well—this is said to be one of the achievements of the Communist Party's 1970s revolution—and the dish is available from stalls throughout the street markets.

1. In a wok or medium-sized nonstick pot, heat 1 tablespoon oil over medium heat. Add the almonds and currants, and stir-fry for 20 seconds. Remove with a slotted spoon and set aside.

2. Using the same wok heat the remaining oil over medium heat, add the cumin and cook for 10 seconds, until aromatic (keep a cover handy to catch any seeds that might fly out). Add the onion and fry for 10 to 15 minutes, until golden brown.

3. Add the carrots, bell pepper, chili and rice, and stir-fry for 5 minutes. Add the turmeric, salt, sugar and water. Bring to a boil, stirring gently once with a wooden spoon. Reduce heat to medium-low, cover and simmer for 30 minutes, until all the water has been absorbed and the rice is in long separated grains.

4. Remove the wok from the heat and add the almonds, currants, and chopped cilantro. Fluff the rice gently with a fork. Transfer to a serving dish and serve with any tomato and cucumber salad.

VARIATION

Afghan Qabeli Pilau

This Afghan specialty *(Qabeli means "much appreciated")* is similar to the Uzbek rice above except for the addition of 1/2 teaspoon ground cinnamon, 1/4 teaspoon ground cloves, 2 black cardamom (to complete the chahar masala).

Servings: 4
Preparation time: 15 minutes
Cooking time: 45 minutes

- 8 tablespoons vegetable oil, butter, or ghee
- 1/2 cup blanched, raw almonds, peanuts, or pine nuts
- 1 cup currants
- 2 teaspoons cumin seeds
- 2 large onion. peeled and thinly sliced
- 1 cup carrots, peeled and shredded
- 1/2 bell pepper, seeded and shredded
- 1 Thai bird or serrano chili, seeded and chopped, or 1/2 teaspoon paprika
- 2 cups long-grain Indian white basmati rice, picked over and washed
- 1/2 teaspoon ground turmeric, or 1/2 teaspoon saffron dissolved in 2 tablespoons hot water
- 2 teaspoons salt
- 1 tablespoon sugar
- 3 cups water
- 2 cups chopped fresh cilantro, parsley or basil

Genoese Dill & Fava Bean Risotto

Servings: 4
Preparation time: 20 minutes
Cooking time: 55 minutes

- 3 pounds fresh or 1 pound frozen fava beans *
- 3 tablespoons vegetable oil
- 1 tablespoon cumin seeds
- 4 cloves garlic, peeled and crushed
- 1 cup chopped fresh dill
- 1/4 cup chopped fresh cilantro or parsley
- 4 cups vegetable stock or water
- 1 sprig rosemary
- 1 tablespoon salt
- 3 tablespoons butter
- 2 shallots, peeled and thinly sliced
- 1 cup Arborio rice (risotto rice), do not wash
- 1/2 cup white wine
- 1/4 teaspoon saffron threads ground and diluted in 2 tablespoons hot water
- 1/2 teaspoon freshly ground black pepper
- 1/2 cup freshly shaved Parmigiano-Reggiano cheese

In the thirteenth century Genoese traders crossed the Mediterranean and the Black Sea. They went eastward through Persia, setting up a trading post in Tabriz, and on, to Beijing and Zhangzhou. According to Marco Polo, Tabriz was an entrepot for goods from Baghdad, Mosul and Hormuz (Bandar Abbas). It is interesting to note that this recipe is still popular, with slight variations, in both Italy and Iran.

1. Shell the beans and remove their outer skin. If using frozen beans, soak in warm water for 10 minutes, then remove the outer skin.

2. Heat 1 tablespoon oil in a large skillet, over medium heat until very hot, and add the cumin seeds. Cook for 10 seconds until aromatic (keep a cover handy to stop any seeds from flying out). Add the garlic, fava beans, dill and cilantro, and stir-fry for 2 minutes. Set aside.

3. Bring 4 cups vegetable stock, a sprig of rosemary and 1 tablespoon salt to a boil and keep warm.

4. Heat 2 tablespoons oil and 1 tablespoon butter in a wok or heavy medium-sized pot. Add the shallots and stir-fry over medium heat for 5 minutes, until golden brown.

5. Add the rice and stir-fry for 1 minute. Add the wine and cook until the wine evaporates (about 3 minutes).

6. Add the warm vegetable stock to the rice gradually, 1/2 cup at a time, stirring constantly after each addition. As each 1/2 cup of stock is absorbed add another, until all the stock has been absorbed and the rice is tender and creamy (30 to 45 minutes).

7. Add the saffron water, pepper, and fava bean and dill mixture and stir-fry for 5 minutes, until the saffron has thoroughly blended with the rice.

8. Add the remaining butter, sprinkle the cheese, season to taste and serve immediately.

Fertile Crescent Bulgur & Mung Bean Pilaf

Bulgur has been made in the Fertile Crescent—that vast swathe of the Middle East where farming began in the 9th millennium BCE—since ancient times. Bulgur is created by removing the husk of the wheat and steaming, drying, and crushing the berries. It was replaced as a staple, in many of the countries along the Silk Road, by rice or noodles.

1. Combine the mung beans, 4 cups water and 1/2 teaspoon salt in a medium-sized saucepan and bring to a boil. Reduce heat, partially cover and cook over medium heat for 15 minutes, until beans are almost tender. Drain and set aside.

2. Meanwhile, heat the oil in a wok or medium-sized pot until very hot. Add the cumin and cook for 10 seconds, until aromatic (keep a cover handy to stop any seeds from flying out). Add the onion and fry for 10 to 15 minutes until golden brown. Add the ginger, garlic, chili and bulgur, and stir-fry for 2 minutes, until the bulgur browns lightly. Add 2 teaspoons salt, pepper, turmeric, tomato, mung beans and 2 cups water. Stir gently once and bring to a boil.

3. Reduce heat to medium-low, cover and cook for 20 minutes, or until all the liquid has been absorbed. Add the dill and butter, and fluff gently with a fork.

4. Serve with yogurt.

Variation

Uzbek Mung Bean & Apricot Pilau

In step 2 above, replace the bulgur with the following: 2 cups Indian basmati rice washed per master recipe on page 136, 1/2 cup dried apricots (chopped), 1/2 teaspoon ground cinnamon, 1/2 teaspoon ground cumin, 1/2 teaspoon ground cardamom, 1/4 teaspoon ground cloves

Baghdad Bulgur & Lentil Pilaf

You can substitute lentils for the mung beans.

Indian Millet & Mung Bean Pilaf

You can substitute 1 cup pearl millet for the bulgur.

Servings: 4
Preparation time: 20 minutes
Cooking time: 50 minutes

- 1 cup mung beans, picked over and washed
- 4 cups water
- 2 1/2 teaspoons salt
- 1/4 cup vegetable oil, butter or ghee
- 2 tablespoons cumin seeds
- 2 large onions, peeled and thinly sliced
- 1-inch fresh ginger, peeled and grated
- 2 cloves garlic, crushed and peeled
- 2 Thai bird or serrano chilies, seeded and chopped
- 2 cups coarse bulgur wheat
- 1/2 teaspoon freshly ground black pepper
- 1/2 teaspoon ground turmeric
- 1 large fresh tomato, peeled and sliced

Garnish
- 1 cup chopped fresh dill, parsley, cilantro, or basil
- 1 tablespoon butter

Note

Do not confuse bulgur with cracked wheat. Bulgur is pre-steamed and needs very little cooking whereas cracked wheat must be cooked in water.

Susa Polow with Lentils, Currants & Dates

Servings: 4
Preparation time: 20 minutes
Cooking time: 55 minutes

- 2 cups long-grain Indian rice
- 1 cup lentils, picked over and rinsed
- 2 1/2 teaspoons salt
- 1/2 cup vegetable oil, butter or ghee
- 1 teaspoon cumin seeds
- One 4-inch cinnamon sticks
- 2 cardamom pods
- 2 medium onions, peeled and thinly sliced
- 2 cups currants
- 2 cups pitted dates, halved
- 1 orange rind
- 2 tablespoons sugar
- 1/2 teaspoon freshly ground black pepper
- 3 cups vegetable stock* or water
- 1 teaspoon ground saffron dissolved in 2 tablespoons hot water (optional)*

Susa was the capital of Elam and the starting point of the 1,500 mile Persian Royal Road that linked the ancient Persian capital with Anatolia and the Aegean Sea. According to the Greek historian Herodotus, royal messengers were stopped by "neither snow, nor rain, nor heat, nor gloom of night" and traversed the entire road in nine days thanks to a system of relays. Normal travel time was about three months. A nourishing rice dish like this might might have made the journey seem more pleasant and quicker.

1. Pick over and wash the rice per the Gilani Smothered Rice master recipe on page 136.

2. Boil the lentils in 3 cups water and 1/2 teaspoon salt for 15 minutes over high heat. Drain.

3. Heat 1/4 cup oil in a wok or medium-sized nonstick pot, over medium heat, until very hot. Add the cumin, cinnamon and cardamom, and cook for 20 seconds, until aromatic (keep a cover handy to stop any seeds from flying out).

4. Add the onion and fry for 15 minutes, until golden brown. Add rice, currants, dates, orange rind, sugar, 2 teaspoons salt, pepper and 3 cups water, and bring to a boil. Cover and simmer over medium heat for 20 minutes, until all the water has been absorbed.

5. Add the lentils to the rice and fluff gently with a fork. Mix the remaining oil with the saffron water and drizzle over the rice. Cover and cook for 15 minutes longer, then remove from heat and let stand for 10 minutes without uncovering.

6. Transfer to a serving platter and serve with a green salad.

VARIATION

Armenian Wedding Pilavi

Add 1 cup dried apricots (chopped), 1/2 cup pitted prunes and 1/2 cup blanched almonds in step 4, at the same time as the currants and dates.

Yazdi Polow with Eggplant & Pomegranate

Servings: 4
Preparation time: 20 minutes
Cooking time: 55 minutes

- 2 cups long-grain white basmati rice
- 4 Chinese eggplants (about 1 1/2 pounds); if using other types of eggplant, peel and remove bitterness*
- 8 tablespoons vegetable oil, butter or ghee
- 1 large onion, peeled and thinly sliced
- 1 teaspoon cumin seeds or mustard seeds
- 4 cloves garlic, peeled and crushed
- 1 hot red chili, seeded and sliced
- 2 teaspoons salt
- 1 teaspoon freshly ground black pepper
- 1 tablespoon sugar
- 1 tablespoon pomegranate paste*
- 2 cups water
- 1 cup tomato sauce

GARNISH
- 1 cup fresh basil or mint leaves
- 1 cup fresh pomegranate seeds (1 large pomegranate)*
- 2 tablespoons rose petals

Marco Polo visited Yazd on his journey from Italy to China in the thirteenth century. Yazd was at the intersection of the trade routes that linked China, India and the West, and continues to be a center for silk in Iran. It is also the last center of Zoroastrian Iran. Although very much in the desert, Yazd is fed by a system of qanats (subterranean aqueducts) that bring water in from a nearby mountain. The almonds and pomegranates of Yazd are the tastiest I have ever eaten.

1. Pick over and wash the rice per the Gilani Smothered Rice master recipe on page 136.

2. Cut the eggplants into 1-inch cubes, rinse and thoroughly blot dry.

3. Heat 4 tablespoons oil in a wok or medium-sized nonstick pot over high heat until very hot. Add the eggplant and fry for 10 minutes until golden brown. Remove the eggplant and set aside.

4. Heat the remaining oil in the same wok, add the onion and fry for 15 minutes, until golden brown. Add the cumin seeds, garlic, chili and rice, and stir-fry for 2 minutes longer. Return the eggplant to the wok.

5. Add the salt, pepper, sugar, pomegranate paste and 2 cups water and stir once gently. Bring to a boil, cover, reduce heat to low and cook for 30 minutes.

6. Remove from heat and uncover. Sprinkle with basil leaves and pomegranate seeds. Fluff the rice gently with a fork.

7. Transfer to a serving dish and serve with yogurt.

VARIATION

Afghan Turnip Pilau

You can substitute 1 pound turnips (peeled and diced into 2-inch cubes) and 1-inch ginger (peeled and grated), for the eggplants.

Rice / 158

Shirazi Baked Saffron Polow with Spinach

Servings: 6
Preparation time: 25 minutes
Cooking time: 2 hours

- 2/3 cup melted butter, ghee or vegetable oil
- 2 medium onions, peeled and thinly sliced
- 4 cloves garlic, peeled and crushed
- 1 teaspoon ground cumin
- 1/4 teaspoon ground cinnamon
- 1/4 teaspoon ground nutmeg
- 1 pound fresh baby spinach, washed and coarsely chopped
- 1 1/2 cups pitted prunes
- 1 cup toasted pine nuts
- 3 cups long-grain white basmati rice
- 3 eggs
- 2 cups plain yogurt
- 1/2 cup plain milk
- 1/2 teaspoon ground saffron threads dissolved in 2 tablespoons hot water
- 1/4 cup candied orange peel, chopped
- 2 teaspoons salt
- 1 teaspoon freshly ground black pepper

SPECIAL UTENSILS
See-through Pyrex baking dish or equivalent (9 by 13 by 2 inches deep)

Shiraz, on the lowlands of the Zagros Mountains, is famous for its poets, its wine and this rice casserole.

1. Heat 2 tablespoons butter in a wok or deep skillet over medium heat. Add the onion and fry for 15 minutes, until golden brown. Add garlic and cumin, and stir-fry for 1 minute. Add the cinnamon, nutmeg and spinach, cover, and cook for 5 minutes until spinach is wilted. Add the prunes and pine nuts. Set aside and allow to cool.

2. Pick over and wash the rice per the Gilani Smothered Rice master recipe on page 136. In a large nonstick pot bring 8 cups water and 2 tablespoons salt to a boil. Add the rice to the pot and boil briskly for 6 minutes. Once the rice rises to the top, it is done. Drain the rice and rinse with 3 cups cold water. Set aside.

3. Preheat oven to 420°F.

4. Combine the eggs, yogurt, milk, saffron water, candied orange peel, 2 teaspoons salt and pepper in a large mixing bowl, and beat for 1 minute.

5. Add half the cooked rice to the yogurt mixture and gently mix with a wooden spoon.

6. Pour 1/4 cup of the butter into a 9-by-13-by-2-inch baking dish, making sure you spread it to cover the bottom and sides of the dish. Add the yogurt rice mixture, then spread the spinach mixture over the rice and top the spinach with the rest of the rice. Pack the rice down firmly with the palms of your hands. Drizzle the remaining butter over the rice. Cover with buttered aluminum foil or a lid.

7. Place the baking dish in the oven and bake for 1 1/4 to 1 1/2 hours, until the crust turns golden brown.

8. Remove the baking dish from the oven and allow to cool, still covered, on a damp surface for 15 minutes to loosen the crust. (This stage is very important; do not uncover until the dish has cooled. If you uncover too early, the rice will not unmold cleanly.)

9. Remove the lid and loosen the edges with a rubber spatula (make sure you go all the way to the bottom). Hold a serving platter tightly over the baking dish, and invert the two together, unmolding the entire mound onto the platter. The rice will emerge as a golden-crusted cake, to be garnished with edible flowers and herbs, then served in wedges.

Herat Noodle & Date Pilau

Herat was a major city at the intersection of the east-west and north-south trade routes linking China, India and the West. It was at Herat that the hardy two-humped Bactrian camels were exchanged for the faster one-humped dromedaries of western Asia and Arabia. Herat was also a meeting place of ingredients from Asia and Arabia, hence this recipe of rice, noodles and dates. During the height of the Silk Road trade one would find, at a caravansary or in the bazaar of Herat, Turkoman nomads as well as Chinese traders and Arab merchants from Baghdad or Damascus. Herat was also a cosmopolitan city where Muslims, Zoroastrians, Nestorians, Christians, Buddhists and Jews commingled. Until the 1880s when it became a part of Afghanistan, Herat was very much a Persian city.

> Servings: 4
> Preparation time: 15 minutes
> Cooking time: 50 minutes
>
> 2 cups long-grain white basmati rice
> 3 cups water
> 8 tablespoons vegetable oil, butter or ghee
> 2 teaspoons salt
> 1/2 pound toasted Persian noodles, broken into 1-inch lengths
> 1 teaspoon cumin seeds
> one 4-inch cinnamon stick
> 2 cardamom pods, crushed
> 1 medium onion, peeled and thinly sliced
> 1/2 cup raisins
> 1 cup Medjool dates, pitted and sliced
> 1 orange rind
> 1/2 teaspoon freshly ground black pepper

1. Pick over and wash the rice per the Gilani Smothered Rice master recipe on page 136.

2. In a medium-sized nonstick pot combine the rice with 3 cups water, 4 tablespoons oil, 2 teaspoons salt and noodles. Bring to a boil, reduce heat to medium, cover, and cook for 20 minutes.

3. Meanwhile, heat 4 tablespoons oil in a wok or deep skillet over medium heat, until very hot. Add the cumin, cinnamon, and cardamom, and cook for 10 seconds, until aromatic (keep a cover handy to stop any seeds from flying out).

4. Add the onion and fry for 15 minutes, until golden brown. Add the raisins, dates, orange rind and pepper.

5. When the rice is done, add the raisin and date mixture to it, and fluff gently with a fork to ensure an even mix.

6. Cover tightly with the lid to prevent steam from escaping. Reduce heat to medium-low and cook for 15 minutes longer.

7. Remove from heat and allow to cool for 5 minutes, still covered.

8. Transfer to a serving dish and serve with a green salad.

VARIATIONS

Armenian Vermicelli Pilavi

To make this festive Armenian rice, substitute 1/2 pound vermicelli for the toasted noodles. Traditionally the vermicelli are fried first, the rice and currants are added, and then the stock. I prefer to make this rice, however, as in the recipe above—the Persian way.

Bulgur with Noodles & Dates

You can substitute 2 cups medium-sized bulgur for the rice.

Rice / 161

Astara Barberry & Cumin Polow

Servings: 4
Preparation time: 20 minutes
Cooking time: 50 minutes

- 2 cups long-grain white basmati rice
- 3 cups water
- 2 teaspoons salt
- 8 tablespoons vegetable oil, butter or ghee
- 2 tablespoons cumin seeds
- 2 cardamom pods, crushed
- 1 medium onion, peeled and thinly sliced
- 1 cup dried barberries, cleaned*
- 1/4 cup sugar
- 1/4 cup toasted pine nuts*
- 1/2 teaspoon ground saffron threads dissolved in 4 tablespoons hot water
- 1 tablespoon rose water

Astara is a city on the southwest coast of the Caspian Sea on the Russia-Iran border. Rice, wheat, corn and vegetables are grown in its rural surroundings, and the lower slopes of the mountains are full of orchards.

1. Pick over and wash the rice per the Gilani Smothered Rice master recipe on page 136.

2. In a medium nonstick pot, combine the rice with 3 cups water, 2 teaspoons salt and 4 tablespoons oil. Cover and cook over medium heat for 20 minutes, gently stirring twice with a wooden spoon to loosen any grains that stick to the bottom.

3. Meanwhile, in a wok or deep skillet, heat 4 tablespoons oil over medium heat, until very hot. Add the cumin and cardamom, and cook for 10 seconds, until they become aromatic (keep a cover handy to stop any seeds from flying out). Add the onion and fry for 15 minutes, stirring occasionally, until golden brown. Reduce heat, add the barberries and sugar, and stir-fry for 10 seconds longer. (Be careful! Barberries burn very easily.) Add the pine nuts and remove from heat.

4. Add the barberry mixture to the rice, and gently fluff with a fork. Drizzle the saffron water and rose water over the rice.

5. Cover firmly with a lid to prevent steam from escaping. Reduce heat to low and cook for 15 minutes longer.

6. Remove from heat and allow to cool for 10 minutes, still covered.

7. Transfer to a serving dish and serve with a vegetable curry braise on pages 183 and 192.

Georgian Pilaf with Tart Cherries

Servings: 4
Preparation time: 35 minutes.
Cooking time: 65 minutes

2 cups long-grain white basmati rice
8 tablespoons vegetable oil, butter or ghee
1 medium onion, peeled and thinly sliced
1-inch fresh ginger, peeled and grated
One 4-inch cinnamon stick
2 cups pitted dried tart cherries
1/4 cup sugar
2 tablespoons lime juice
1/2 teaspoon cayenne, or 1 Thai bird or serrano chili, seeded and chopped
4 cups water
1/2 cup blanched, toasted almonds
1/2 cup shelled unsalted pistachios
2 teaspoons salt
1/4 cup sour cherry syrup*
1/2 teaspoon ground saffron threads, dissolved in 2 tablespoons hot water (optional)

1. Pick over and wash the rice per the Gilani Smothered Rice master recipe on page 136.

2. In a medium-sized nonstick pot, combine the rice with 3 cups of water, 2 tablespoons oil and 2 teaspoons salt, and bring to a boil. Reduce heat, cover and cook over medium heat for 20 minutes.

3. Meanwhile, heat 4 tablespoons oil in a wok or deep skillet over medium heat until very hot. Add the onion, ginger and cinnamon, and fry for 15 minutes, stirring occasionally, until golden brown. Add the dried cherries, sugar, lime juice, cayenne and 1 cup water. Bring to a boil, reduce heat, cover and simmer for 10 minutes. Add the almonds and pistachios. Remove from heat.

4. Add the cherry mixture to the rice and fluff gently. Drizzle the sour cherry syrup, 2 tablespoons oil and the saffron water over the rice. Cover firmly with the lid to prevent steam from escaping. Cook for 20 minutes longer over low heat.

5. Transfer to a serving dish and serve with a green salad.

NOTE

You can substitute 2 cups pitted sour cherries in light syrup, (drained) or 2 cups fresh or frozen pitted sour cherries (cooked with 1/2 cup sugar for 20 minutes over high heat and drained) for the dried tart cherries.

Persian Polow with Green Beans & Tomatoes

Servings: 4
Preparation time: 15 minutes
Cooking time: 45 minutes

- 2 cups long-grain white basmati rice
- 12 tablespoons vegetable oil, butter or ghee
- 1 teaspoon mustard seeds
- One 4-inch cinnamon stick
- 1 large onion, peeled and thinly sliced
- 1 serrano chili, seeded and chopped
- 4 cloves garlic, crushed and peeled
- 1 1/2 pounds fresh green beans, cleaned and cut into half-inch pieces, or 10 ounces frozen green beans
- 3 large fresh tomatoes (1 pound), peeled and sliced, or 3 cups canned tomatoes, drained
- 2 teaspoons salt
- 1 teaspoon freshly ground black pepper
- 2 teaspoons dried Persian lime powder or 2 tablespoons lime juice
- 1/2 teaspoon ground saffron threads dissolved in 2 tablespoons hot water (optional)

Green beans and tomatoes are relatively new along the Silk Road, but they have been incorporated into the cuisines of many of the countries along it and are very popular.

1. Pick over and wash the rice per the Gilani Smothered Rice master recipe on page 136.

2. Heat 4 tablespoons oil in a wok or medium nonstick pot over medium heat until very hot. Add the mustard seeds and the cinnamon, and cook for 10 seconds, until aromatic (keep a cover handy to stop any seeds from flying out). Add the onion and stir-fry for 10 minutes, until translucent. Add the chili, garlic and green beans, and stir-fry for another 5 minutes. Add the rice and stir-fry for 1 minute longer.

3. Add the tomatoes, salt, pepper and lime powder, and stir once gently with a wooden spoon. Cover firmly and cook over low heat for 30 minutes. Drizzle the saffron water and remaining oil over the rice.

4. Remove the pot from the heat and allow to cool, still covered, on a damp surface for 5 minutes to loosen the crust.

5. Transfer to a serving dish and serve with a green salad.

Rice / 164

Caspian Dill & Fava Bean Polow with Baby Garlic

Servings: 4
Preparation time: 45 minutes
Cooking time: 45 minutes

- 2 cups long-grain white basmati rice
- 3 pounds fresh fava bean pods, shelled, or 1 pound frozen fava beans with second skin removed*
- 1/2 cup vegetable oil, butter, or ghee
- 1 teaspoon cumin seeds
- 1 4-inch cinnamon stick
- 1 fresh leek (white and green parts), chopped
- 10 baby garlic (also known as green garlic or sweet fresh garlic), trimmed and chopped, or 4 cloves garlic, crushed and peeled
- 3 cups coarsely chopped fresh dill
- 2 teaspoons salt
- 1/2 teaspoon freshly ground pepper
- 1/4 teaspoon turmeric
- 3 cups vegetable stock* or water
- 4 eggs
- 1/2 cup plain yogurt

1. Pick over and wash the rice per the Gilani Smothered Rice master recipe on page 136.

2. Shell and skin the fresh fava bean pods. Soak frozen ones for a few minutes in warm water, then peel them.

3. Heat 4 tablespoons oil in a wok or medium nonstick pot until very hot. Add the cumin and cinnamon, and stir-fry for 20 seconds, until they become aromatic. Add the leek and garlic, and stir-fry for 1 minute. Add the fava beans, dill, salt, pepper, turmeric and rice, and stir-fry for 1 minute longer.

4. Add 3 cups water, gently stirring once with a wooden spoon. Bring to a boil and cover firmly with the lid to prevent steam from escaping. Reduce the heat to medium and cook for 25 minutes.

5. Drizzle the remaining oil over the rice and break in the eggs. Sprinkle with salt and pepper. Cover and cook for another 15 minutes, until the eggs have firmed up. Remove the pot from heat and allow it to cool, still covered, on a damp surface for 5 minutes to loosen the crust.

6. Transfer to a serving dish and serve with yogurt.

Persian Wedding Polow with Orange Peel

Servings: 4
Preparation time: 40 minutes
Cooking time: 1 hour 15 minutes

- 3 cups long-grain white basmati rice
- 8 tablespoons vegetable oil, butter, or ghee
- 2 cardamom pods
- One 4-inch cinnamon stick
- 1 medium onion, peeled and thinly sliced
- 2 large carrots (about 1/2 pound), peeled and cut into thin strips
- 1 cup slivered orange peel, bitterness removed*
- 1 cup sugar
- 1 cup water
- 1/2 cup unsalted pistachios
- 1/2 cup almonds, toasted
- 1 tablespoon salt
- 1 tablespoon orange blossom water
- 1/2 teaspoon ground saffron threads dissolved in 2 tablespoons hot water (optional)

1. Pick over and wash the rice per the Gilani Smothered Rice master recipe on page 136.

2. Heat 4 tablespoons oil in a wok or deep skillet, over medium heat, until very hot. Add the cardamom and cinnamon and stir-fry for 20 seconds, until they become aromatic. Add the onion and fry for 15 minutes, until golden brown. Add carrots and stir-fry for 2 minutes longer. Add the orange peel, sugar and 1 cup water, and bring to a boil. Cook over medium heat for 15 minutes. Remove from heat. Add the pistachios, almonds. Set aside.

3. Meanwhile, in a medium nonstick pot, combine 3 cups water, 1 tablespoon salt, 2 tablespoons oil and the rice. Cover and cook over medium heat for 15 minutes.

4. Add the orange peel and carrot mixture, stir once gently with a wooden spoon, and drizzle the remaining oil, orange blossom water and saffron water over the rice. Reduce heat, cover firmly to prevent any steam from escaping, and cook over low heat for 30 minutes.

5. Remove from heat and allow to cool, still covered, on a damp surface for 5 minutes to loosen the crust.

6. Transfer to a serving platter and serve with a green salad.

VARIATION

Uzbek Quince Palau

Substitute 3 pounds quince (2 quinces), cored and diced into 2-inch cubes, for the orange peel.

Rice / 166

Levantine Pilaf in Pastry

Servings: 6
Preparation time: 20 minutes
Cooking time: 1 hour 25 minutes

FILLING
- 4 tablespoons vegetable oil, butter or ghee
- One 4-inch cinnamon stick
- 2 tablespoons cumin seeds
- 2 cardamom pods
- 1 teaspoon coriander seeds
- 2 large onions, thinly sliced
- 2/3 cup blanched almonds
- 2 large carrots (1/2 pound), peeled and thinly sliced
- 1/2 cup dried apricots, chopped
- 1 cup white basmati rice
- 1 cup toasted Persian noodles, or vermicelli, snipped into 4-inch pieces, or any other noodle
- 3 cups water
- 2 teaspoons salt
- 4 tablespoons sugar
- 1/2 teaspoon freshly ground pepper
- 1 cup raisins
- 1 cup milk
- 1 tablespoon rose water

PASTRY
- 10 sheets filo pastry (take the package out of the freezer and leave at room temperature for 2 hours)
- 3/4 cup butter or ghee, melted
- 1 egg yolk for the glaze

NOTE
Cover the filo while working to prevent it from drying.

1. Heat 4 tablespoons oil in a wok or deep skillet over medium heat until very hot. Add the cumin, cinnamon, cardamom and coriander, and cook for 10 seconds, until they become aromatic (keep a cover handy to stop any seeds from flying out). Add the onions and stir-fry for 10 minutes, until translucent. Add the almonds, carrots, apricots, rice and noodles and stir-fry for 1 minute longer.

2. Add 3 cups water and the salt and bring to a boil. Reduce heat to medium, cover and cook for 15 minutes. Add the sugar, pepper, raisins, milk and rose water, cover and cook for 15 minutes longer. Remove from heat and allow to cool.

3. Preheat oven to 400°F.

4. Brush a 12-inch-diameter baking dish with some melted butter.

5. Lay the first sheet of filo pastry in the baking dish (allow the ends to hang well over the edges) and brush it with melted butter. Repeat this for 10 more sheets of filo pastry, laying one over the other.

6. Place the filling in the center of the baking dish on top of the layers of filo pastry. Fold the filo pastry across and over the top of the filling. Place a sheet of filo pastry over the top and tuck in any overlapping edges. Use your hands to form a round, smooth surface and brush the top of the pastry with the egg yolk.

7. Bake in the center of the preheated oven for 40 minutes, until the crust is crisp and golden.

8. Remove from oven and cut into wedges. Serve hot with a green salad.

Rice Type & Cooking Method Table

Type of Rice	Cups Rice	Cups Water	Teaspoons Salt	Tablespoons Oil/Butter	Cooking Style
Smothered white basmati rice	2	3 1/2	2	2	Pick over rice. Wash the rice in a container in warm water at least 5 times, changing water. Drain. Add cold water, salt, oil. Bring to a boil, stir gently, reduce heat, cover tightly, cook over medium heat for 30 minutes. Page 136.
Persian-style golden crust long-grain white basmati (Chelow)	3	8	6	8	Wash thoroughly, bring water to a boil, add salt and rice, parboil for 6 to 10 minutes until rice rises. Drain and rinse with cold water. Add 4 tablespoons oil and 1/2 cup milk to the bottom of the pot, add the rice, pour remaining oil on top, cover tightly and cook over medium heat for 10 minutes and low heat for 50 minutes. Page 138.
Rice cooker method for white basmati	3	4	2	4	Wash rice thoroughly, combine all the ingredients in the rice cooker pot. Stir with a wooden spoon for 1 minute gently plug in rice cooker and cook for 30 minutes. Unplug. For a golden crust leave plugged in for 90 minutes. Page 137
White basmati pilaf	2	3 (warm vegetable stock or warm water)	2	4	In a medium nonstick pot, heat 4 tablespoons oil, add onion and stir-fry for 10 minutes. Add garlic, spices and rice and stir-fry for another 5 minutes or until the rice grains become opaque. Add salt, pepper and warm vegetable stock and bring to a boil. Reduce heat, cover tightly and cook for 30 minutes over medium-low heat. Page 144.
Stir-fry Chinese rice	4 (cooked rice)	0	1	4	Heat the oil in a wok. Add your favorite vegetables and stir-fry for 2 minutes. Add the cooked rice and salt and pepper. Stir-fry, breaking the lumps with the back of a slotted spoon until the rice has been heated. Add scrambled eggs, 2 tablespoons sesame oil and fresh chopped scallion. Page 151.
Arborio rice (risotto)	2 (unwashed)	5 1/2 (boiling stock)	1	5	Do not wash rice. Heat 2 tablespoons oil. Stir-fry onion, garlic and rice. Add wine, cook for 5 minutes, gradually add boiling stock (1 cup at a time), stirring constantly about 45 minutes until stock is absorbed. Page 154.
Long-grain brown basmati	2	4 (warm vegetable stock)	2	4	Pick over rice. Wash the rice in a container, in warm water, 2 times, Drain. Add water, salt and oil. Bring to a boil, stir gently, reduce heat, cover tightly and cook over medium heat for 40 minutes. Page 144.
Long-grain Thai sticky rice (long-grain, sweet glutinous rice), steamer method	2	4 (soak in water over night, drain)	-	-	Cover tightly and steam over 2 layers of cheese cloth for about 45 minutes (over high heat), until soft. Page 141.
Long-grain Thai sticky rice (long-grain, sweet glutinous rice), pot method	2	3	-	-	Wash rice thoroughly. Boil water, add drained rice, bring back to a boil, cover tightly, reduce heat to low and cook for 30 minutes. Page 141.
Japanese short-grain rice	2	2 1/2	-	-	Wash thoroughly, add water, cover tightly and bring to a boil, reduce heat to low, cook for 30 minutes, remove from heat and allow to sit for 10 minutes undisturbed. Page 140.
Black sweet wild rice (rice-like grass)	2	4	2	2	In a fine-mesh sieve, rinse rice with cold water. In a large pot, bring rice and water to a boil. Reduce heat to medium, cover and cook for 35 minutes. Reduce heat to low, add salt and oil, stir gently, cover tightly, and steam over very low heat for 25 minutes longer. Page 145.

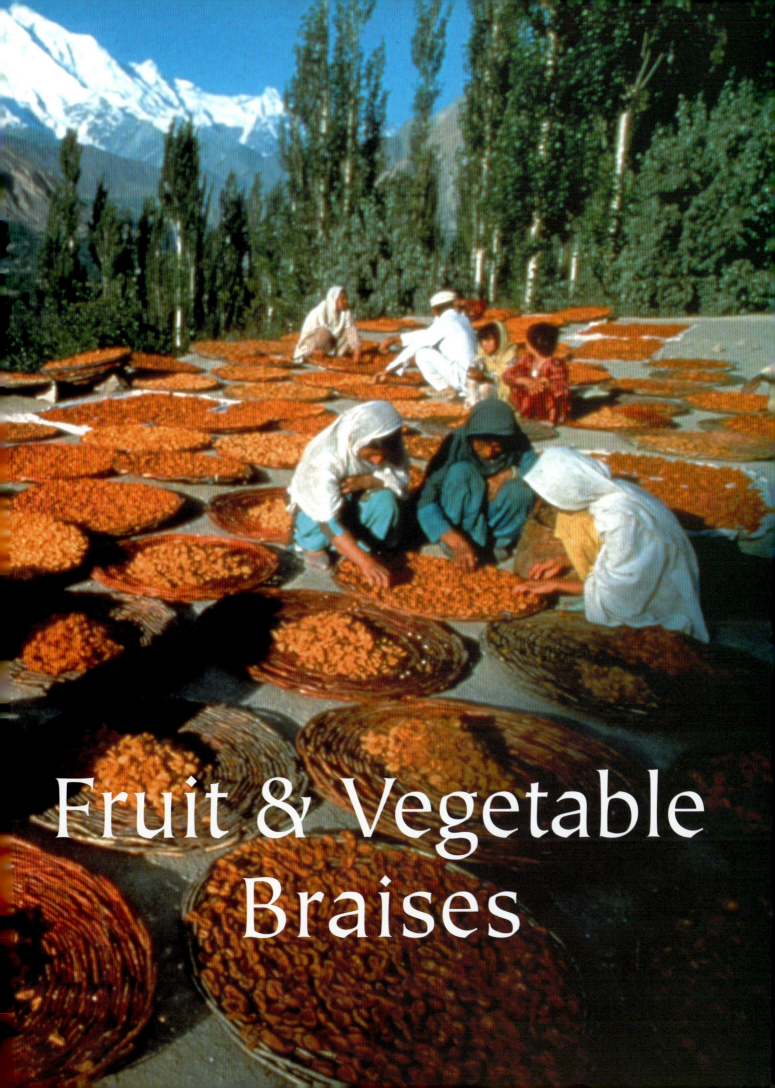

Fruit & Vegetable Braises

Caspian Fava Bean Braise with Garlic & Dill

Servings: 4
Preparation time: 15 minutes
(8 hours soaking for dried fava beans)
Cooking time: 35 minutes

- 3 pounds fresh, frozen, or 2 cups dried skinless fava beans
- 3 tablespoons vegetable oil, butter or ghee
- 2 bulbs garlic, peeled and crushed, or 4 cups fresh, chopped baby garlic (white and green)
- 2 cups chopped fresh dill or 1/4 cup dried
- 2 teaspoons salt
- 1 teaspoon pepper
- 1/2 teaspoon sugar
- 1/2 teaspoon turmeric powder
- 2 tablespoons fresh lime juice
- 2 cups water
- 6 large eggs

NOTE

For a more Italian flavor, in step 3 substitute 1/2 cup blanched, toasted almonds for the eggs. There is no need to simmer for 5 minutes at the end.

For a more Turkish flavor, substitute 2 cups of labneh (thick or drained yogurt)* for the eggs in step 3. There is no need to simmer for 5 minutes at the end.

This braise is one of the most popular dishes in Gilan, by the Caspian Sea. There, it is made from a short-tailed fava bean indigenous to the Caspian, but you can use fresh, frozen or dried fava beans available in local grocery stores or specialty markets.

1. If you use fresh fava beans, first break the green pods (the outer shells) and then skin the beans. If you use frozen beans, soak in warm water for 5 minutes before skinning the beans. For dried fava beans, first pick over for grit, then soak in 8 cups warm water for at least 8 hours. Drain and rinse.

2. Heat the oil in a wok or deep skillet over medium heat until very hot. Add the garlic and stir-fry for 1 minute. Add the fava beans, dill, salt, pepper, sugar, turmeric and lime juice, and stir-fry for 5 minutes. Add 2 cups water and bring to a boil. Reduce heat, cover and simmer over medium-low heat for 15 to 20 minutes or until the beans are tender. Adjust seasoning to taste.

3. Break the eggs gently over the beans, cover and allow to simmer for 5 to 8 minutes, until the eggs are set.

4. Serve immediately over plain rice, pasta or couscous.

Athenian Artichoke & Pearl Onion Braise

Servings: 4
Preparation time: 25 minutes
Cooking time: 35 minutes

1. If using fresh artichokes, wash them under running water and cut off the stem close to the base. Remove the tough outer leaves and trim carefully around the base. Use scissors to cut off about 1 inch from the top. Trim any remaining leaves and scoop out choke and pink thorny leaves from center. Place 1/2 cup lime juice and a few lime slices in a large container, and fill with cold water. Place each artichoke heart in the container to prevent discoloration. When ready to use, drain, rinse thoroughly and pat dry. If using frozen artichokes, just thaw. If using artichokes in jars, just drain.

2. Heat the oil in a wok or deep skillet over medium heat, until hot. Add the onions, carrots, potatoes, fava beans, artichokes, salt, pepper and sugar, and stir-fry for 20 seconds. Pour in 2 1/2 cups water, bring to a boil, cover and simmer over medium heat for 20 minutes.

3. Add the cornstarch, saffron and dill, and cook for another 15 minutes. Check to see if the vegetables are tender. Adjust seasoning to taste.

4. Transfer to a serving dish, drizzle with olive oil and serve with rice, couscous or bread.

- 8 fresh artichokes, 1 package frozen (9 ounces), or 1 jar artichoke hearts
- 1/2 cup fresh lime juice and a few lime slices
- 4 tablespoons olive oil
- 15 pearl onions, peeled
- 2 large carrots, peeled and sliced
- 8 small golden potatoes, peeled
- 1 cup fresh fava or soy beans, outer shells (pods) and second skins removed, or frozen fava beans, soaked in warm water for 5 minutes and skinned
- 1 1/2 teaspoons salt
- 1 teaspoon freshly ground black pepper
- 1 teaspoon sugar
- 2 1/2 cups water
- 1 tablespoon cornstarch, dissolved in 2 tablespoons cold water
- 1/4 teaspoon ground saffron dissolved in 1 tablespoon hot water
- 1/2 cup chopped fresh dill

GARNISH
- 1/4 cup olive oil

Isfahani Green Bean & Tomato Braise

Servings: 4
Preparation time: 15 minutes
Cooking time: 30 minutes

- 4 tablespoons vegetable oil, butter or ghee
- 1 tablespoon mustard seeds
- 1 large onion, peeled and thinly sliced
- 1 pound fresh green beans, washed, trimmed and cut in halves
- 2 cloves garlic, peeled and crushed
- 1 bird or serrano chili, seeded and chopped, or 1/4 teaspoon chili paste
- 1 teaspoon salt
- 1/2 teaspoon freshly ground black pepper
- 1/2 teaspoon sugar
- 2 tablespoons fresh lime juice
- 3 large fresh tomatoes, sliced, or 2 cups canned whole tomatoes
- 1/2 chopped fresh cilantro (optional)

Both green beans and tomatoes are South and Central American plants, which arrived in Spain during the 16th century and spread far along the trade routes. The French word for green bean (haricot); and the various words for tomato are derived from their Aztec names. Indian cooks, long expert in adapting the foods that trade brought, immediately incorporated them into their cuisines. This dish is popular in southern India and Iran.

1. Heat 4 tablespoons oil in a wok or deep skillet, over medium heat, until very hot. Add the mustard seeds and cook for 10 seconds (keep a cover handy to stop any seeds from flying out). Add the onion and stir-fry for 10 minutes, until translucent. Add the green beans, garlic and chili, and stir-fry for 1 minute longer.

2. Add the salt, pepper, sugar, lime juice and tomatoes. Cover and simmer over medium heat for 15 to 20 minutes, stirring occasionally, until the beans are tender.

3. Adjust seasoning to taste. Add the cilantro, cover and keep warm until ready to serve.

4. Serve with rice, couscous, pasta or bread.

Elam Kidney Bean & Lime Braise

Servings: 4
Preparation time: 25 minutes plus 2 hours for soaking beans
Cooking time: 1 3/4 hours

- 6 tablespoons vegetable oil, butter or ghee
- 1 small onion, peeled and thinly sliced
- 4 cloves garlic, peeled and crushed
- 1 Thai bird or serrano chili, seeded and chopped
- 4 cups finely chopped fresh parsley
- 1 cup finely chopped fresh leeks, garlic chives or scallions
- 1 cup finely chopped fresh coriander
- 1 cup chopped fresh fenugreek leaves or 3 tablespoons dried fenugreek flakes
- 1 1/2 teaspoons salt
- 1 teaspoon freshly ground black pepper
- 1/2 teaspoon ground turmeric
- 4 whole dried Persian limes, pierced
- 2/3 cup dried kidney beans, picked over and soaked in 4 cups water for at least 2 hours and drained
- 4 1/2 cups water
- 4 tablespoons fresh lime juice
- 1/2 teaspoon ground saffron threads dissolved in 1 tablespoon hot water

NOTE

You may substitute drained canned beans for the kidney beans. Reduce the water in step 2 to 1 cup and eliminate the cooking time in that step.
Also, you may substitute black beans or yellow split peas for the kidney beans.

Elam was an ancient civilization in what is modern-day Khuzistan in southern Iran. We know from Babylonian culinary tablets that this area (around Susa and Anshan) was a source for some of the herbs and spices used in Mesopotamian cuisine as far back as 3,700 years ago. The Elamites artistic pottery featuring dishes shaped as stylized animals and birds, hints at a sophisticated approach to cuisine.

1. Heat 6 tablespoons oil in a wok or deep skillet, over medium heat, until very hot. Add the onion and stir-fry for 10 minutes, until translucent. Add the garlic, chili, parsley, leeks, coriander and fenugreek, and fry for 20 minutes longer, stirring occasionally, until aromatic (this is important if you want the tastiest braise). Add the salt, pepper, turmeric, limes and beans, and stir-fry for 2 minutes.

2. Pour in 4 1/2 cups water and bring to a boil. Reduce heat to low, cover and simmer for 30 minutes, stirring occasionally.

3. Add the lime juice and saffron water, cover partially and simmer over medium-low heat for 30 to 40 minutes, stirring occasionally, until the beans are tender.

4. Adjust seasoning to taste. Cover and keep warm until ready to serve.

5. Serve hot with plain rice.

Fruit & Vegetable Braises

Uzbek Apple & Tart Cherry Braise

Servings: 4
Preparation time: 20 minutes
Cooking time: 40 minutes

- 5 tablespoons vegetable oil, butter or ghee
- 1/2 cup blanched almonds
- 1/2 cup pitted, dried tart cherries
- 6 tart cooking apples (about 2 pounds), peeled, cored and cut into 1-inch cubes and sprinkled with 2 tablespoons lime juice to prevent discoloration
- 1 small onion, peeled and thinly sliced
- 1 teaspoon salt
- 1/2 teaspoon freshly ground black pepper
- 1/4 teaspoon ground cinnamon
- 1/4 teaspoon ground cardamom
- 2 tablespoons curry powder
- 2 cups apple juice
- 1 tablespoon sugar (optional)

1. Heat 1 tablespoon oil in a wok or deep skillet over medium heat, until very hot. Add the almonds and cherries, and stir-fry for 20 seconds. Remove the almonds and cherries using a slotted spoon. Set aside.

2. Add 2 tablespoons oil to the same wok; when hot, add the apples and fry for 20 minutes until golden brown, stirring occasionally. Remove from the wok and set aside.

3. Add the remaining oil and the onion to the wok, and fry for 10 to 15 minutes, until golden brown.

4. Add the salt, pepper, cinnamon, cardamom, curry powder, apple juice and sugar, and bring to a boil. Return the apples to the wok, cover and simmer for 10 minutes over medium-low heat, stirring occasionally.

5. Taste the braise. It should taste sweet and sour. Adjust seasoning, adding sugar or lime juice to taste.

6. Just before serving, transfer the sauce to a serving dish, sprinkle the almonds and cherries over the sauce, and serve hot with rice, pasta or couscous.

On the road from Samarkand to Bokhara, an Uzbek woman (with her family) carry the apples they have picked using an age-old transportation system.

Fruit & Vegetable Braises / 180

Horn of Africa Okra & Eggplant Braise with Unripe Grapes

Okra originated somewhere around the Horn of Africa and was spread through the spice route to the rest of the world. In the American south it is used to make gumbo. It is a relatively recent arrival in China, but it has been very popular in Indian cooking and the cooking of the central part of the Silk Road region from ancient times.

1. Place the okra in a container, and cover with water and 2 tablespoons vinegar. Let stand for 20 minutes, then rinse with cold water and pat dry. If using frozen okra, follow package instructions.

2. Meanwhile, heat 3 tablespoons oil in a wok or deep skillet over medium heat, until very hot. Fry the eggplant (one layer at a time in the wok or skillet) on both sides, until golden brown. Remove from the wok and set aside.

3. Add the remaining oil to the same wok. When very hot, add the cumin, coriander and cinnamon, and cook for 10 seconds, until aromatic (keep a cover handy to stop any seeds from flying out). Add the onion and stir-fry for 10 minutes, until translucent. Add the garlic, chilies, bell pepper and okra, and stir-fry for 2 minutes.

4. Add the tomatoes, unripe grapes, lime juice, salt, pepper, turmeric, and sugar. Gently arrange the fried eggplant over the top and bring to a boil. Reduce heat to low, cover and simmer for 10 to 15 minutes, until the vegetables are tender.

5. Remove from heat and adjust seasoning to taste.

6. Serve hot with rice, pasta or couscous.

Servings: 4
Preparation time: 30 minutes
Cooking time: 30 minutes

- 1 pound fresh or frozen okra, rinsed and fuzz removed
- 2 tablespoons vinegar
- 5 tablespoons vegetable oil, butter or ghee
- 1 pound Chinese eggplant, sliced lengthwise into 1/4-inch strips
- 1 teaspoon cumin seeds
- 1 teaspoon coriander seeds
- One 3-inch cinnamon stick
- 1 medium-sized onion, peeled and thinly sliced
- 4 cloves garlic, peeled and crushed
- 2 red hot chilies, seeded and chopped
- 1/2 red bell pepper, chopped
- 4 fresh tomatoes, peeled and chopped, or 2 pounds canned tomatoes
- 1 cup unripe grapes* or 1 tablespoon pomegranate paste
- 2 tablespoons fresh lime juice
- 1 1/2 teaspoons salt
- 1 teaspoon freshly ground black pepper
- 1/4 teaspoon turmeric
- 1 teaspoon sugar

NOTE

*If you don't use Chinese eggplants, bitterness must be removed.**

Gujarati Potato Braise

Servings: 4
Preparation time: 30 minutes
Cooking time: 50 minutes

- 1/2 cup vegetable oil, butter or ghee
- 4 large potatoes (about 2 pounds), peeled and cut into 1-inch cubes
- 2 teaspoons fennel seeds
- 1 teaspoon coriander seeds
- 1 teaspoon poppy seeds
- 2 cardamom pods
- 1 small onion, peeled and thinly sliced
- 2 cloves garlic, peeled and crushed
- 1 hot green chili, seeded and chopped
- 1/2-inch fresh ginger, peeled and crushed, or 1/4 teaspoon ginger powder
- 1 teaspoon salt
- 1 large tomato, peeled and sliced, or 1/2 cup tomato puree
- 1 1/2 cups plain yogurt
- 1/2 teaspoon sugar
- 1/2 cup blanched almonds, toasted and coarsely chopped
- 1/2 cup cilantro, chopped

Although the potato was introduced to India only in the sixteenth century by Portuguese traders (along with cashews, papaya, guava and tobacco), it quickly became very popular, especially in the Gujarat region, where two-thirds of the population are vegetarian.

1. Heat 4 tablespoons oil in a wok or deep skillet over medium heat, until very hot. Add the potatoes and fry for 15 to 20 minutes, stirring occasionally, until golden brown and tender. Remove from the wok and set aside.

2. Add 4 tablespoons oil to the same wok; when very hot, add the fennel, coriander, poppy and cardamom, and cook for 10 seconds until aromatic (keep a cover handy to stop any seeds from flying out). Add the onion and fry for 10 to 15 minutes, until golden brown. Add the garlic, chili, ginger and salt, and stir-fry for 20 seconds.

3. Add the tomatoes and bring to a boil. Reduce heat to very low.

4. Beat the yogurt with 1/2 teaspoon sugar for 5 minutes (you can use a food processor). Gradually add the yogurt to the wok on very low heat, stirring constantly (to prevent curdling) for 5 minutes. Adjust seasoning, cover and keep warm. Just before serving, arrange the potatoes on top and sprinkle with toasted almonds and cilantro.

5. Serve with rice, pasta or, in traditional Gujarati style, pan bread and a green salad.

Bombay Mushroom Curry

Servings: 4
Preparation time: 15 minutes
Cooking time: 40 minutes

- 4 tablespoons vegetable oil, butter or ghee
- 1/2 cup blanched almonds
- 1/4 cup raisins
- 2 small onions, peeled and thinly sliced
- 2 cloves garlic, peeled and sliced
- 1 teaspoon coriander seeds
- 1-inch fresh ginger, peeled and grated
- 1 bay leaf
- 2 Thai bird or serrano chilies, sliced
- 1 pound mushrooms, sliced
- 1 cup chopped celery
- 2 teaspoons salt
- 1/4 teaspoon freshly ground black pepper
- 2 teaspoons hot curry powder
- 2 teaspoons garam masala
- 1 large tomato, peeled and sliced
- 1 1/2 cups plain yogurt
- 2 teaspoons cornstarch dissolved in 2 tablespoons cold water
- 3 egg yolks (optional)

GARNISH
- 1/4 cup chopped fresh cilantro

1. In a wok or deep skillet, heat 2 tablespoons oil over medium heat, until very hot. Add the almonds and raisins, and stir-fry for 20 seconds. Remove with a slotted spoon and set aside.

2. Heat the remaining oil in the same wok, until very hot. Add the onions and stir-fry for 10 minutes, until translucent. Add the garlic, coriander, ginger, bay leaf and chilies, and stir-fry for 1 minute. Add the mushrooms and celery, and cook for 5 minutes. Add the salt, pepper, curry powder, garam masala and tomato. Cover and cook over very low heat for 10 minutes.

3. Meanwhile, in a mixing bowl, combine the yogurt, cornstarch and egg yolks. Beat, in one direction, for 5 minutes (you can use a food processor).

4. Just before serving, gradually add the yogurt mixture to the wok over very low heat, stirring constantly (to prevent curdling). .

5. Adjust seasoning to taste, cover and keep warm.

6. Transfer to a serving dish, garnish with the almonds and raisins from step 1, and cilantro, and serve hot with rice, pasta or couscous.

Fruit & Vegetable Braises

Gilani Jujube, Walnut & Pomegranates Braise

Servings: 4
Preparation time: 15 minutes
Cooking time: 55 minutes

- 1/2 pound toasted walnuts (about 2 cups)
- 1/2 cup pomegranate paste diluted in 3 cups water (or use 4 cups fresh pomegranate juice)*
- 4 tablespoons sugar
- 1/4 teaspoon ground cinnamon
- 1 teaspoon ground cumin
- 1 teaspoon salt
- 1/4 teaspoon freshly ground black pepper
- 2 tablespoons vegetable oil, butter or ghee
- 1 small onion, peeled and thinly sliced
- 1-inch fresh ginger, peeled and grated, or 1/2 teaspoon ginger powder
- 4 cloves garlic, crushed and peeled
- 1/2 cup dried figs
- 1/2 cup dried apricots
- 1/2 cup dried tart cherries
- 1 cup dried jujubes, pitted*

GARNISH
- 1/2 cup pomegranate seeds (optional)

The jujube, sometimes called the Chinese date, is a rich red, round fruit about the size of a cherry or slightly larger. It has been known for its taste and medicinal properties from China to the Mediterranean since antiquity. It is a classic Silk Road fruit, very popular from China to Iran. In China it is often used in soup and preserves, and most importantly as a tea. In Iran, it is eaten both as a children's snack and as medicine in the form of a tea. This sweet and sour dish is typical in the Gilan region of the Caspian Sea.

1. Finely grind the walnuts in a food processor. Add the diluted pomegranate paste, sugar, cinnamon, cumin, salt and pepper, and mix well to create a smooth and creamy sauce.

2. Heat the oil in a wok or deep skillet over medium heat, until very hot. Add the onions and stir-fry for 10 minutes, until translucent. Add the ginger, garlic, figs, apricots, tart cherries and jujubes, and stir-fry for 2 minutes longer.

3. Transfer the sauce from the food processor to the wok, cover and simmer over low heat for 40 minutes, stirring occasionally with a wooden spoon to prevent the nut sauce from burning.

4. Taste the sauce and adjust for seasoning and thickness; it should be sweet and sour. Add more pomegranate paste for sourness or sugar for sweetness. If the sauce is too thick, thin it with hot water. Cover and keep warm until ready to serve. Just before serving, garnish with pomegranate seeds.

5. Serve hot with rice, pasta, bulgur or couscous.

Isfahani Quince & Pomegranate Braise

Variations of this recipe, mentioned as being Persian in thirteenth century Arab cookbooks, were taken by the Arabs to Spain and Europe.

1. Wash but do not peel the quinces. Core, cut into quarters, remove seeds and cut into 1-inch cubes. Soak in a container of cold water with 2 tablespoons vinegar to prevent discoloring.

2. Finely grind the almonds in a food processor. Add the diluted pomegranate paste, honey, cinnamon, salt, pepper, rose water and saffron water, and mix well to create a smooth and creamy sauce. Set aside.

3. Drain the quince cubes and pat dry.

4. Heat 3 tablespoons oil in a wok or deep skillet over medium heat, until very hot. Add the quince, onion and ginger, and fry for 20 minutes, stirring occasionally, until the quince is golden brown.

5. Stir in the almond sauce and bring to a boil. Reduce heat to very low, cover and simmer for 35 minutes, stirring occasionally, until the quince is tender.

6. Adjust seasoning to taste by adding honey or pomegranate paste. Cover and keep warm.

7. Just before serving, garnish with pomegranate seeds and almonds. Serve hot with rice, pasta or bulgur.

Servings: 4
Preparation time: 20 minutes
Cooking time: 55 minutes

- 3 medium quinces (about 2 pounds)
- 2 tablespoons vinegar
- 2 cups (1/2 pound) toasted blanched almonds
- 1/3 cup pomegranate paste diluted in 2 1/2 cups water
- 2 tablespoons honey
- 1/4 teaspoon ground cinnamon
- 1 teaspoon salt
- 1/4 teaspoon freshly ground black pepper
- 1 tablespoon rose water
- 1/4 teaspoon ground saffron dissolved in 1 tablespoon hot water (optional)
- 3 tablespoons vegetable oil, butter or ghee
- 1 medium onion, peeled and thinly sliced
- 1/2-inch fresh ginger, peeled and grated

GARNISH

- 1 cup fresh pomegranate seeds (about 1 pomegranate)
- 2 tablespoons blanched almonds, sliced and toasted

NOTE

You may substitute 2 cups toasted walnuts for the almonds.

Kurdish Rhubarb Braise with Aromatic Herbs

Servings: 4
Preparation time: 30 minutes
Cooking time: 1 hour 10 minutes

- 4 tablespoons vegetable oil, butter or ghee
- 1 small onion, peeled and thinly sliced
- 4 cloves garlic, crushed and peeled
- 1 red hot chili, seeded and chopped, or 1/2 teaspoon chili paste
- 3 cups chopped fresh parsley
- 1/2 cup chopped fresh mint or 2 tablespoons dried mint
- 1/2 cup chopped fresh chives
- 1/2 cup chopped fresh dill
- 1/2 cup chopped fresh cilantro
- 2/3 cup yellow split peas, picked over and rinsed
- 2 teaspoons salt
- 1/2 teaspoon freshly ground black pepper
- 1/4 teaspoon ground turmeric
- 3 1/2 cups vegetable stock* or water
- 1 fresh tomato, peeled and sliced
- 1/2 teaspoon ground saffron diluted in 2 tablespoons hot water
- 2 tablespoons fresh lime juice
- 2 tablespoons sugar
- 1 pound fresh or frozen rhubarb, cut into 2-inch pieces

Rhubarb, which appears to have originated in eastern Asia, has been valued since antiquity in China as well as classical Greece, Rome and Iran for its medicinal properties: It is said to cleanse the blood and purify the system. It is also delicious to eat. It grows well in high, cold climate zones such as the Himalayas or the Pir Omar Mountains of Kurdistan, where this dish originated in the camps of Kurdish mountain nomads.

1. Heat 4 tablespoons oil in a wok or deep skillet, over medium heat, until very hot. Add the onion and stir-fry for 5 minutes, until translucent. Add the garlic, chili, parsley, mint, chives, dill and cilantro, and fry for 15 minutes, stirring occasionally, until aromatic.

2. Add the split peas, salt, pepper and turmeric, and stir-fry for 2 minutes.

3. Pour in 3 1/2 cups stock and bring to a boil. Reduce heat to medium, cover and simmer for 20 minutes, stirring occasionally.

4. Add the tomato, saffron, lime juice and sugar, and bring back to a boil. Reduce heat to low, arrange the rhubarb on top and around the wok, cover and cook for 10 to 15 minutes until the rhubarb is soft but not to the point of falling apart.

5. Adjust seasoning to taste. If the braise is too sour, add 1 tablespoon sugar.

6. Serve hot with rice, pasta or bulgur.

Uzbek Sweet & Sour Carrot & Raisin Braise

1. Heat 2 tablespoons oil in a wok or deep skillet over medium heat, until very hot. Add the pistachios and raisins, stir-fry for 20 seconds, remove from the wok and set aside.

2. Heat the remaining oil in the same wok; when hot, add the onions and fry for 15 minutes, stirring occasionally, until golden brown. Add the garlic, chili and carrots, and cook over medium heat for 10 minutes.

3. Add the salt, pepper, cinnamon, cumin, saffron, sugar, tomatoes, tomato paste, and stir-fry for 5 minutes. Add 1/2 cup vegetable stock, and bring to a boil. Reduce heat to medium, cover and cook for 15 minutes, stirring occasionally.

4. Check the carrots for tenderness. Adjust seasoning. Cover and keep warm until ready to serve.

5. Just before serving, sprinkle the raisin and pistachio mixture over the top, and serve hot with rice, pasta or couscous.

Servings: 4
Preparation time: 10 minutes
Cooking time: 45 minutes

- 1/2 cup vegetable oil, butter or ghee
- 1 cup unsalted pistachios, shelled
- 1 cup raisins
- 1 large onion, peeled and very thinly sliced
- 1 clove garlic, peeled and crushed
- 1 green chili pepper (cubenelle)
- 1 pound carrots, peeled and sliced
- 1 teaspoon salt
- 1 teaspoon freshly ground black pepper
- 1/2 teaspoon ground cinnamon
- 1/2 teaspoon ground cumin
- 1/4 teaspoon ground saffron threads dissolved in 1 tablespoon hot water (optional)
- 1 teaspoon sugar
- 1 large tomato peeled and sliced
- 1 teaspoon tomato paste
- 1/2 cup vegetable stock* or water

The Stranger at the Gate

Among the oldest of tales is this Greek one: It happened that the gods Zeus and Hermes assumed mortal form to wander the mountains of Phrygia (now Turkey), stopping at farmhouses for something to eat and a place to rest. The Phrygians, however, were mean spirited and suspicious. They bolted their doors against strangers. Only one house welcomed the travelers. It was a tiny, poor, thatched house, home to the elderly Baucis and her husband Philemon. The old people invited the strangers to rest and chatted kindly with them as Baucis bustled about, preparing a meal.

It was the best meal they could offer. First Baucis spread out olives, pickles, endives, radishes and baked eggs. There was wine—not very good—served from an earthenware bowl. Then the guests ate apples, grapes, nuts, figs and plums. Last was the couple's treasure: A golden comb of honey from their hive.

Toward the end of the meal the hosts noticed that the wine bowl never emptied, a sign that gods were present. Terrified, Baucis and Philemon apologized for the humble fare. They even offered to slaughter their one goose for their guests.

Zeus and Hermes spared the bird, but not the Phrygians. All the valley—all the rich farmhouses, fields and orchards—vanished beneath a lake. Only Baucis and Philemon's house, standing alone on a hill, survived, and it was changed into a temple of marble and gold.

Smiling, Zeus told the old people that they might ask for any gift. Devout as well as generous, they asked to serve the gods as priests in the temple. They also asked that they might die at the same time, so that neither would have to mourn.

That is what happened. For some years, the couple served the temple. When it came their time to die, Baucis was transformed into a lime tree and Philemon into an oak. The trees could be seen for years, entwined outside the temple.

Almost every culture has a tale of gods in disguise seeking hospitality, for in almost every culture, the guest is sacred. He is "dear to God" or "God's friend," as Iranians say, and must be welcomed.

The sign of welcome is always food and drink. In medieval Europe, the food was bread and salt. In China the drink was tea. In Iran it was (and is) fresh herbs, bread and cheese. In the regions along the Silk Road, hospitality traditionally meant bread and yogurt, although in more recent times the custom has been to serve tea with preserved fruits or jam: An ever-steaming samovar greets visitors to most houses in central Asia.

Whatever the food, the rules of hospitality say it must be the best the hosts can provide—and it must be given without asking, assuming a visitor to be hungry: A guest who is asked whether he wants something to eat is bound to answer that he does not (the host should insist). The host's other duty is to be as entertaining as he can. If he is rich (or talented) he may provide music, for instance. Even if he is as poor as the old couple in the story, he can offer friendly conversation, as they did. As for the guest, he must be appreciative of all that is given.

Generosity and appreciation form a bond between guest and host, and it is the breaking of bread together that seals the bond. Once they have dined, it might be said, their spirits are entwined, like the lime tree and the oak in the legend.

Persian Butternut Squash Braise

Servings: 4
Preparation time: 35 minutes
Cooking time: 40 minutes

- 5 tablespoons vegetable oil, butter or ghee
- 1 cup walnuts, shelled
- One 3-inch cinnamon stick
- 2 whole cloves
- 2 small onions, peeled and thinly sliced
- 2 pounds butternut squash, peeled and cut into 2-inch cubes
- 1 teaspoon salt
- 1/2 teaspoon freshly ground black pepper
- 2 tablespoons sugar
- 1 tablespoon fresh lime juice
- 1 cup pitted prunes or dried golden plums*
- 1 1/2 cups vegetable stock* or water

1. Heat 3 tablespoons oil in a wok or deep skillet over medium heat, until very hot. Add the walnuts and stir-fry for 10 seconds. Remove from the wok and set aside.

2. Heat the remaining oil, in the same wok, until very hot, add the cinnamon and cloves, and cook for 10 seconds, until aromatic. Add the onions and butternut squash, and fry for 15 minutes, stirring occasionally, until the butternut squash is golden brown.

3. Add the salt, pepper sugar, lime juice, prunes and vegetable stock. Bring to a boil, reduce heat to low, cover and simmer for 15 to 20 minutes, until the squash is tender.

4. Just before serving, sprinkle the walnuts over the top. Serve hot with rice, bread, pasta or couscous.

Fruit & Vegetable Braises

Samarkand Golden Peach Braise

Servings: 4
Preparation time: 30 minutes
Cooking time: 1 hour 15 minutes

5 firm peaches
1 tablespoon fresh lime juice
4 tablespoons vegetable oil, butter or ghee
1 small onion, peeled and thinly sliced
2 cloves garlic, crushed and peeled
1/2-inch fresh ginger, peeled and grated
1 teaspoon ground coriander
1/4 teaspoon cinnamon
1 tablespoon sugar
1 teaspoon salt
1/2 teaspoon freshly ground black pepper
1 Thai bird or serrano chili, seeded and chopped, or 1/8 teaspoon cayenne
2/3 cup yellow split peas
1/4 cup chopped fresh parsley or mint

It is often thought that peaches came from Persia, because their name in most languages derives from the Latin persicum malum, *or "Persian apple." Actually, it is now fairly certain that peaches originated in China but thrived when introduced to the West. No doubt the name derives from the fact that Alexander the Great sent peaches to Greece after his Persian conquests. The Romans spread them to the rest of Europe, and the Spanish to the Americas. As for the Chinese, they eagerly imported new varieties developed in the West, among them peach trees that produced yellow fruit the size of goose eggs. These were the "golden peaches of Samarkand" that grew in the imperial gardens of Changan (Xian) during the T'ang dynasty in the seventh to tenth century.*

1. Wash the peaches well to remove the fuzz. Remove the pits and cut the peaches into 1-inch wedges. Sprinkle with lime juice (to prevent discoloring) and set aside.

2. Heat the oil in a wok or deep skillet over medium heat, until very hot. Add the onion and fry for 15 minutes, until golden brown. Add the garlic, ginger, coriander, cinnamon, sugar, salt, pepper, chili and split peas, and stir-fry for 1 minute longer.

3. Pour in 2 1/2 cups water and bring to a boil. Reduce heat to low, cover and simmer for 20 minutes.

4. Add the peaches. Cover and simmer over medium-low heat for 10 to 15 minutes, until the peas and peaches are tender.

5. The sauce should taste sweet and sour. Adjust seasoning to taste by adding sugar or lime juice as necessary.

6. Just before serving, sprinkle with the parsley. Serve hot with rice or couscous.

Indian Cauliflower & Potato Curry

Servings: 4
Preparation time: 15 minutes
Cooking time: 1 hour 15 minutes

- 6 new potatoes (1 pound), scrubbed, washed, and halved
- 4 tablespoons vegetable oil, butter or ghee
- 1 teaspoon cumin seeds
- 1 teaspoon coriander seeds
- 1 medium onion, peeled and sliced
- 1-inch fresh ginger, peeled and grated
- 2 cloves garlic, crushed and peeled
- 1 Thai bird or serrano chili, seeded and chopped
- 1 medium cauliflower head, cut into small florets
- 2 large tomatoes, peeled and sliced
- 1 teaspoon salt
- 1 teaspoon freshly ground black pepper
- 1/4 teaspoon sugar
- 1 teaspoon curry powder
- 1 cup frozen peas (optional)

GARNISH
- 1/4 cup chopped fresh cilantro
- 1 cup yogurt, drained

Traditionally, this dish is made for wedding banquets and without onion or garlic, but I prefer to include them.

1. Place the potatoes in a medium-sized pot, cover with water and cook over medium heat for 25 to 30 minutes, until almost tender. Drain and set aside.

2. Meanwhile, heat the oil in a wok or deep skillet over medium heat, until very hot. Add the cumin and coriander, and cook for 10 seconds, until aromatic (keep a cover handy to stop any seeds from flying out). Add the onion and stir-fry for 5 minutes, until translucent. Add the ginger, garlic, chili and cauliflower, and stir-fry for 5 minutes.

3. Add the tomatoes, salt, pepper, sugar and curry powder. Cover and simmer over medium heat for 20 minutes.

4. Add the potatoes and peas, and stir gently. Cover and cook, over medium-low heat, for 10 to 15 minutes, until potatoes are cooked. Adjust seasoning to taste.

5. Transfer to a serving bowl and sprinkle with cilantro. Serve with yogurt over bread or rice.

Sichuan Spicy Stir-Fry Tofu

Servings: 4
Preparation time: 30 minutes
Cooking time: 15 minutes

SAUCE

- 1 tablespoon cornstarch, dissolved in 1/4 cup cold water
- 2 tablespoons soy sauce
- 3 tablespoons rice vinegar
- 1 tablespoon sugar
- 2 teaspoons salt
- 1/2 teaspoon toasted Sichuan pepper, ground
- 1/2 teaspoon hot chili paste
- 1 tablespoon toasted sesame oil
- 2 fresh scallions, shredded

TOFU

- 6 tablespoons peanut oil
- 1 pound firm tofu (bean curd), wrapped in 3 layers of paper towels (to absorb excess water) and allowed to sit for 10 minutes, then sliced into 2-by-3-inch cubes
- 1 Chinese eggplant, shredded
- 4 cloves garlic, crushed and peeled
- 1-inch fresh ginger, peeled and grated
- 4 baby bok choy, washed, trimmed and cut into quarters (lengthwise)

I adapted this recipe, which uses the classical Sichuan cooking ingredients of chili pepper, Sichuan pepper and sesame oil, from a wonderful vegetarian meal I had at the Wenshu Monastery in Chengdu. In the traditional Chinese su style, we were served all kinds of delicious vegetarian dishes, including a whole fish made from doufu (tofu).

1. Combine the cornstarch, soy sauce, vinegar, sugar, salt, Sichuan pepper, chili paste, sesame oil and scallions in a small bowl, and set aside.

2. Heat 4 tablespoons peanut oil in a wok or deep skillet over medium heat, until very hot. Arrange the tofu pieces in a single layer in the wok and fry on all sides, until golden brown. Remove from the wok and set aside.

3. Add the remaining oil to the same wok. When hot, add the eggplant, garlic and ginger, and stir-fry for 2 minutes, until the eggplant is golden brown. Add the sauce, bok choy and tofu to the wok. Reduce heat to low, cover and simmer for 5 to 10 minutes, until the bok choy are tender. Adjust seasonings to taste.

4. Serve with rice, bulgur or pasta.

VARIATION

Indonesian Stir-Fry Tempeh

You may substitute an 8-ounce package of tempeh (fermented and spiced soybeans), cut into 2-inch slices, for the tofu. Reduce the salt in the ingredients to 1 teaspoon.

Caspian Eggplant & Aromatic Herbs Braise

Servings: 4
Preparation time: 15 minutes
Cooking time: 50 minutes

- 8 Chinese eggplants (2 pounds) or 2 large regular eggplants, peeled and bitterness removed*
- 1/2 cup olive oil
- 4 cloves garlic, peeled and crushed
- 2 cups (1/2 pound) toasted walnuts
- 1/4 cup pomegranate paste* diluted in 2 1/2 cups water, or 3 cups fresh pomegranate juice (4 pomegranates)
- 1 tablespoon honey
- 2 teaspoons ground cumin
- 1/4 teaspoon ground cinnamon
- 1 teaspoon salt
- 1/4 teaspoon pepper
- 1/4 teaspoon turmeric
- 1 Thai bird or serrano chili, chopped or 1/4 teaspoon chili paste or cayenne
- 1 cup chopped fresh parsley
- 1 cup chopped fresh cilantro
- 1/2 cup chopped scallions

1. Remove the stalks from the eggplants and slice them into 1/4-inch-thick-by-3-inch lengths.

2. Arrange the eggplant slices on an oiled baking sheet and brush both sides with a little oil. Cook each side under the broiler for 2 minutes or until golden brown (alternately, you can bake the eggplant slices in a 500°F preheated oven for 15 minutes).

3. In a food processor, grind the garlic, walnuts, diluted pomegranate paste, honey, cumin, cinnamon, salt, pepper, turmeric, chili, parsley, cilantro and scallions until you have a smooth sauce.

4. Preheat the oven to 350°F.

5. Arrange one layer of eggplant slices in a deep, nonreactive 9-by-9-inch baking dish and spread a layer of the walnut sauce on top. Then place another layer of eggplant over the top. Continue, alternating eggplant slices and walnut sauce layering, until you have used all the eggplant slices.

6. Cover and bake for 45 minutes. Adjust seasoning to taste. If it is too sour, add a little honey.

7. Serve with rice, pasta or bulgur.

Pasta, Pizza & Bread

Neapolitan Pasta with Tomato Sauce (Master Recipe)

Servings: 2 to 4
Preparation time: 5 minutes
Cooking time: 25 minutes

2 tablespoons olive oil
4 cloves garlic, crushed and peeled
1 bird or serrano chili, chopped
2 bay leaves
1 teaspoon salt
1/2 teaspoon freshly ground black pepper
3 large tomatoes (about 2 pounds), peeled and sliced, or one 28-ounce can of Italian plum tomatoes
8 ounces spaghetti
1 tablespoon butter
1/2 cup freshly grated Parmigiano-Reggiano cheese
1/2 cup fresh basil leaves

NOTE

You can use other noodles, including fettuccine, capellini or reshteh (fettuccini-like 1/4-inch flat Persian noodles) as well as any of the Asian noodles.

Do not add salt to the water when preparing Asian noodles.

You can also make this pasta with any of the sauces listed on the pages that follow.

1. Bring 5 quarts water to a rolling boil in a large steamer (a steamer makes draining and adding the pasta to the sauce easier, but you can also use any large pot).
2. Meanwhile, prepare the sauce. In a wok or large skillet, heat 2 tablespoons oil over medium heat. Add garlic, chili, bay leaves, salt and pepper, and stir-fry for 30 seconds. Add tomatoes and cook for 10 minutes over medium heat. Turn off the heat and allow to stand until the noodles are ready.
3. When the water for the noodles has come to a full boil, add 2 tablespoons salt and the noodles. Stir once and boil for 2 to 10 minutes (depending on the type of noodle and whether you prefer a firmer or softer noodle). Test for doneness.
4. Drain the pasta, reserving 1/4 cup liquid, then add both pasta and liquid to the sauce.
5. Add the butter, toss well and serve on heated plates. Garnish with grated Parmigiano-Reggiano cheese and fresh basil.

A NOTE ON COOKING ASIAN NOODLES

Rice Stick Noodles (Vermicelli)
Soak 1 pound of noodles in a container of warm water for 15 to 20 minutes, until soft. Drain. Snip in half using scissors. Rinse with cold water and shake well to remove all excess water and starch. Do not soak for longer as the noodles will become too soft.

Cellophane Noodles (Mung Bean Noodles)
Bring 5 quarts water to a boil. Meanwhile, soak 1 pound of cellophane noodles in a container of cold water for 20 minutes, until soft. Drain. Snip in half using scissors. Drop the noodles in the boiling water for 1 minute or until the water comes back to a boil. Drain immediately and rinse well with cold water to stop cooking.

Thai Noodles (1/4-Inch Flat Rice Noodles)
Bring 5 quarts water to a boil in a large steamer (steamer makes it easy to drain and rinse). Add 8 ounces of Thai noodles, turn off the heat and allow to soak in the boiling water for 1 minute. Drain and rinse.

Chinese Egg Noodles (Wheat Noodles)
Bring 5 quarts water to a rolling boil in a large steamer. Add the noodles and boil for a few minutes until the strands can be pulled apart with chop sticks.

Sicilian Mushroom, Saffron Cream Sauce

1. In a wok or large skillet heat 2 tablespoons oil over medium heat. Add the garlic and stir-fry for 20 seconds. Add the mushrooms and fry for 5 minutes. Add the broccoli, salt, pepper, nutmeg and chili, and stir-fry 2 minutes longer. Add the wine and cook until all the liquid has evaporated.

2. Just before serving, add spaghetti or your favorite pasta (cooked per the master recipe for Neapolitan pasta on page 198), 1/4 cup pasta liquid, cream, butter, cheese and basil. Toss thoroughly, adjust seasoning to taste and serve right away.

Servings: 2 to 4
Preparation time: 15 minutes
Cooking time: 10 minutes

- 2 tablespoons oil
- 4 cloves garlic, crushed and peeled
- 1/2 pound fresh shitake mushrooms, washed and sliced
- 1/2 pound broccoli, washed and separated into small florets
- 1/2 teaspoon salt
- 1 teaspoon freshly ground black pepper
- 1 teaspoon ground nutmeg
- 1/2 teaspoon red chili paste or red hot pepper flakes
- 1/2 cup white wine
- 8 ounces spaghetti or your favorite pasta
- 1 cup cream mixed with 1/4 teaspoon ground saffron threads dissolved in 1 tablespoon hot water
- 1 tablespoon butter
- 1/2 cup freshly grated Parmigiano-Reggiano cheese
- 1/3 cup fresh Thai basil leaves

Silk Road Noodle Sauces

Servings: 2 to 4
Preparation time: 10 minutes
Cooking time: 10 minutes

- 6 cloves garlic, peeled and crushed
- 1/2 cup shelled, unsalted pistachios* (or pine nuts or walnuts), ground
- 2 1/2 cups fresh basil leaves, finely chopped
- 1/4 cup olive oil
- 1/2 teaspoon kosher salt
- 1/2 teaspoon freshly ground black pepper
- 1 teaspoon ground cumin (optional)
- 1/2 teaspoon red chili paste
- 1/4 cup freshly grated Parmigiano-Reggiano cheese

BIRJANDI CUCUMBER & PISTACHIO SAUCE (PESTEH BANEH)
- 1 cup shelled pistachios, picked over and rinsed
- 1 cup shelled walnuts, picked over and rinsed
- 1/2 cup fresh basil leaves
- 1/2 cup fresh mint
- 1/4 cup fresh tarragon
- 1 teaspoon salt
- 1 teaspoon freshly ground pepper
- 1 cup boiling water
- 1 pita bread toasted
- 1 seedless cucumber, peeled and thinly sliced

BIRJANDI WHEY SAUCE (QORUT)
- 1 cup liquid whey (kashk)*
- 2 cups shelled walnuts, picked over and rinsed
- 5 cloves garlic, peeled
- 1 tablespoon dried mint
- 1/2 teaspoon salt
- 1 teaspoon freshly ground pepper
- 1/2 cup boiling water

These various topping can be used with 1/2 pound of your favorite noodles. Each is for 2 to 4 servings and can be made in about 15 minutes.

Persian Pistachio Sauce

1. To make the sauce, grind (by pulsing) all the ingredients for the sauce in a food processor until you have a grainy sauce. Adjust seasoning to taste. Transfer to a large serving dish, cover and set aside.

2. Just before serving, add your favorite pasta (cooked per master recipe), Toss thoroughly, adjust seasoning to taste, garnish with a few sprigs of basil, some flowers petals and two table spoons pistachios, and serve right away.

Birjandi Cucumber & Pistachio Sauce

Both recipes below are traditionally made as a soup with tiny wild pistachios first ground with water and then drained. I have adapted them using regular pistachios and turned them into sauces. The recipes come directly from the Sepehri family in Birjand. Birjand is an ancient town in eastern Iran on low hills surrounded by desert. It was a caravan town on the Silk Road but has kept its traditionally Iranian cuisine, which has much in common with Afghan cuisine.

1. Puree all the ingredients (except the cucumber) in a food processor and adjust seasoning to taste.

2. Just before serving, add your favorite pasta (cooked per the master recipe) and the cucumber. Toss thoroughly, adjust seasoning to taste and serve right away.

Birjandi Whey Sauce

1. Purée all the ingredients in a food processor and transfer to a medium saucepan. Cook over very low heat, stirring constantly, for 5 to 10 minutes, until thoroughly blended. Adjust seasoning to taste.

2. Just before serving, add your favorite pasta (cooked per the master recipe). Toss thoroughly, with stir-fried zucchini and eggplant. Adjust seasoning to taste and serve right away.

Pasta, Pizza & Bread

Silk Road Sauces (Continued)

Servings: 2 to 4
Preparation time: 10 minutes
Cooking time: 20 minutes

- 4 tablespoons vegetable oil, butter or ghee
- 2 medium onions, peeled and thinly sliced
- 1 clove garlic, crushed and peeled
- 1/2 cup walnuts, coarsely chopped
- 1/2 cup currants
- 1 large pita loaf, toasted and cut into 1-inch pieces
- 2 cups plain yogurt, beaten with 1 teaspoon salt and 1/2 teaspoon freshly ground pepper

AFGHAN SPICY YOGURT SAUCE

- 4 tablespoons olive oil
- 1 teaspoon coriander seeds
- 1 teaspoon fennel seeds
- 1 teaspoon cumin seeds
- 1 bird or serrano chili, seeded and sliced
- 1 onion, peeled and thinly sliced
- 1 clove garlic, crushed and peeled
- 1/2 cup ground walnuts
- 1 large tomato, peeled and sliced
- 1 teaspoon salt
- 1/2 teaspoon freshly ground black pepper
- 1 cup fresh mint leaves
- 2 cups yogurt and 1 teaspoon cornstarch, beaten for 5 minutes, clockwise

GREEK GARLIC & ALMOND SAUCE

- 3 cloves garlic, roasted and peeled
- 1 cup blanched almonds
- 1 pita bread, chopped and soaked in 1/2 cup water
- 1/2 teaspoon salt
- 1/2 teaspoon fresh ground pepper
- 1/2 cup virgin olive oil
- 2 tablespoons fresh lime juice
- 2 tablespoons vinegar

Traditionally this Afghan yogurt sauce, called qoruti and the shurba recipe below are used as a dip or a soup, but I find that they also make excellent pasta toppings.

Afghan Yogurt & Bread Sauce (Qoruti)

Heat oil in a wok or large, deep skillet over medium heat. Add the onions and fry for 15 minutes, until golden brown. Add garlic and stir-fry for 1 minute. Add currants, walnuts and bread, and stir-fry for 10 seconds. Remove from heat and gradually stir in the yogurt. Adjust seasoning to taste.

Afghan Spicy Yogurt Sauce (Shurba)

Heat the oil in a wok over medium heat until very hot. Add all the seeds and cook for 10 seconds, until aromatic (keep a cover handy to stop the seeds from flying out). Add the chili and onion, and fry for 15 minutes, until golden brown. Add the garlic and walnut, and stir-fry for 20 seconds. Reduce heat to very low. Add all the remaining ingredients except the yogurt. Cook for 5 minutes, then gradually add the yogurt stirring constantly for 5 minutes to prevent the yogurt from curdling. Remove from heat and adjust seasoning to taste.

VARIATION

The Kurdish sauce below is called Tarkhineh, a name also used for the disks of fermented bulgur and yogurt used by the Kurds.

Kurdish Bulgur Sauce (Tarkhineh)

In the Afghan spicy sauce, replace the walnuts and the tomatoes with 1 cup fine bulgur soaked in 1/2 cup of warm water for 45 minutes and drained.

In certain regions of Greece, the pita bread in the recipe is replaced with mashed potato.

Greek Garlic & Almond Sauce (Skorthalia)

1. In a food processor, blend the garlic, almonds, soaked bread, salt and pepper until smooth.

2. Gradually add the olive oil and pulse until it is thoroughly blended.

3. Drizzle with the lime juice and vinegar, and adjust seasoning to taste.

4. Just before serving, add your favorite pasta (cooked per the master recipe). Toss thoroughly, adjust seasoning to taste and serve right away.

Syrian Tahini Sauce (Tarator)

1. To make the sauce, mix the tahini paste (be sure to shake the bottle of the tahini paste before using) and lime juice in a food processor, until you have a thick paste. Gradually add the water and the rest of the ingredients, except the pomegranate and basil. Adjust seasoning to taste.

2. Just before serving, add your favorite pasta (cooked per the master recipe for Neapolitan pasta on page 198. Transfer to a large bowl and garnish with 1/2 cup pomegranate seeds and 1/2 cup basil leaves or parsley.

Thai Stir-Fry Coconut Sauce (Pad Thai Sauce)

Heat the oil in a wok over medium heat until very hot. Add all the ingredients and cook for 3 to 5 minutes, stirring constantly, until you have a thick sauce. Adjust seasoning to taste (add more sugar if too sour).

Vietnamese Peanut Sauce (Nuocleo)

1. Heat the oil in a wok over medium heat until very hot. Add the garlic, chili and ginger, and stir-fry for 20 seconds. Add the rest of the ingredients, stirring constantly with a wooden spoon for 5 minutes, until you have a smooth sauce.

2. Just before serving, add your favorite pasta (cooked per the master recipe). Toss thoroughly, adjust seasoning to taste, garnish with basil and serve right away.

Servings: 2 to 4
Preparation time: 10 minutes
Cooking time: 5 minutes

- 1 cup tahini (sesame) paste
- 1/4 cup fresh lime juice
- 1/2 cup boiling water
- 2 cloves garlic, peeled & crushed
- 1 teaspoon olive oil
- 1 teaspoon salt
- 1/2 teaspoon chili paste
- 1 teaspoon ground cumin
- 1/2 cup pomegranate seeds
- 1/2 cup basil leaves

THAI COCONUT SAUCE

- 2 tablespoons oil
- 1/2 cup tamarind paste*
- 2 cups unsweetened coconut milk*
- 1 shallot, peeled and thinly sliced
- 1 tablespoon bean paste
- 2 tablespoons brown sugar
- 1/2 teaspoon cayenne
- 2 scallions, shredded

VIETNAMESE PEANUT SAUCE

- 2 tablespoons peanut oil
- 2 cloves garlic, peeled and crushed
- 1 bird or serrano chili, chopped, or 1 teaspoon cayenne
- 1/4-inch fresh ginger, peeled and grated
- 2 teaspoons hot curry powder
- 2 cups plain soy or coconut milk (if using canned, shake well)
- 2 tablespoons peanut butter
- 2 teaspoons soy sauce
- 4 tablespoons rice vinegar
- 2 teaspoons brown sugar
- 1 teaspoon salt
- 1/2 teaspoon freshly ground black pepper
- 1 teaspoon cornstarch, dissolved in 1/4 cup water

GARNISH

- 1/4 cup fresh Thai basil leaves

Afghan Garlic Chive Ravioli with Yogurt Sauce (Ashak)

Servings: 6
Preparation time: 15 minutes
Cooking time: 30 minutes

FILLING

- 1 pound firm tofu (removed from the package, drained, wrapped with a few layers of paper towel, all juice squeezed out and crumbled)
- 4 cups chopped scallions, garlic chives (gandana) or leeks
- 2 tablespoons vegetable oil
- 2 teaspoons salt
- 1 teaspoon ground coriander
- 1 teaspoon freshly ground pepper
- 1 teaspoon chili paste

WRAPPERS

- 1 package ready-made wonton wrappers removed from the package and covered with a dish towel to prevent drying
- 2 tablespoons olive oil

YOGURT SAUCE (CHAKA)

- 2 cups plain yogurt (drained) or whey*
- 1 clove garlic, crushed, peeled and chopped
- 1 tablespoon dry mint or 1 cup fresh mint
- 1 teaspoon salt
- 1/2 teaspoon freshly ground pepper

Ashak is a ravioli-like pasta traditionally filled with ground meat and gandana (similar to garlic chives), and served with a yogurt sauce. Here, I have replaced the ground meat with tofu.

1. In a bowl, mix all the ingredients for the filling with a rubber spatula until you have a grainy paste. Set aside.

2. To make the yogurt sauce, combine all the ingredients for the sauce in a mixing bowl and set aside.

3. To make the ashak, place 2 heaping teaspoons of the filling in the center of a wrapper and moisten the edge with a little water. Fold the wrapper over to form a triangle, and pinch and crimp to seal. Place the finished ashaks, separated from each other, on a baking sheet lined with parchment paper. Cover the ashaks with a dish towel as you work so that they do not dry out.

4. To cook the ashak, bring 8 cups of water to a boil in a medium-sized pot. Add 1 teaspoon salt and 1 tablespoon olive oil. Add 10 ashaks at a time, and stir gently to prevent the ashaks from sticking together. Reduce heat to low and allow them to simmer for about 10 minutes until they float to the surface. Gently remove the ashaks using a slotted spoon, set aside and continue this procedure until you have cooked all the ashaks. Drizzle 1 tablespoon olive oil over the ashaks.

5. Just before serving, place half the yogurt sauce in a serving dish, place the ashaks over it and cover them with the remaining yogurt sauce.

HOMEMADE WRAPPER

It is very easy to make this wrapper at home, and I prefer to do it in this way: Place 3 cups flour in a mixing bowl and gradually stir in 1 cup water. Knead for 5 minutes until you have a soft dough that does not stick to your hands. Cover and allow to rest at room temperature for 30 minutes. Roll the dough into a long cylinder and divide it into 32 pieces. Roll out each piece into a 3-inch disk. Cover the pieces to prevent drying while you prepare your filling.

Greek Spinach & Leek Pie in Filo Pastry (Spanakopita)

1. Unwrap the filo sheets and stack them on a dish cloth. Cover the stack with another cloth and place a moist cloth over the top of the stack. This will prevent the filo from drying out while you are working with it.

2. To make the filling, heat 2 tablespoons of butter in a wok or deep skillet over medium heat, add the shallots and leeks, and stir-fry for 5 minutes until the shallots are translucent. Add the spinach, cover and cook for 5 minutes. Uncover and continue cooking until all excess juice has evaporated (be careful not to burn the spinach). Remove from heat, transfer to a mixing bowl and allow to cool.

3. Paint a 10-by-12-inch baking sheet with butter. Line the baking sheet with parchment paper, brush with butter, add one layer of filo pastry and brush lightly with butter. Repeat until you have 6 layers of filo sheets.

4. Combine the herbs, spices, cheeses and egg with the spinach and leek mixture.

5. Carefully spread the spinach mixture on top of the filo sheets; start in the center and spread evenly.

6. Place a layer of filo pastry on top of the spinach mixture and brush lightly with butter. Repeat until there are 6 layers of filo pastry covering the spinach.

7. Preheat the oven to 350°F.

8. With a sharp knife, cut the pie into 2-inch squares. Pour the glaze over the top and allow to set for 15 minutes.

9. Bake for 35 minutes, until the top is golden brown.

10. Remove from the oven and allow to cool for a few minutes. Transfer to a serving dish.

Makes one 10-by-12-inch baking sheet of pastry
Preparation time: 30 minutes plus 15 minutes setting time for the glaze
Cooking time: 45 minutes

4 tablespoons butter (melted), vegetable oil or ghee
8 shallots, peeled and chopped
4 fresh leeks, chopped (white and green)
1 1/2 pounds fresh spinach leaves, washed and coarsely chopped (or 8 ounces frozen spinach, chopped)
1/4 cup chopped fresh dill
1/2 cup chopped fresh arugula
1 teaspoon freshly ground black pepper
1 cup ricotta cheese
1/3 cup grated Parmesan cheese
1/2 pound crumbled feta cheese
2 eggs
1 teaspoon hot red chili flakes
1/2 teaspoon salt
1/2 teaspoon pepper

GLAZE
Mixture of 1 egg and 1 cup milk

FILO
1 package filo pastry sheets (left out of the freezer for at least 2 hours)
1 cup butter or ghee

Sicilian Fava Bean, Garlic & Dill Crostata

Makes one 10-inch tart
Preparation time: 20 minutes, plus 30 minutes for refrigeration
Cooking time: 1 hour 5 minutes

HOMEMADE DOUGH
- 1 1/2 cups all-purpose unbleached flour
- 1/2 teaspoon salt
- 1/2 cup butter, diced or olive oil
- 1 egg
- 3 to 4 tablespoons ice water

FILLING
- 1 tablespoon vegetable oil, butter or ghee
- 1 medium onion, peeled and thinly sliced
- 4 cloves garlic, peeled and crushed
- 2 pounds fresh fava beans (in the pod), shelled and removed from the outer layer of skin, or 1 pound frozen fava beans soaked in warm water for a few minutes and outer skin peeled off
- 1 cup chopped fresh dill
- 1 teaspoon salt
- 1 teaspoon freshly ground pepper
- 1/8 teaspoon sugar
- 2 eggs
- 1 1/4 cups heavy cream or soy milk
- 1/3 cup grated Parmesan cheese

NOTE
You may replace the homemade dough with 8 ounces of ready-made frozen puff pastry, thawed and rolled out to an 11-inch circle.

The mixture of fava beans, garlic, and dill is ubiquitous throughout the countries of the Silk Road region. This Sicilian crostata (a simple crust, filled with fruit or savory), for example, is made with shortcrust, whereas in the Caspian region, the base for the same filling is lavash bread.

1. To make the homemade dough, combine the flour and salt in a food processor and pulse several times. Add the butter and pulse. Add the egg and pulse. Add the ice water, a little at a time, and mix for 20 seconds until the dough is just holding together but has not yet formed a ball. Gather the mixture with your hands and roll out on a cool, floured surface to an 11-inch circle. Roll the dough over the rolling pin and transfer to the tart pan to make a shell.

2. Prick the shell with a fork a few times, line it with heavy duty aluminum foil and chill in the refrigerator for 30 minutes or several hours (or you can freeze it for up to 3 weeks).

3. To bake the shell, preheat the oven to 425°F. Remove the shell from the refrigerator, place it on a baking sheet still wrapped in aluminum foil, and bake for 15 minutes. Remove from the oven and remove the foil.

4. To make the filling, heat the oil in a wok or deep skillet over medium heat. Add the onion and stir-fry for 5 minutes or until translucent. Add the garlic, beans, dill, salt, pepper, and sugar and stir-fry for 5 minutes longer. Remove from heat and allow to cool.

5. In a mixing bowl, whisk the eggs, cream, and 1/4 cup cheese. Add the bean mixture and blend thoroughly. Fill the shell with the filling and top with the remaining cheese.

6. Reduce the oven temperature to 375°F and return the tart to the oven. Bake for 30 to 40 minutes longer or until the crust is golden brown.

7. Remove from the oven and allow to cool before serving.

Mosul Bulgur Patties with Walnut & Pomegranate (Kibbeh)

Mosul, sited on the road that linked Syria and Anatolia with Persia, was the principal city of northern Mesopotamia in the early centuries of our era, and among the things it was famed for were patties such as these. In fact, the patties can be found throughout the Silk Road region. In Lebanon, Egypt, and Syria they are called kibbeh; in southern Iraq and Iran kubba; elsewhere in Iran they are known as chabab or kuefta. The Turks call the dish koftesi. The many variants of the name all describe a pounded mixture of grains such as rice or bulgur—often combined with meat—with a filling of fruit, nuts, cheese, or eggs. The mixture can be shaped into a 3-inch torpedo, a round ball, or a flat patty; it may be deep fried, grilled, steamed, baked, or poached in broth to produce a crisp outer shell and a juicy, spicy interior. The recipe below describes the simplest way of making the patties. If you're feeling adventurous, you might want to try the more elaborate traditional version offered as a variation.

Servings: 4
Preparation time: 10 minutes, plus 20 minutes for refrigeration
Cooking time: 1 hour

SHELL
- 2 large potatoes (about 1 pound), boiled and peeled
- 1 egg
- 2 cups fine grain bulgur, soaked in 3/4 cup warm water for 15 minutes
- 1/3 cup unbleached all-purpose flour or bread crumbs
- 1 medium onion, peeled and sliced
- 2 teaspoons salt
- 1 teaspoon freshly ground black pepper
- 2 teaspoons ground cumin
- 1 tablespoon vegetable oil
- 2 teaspoons pomegranate paste*
- 1/2 cup chopped fresh cilantro or parsley

FILLING
- 2 tablespoons vegetable oil, butter or ghee
- 2 medium onions, peeled and thinly sliced
- 2 cloves of garlic, peeled and crushed
- 1 cup pine nuts, walnuts or pistachios, finely chopped
- 1 teaspoon salt
- 1/2 teaspoon pepper
- 1 teaspoon chili paste or cayenne
- 1/2 teaspoon cinnamon
- 1/2 teaspoon ground cumin
- 2 tablespoons pomegranate paste
- 4 cups oil for frying

GARNISH
- 1 tomato chopped
- 1 cup shredded lettuce
- 1/4 cup tahini paste

1. To prepare the shell, place the cooked potatoes and the rest of the ingredients for the shell in a food processor and mix until you have a soft dough. Cover and refrigerate for 20 minutes.

2. To prepare the filling, heat the oil in a wok or deep skillet over medium heat. Add the onion and stir-fry for 5 minutes until translucent. Add the garlic, pine nuts, salt, pepper, chili paste, cinnamon, cumin and pomegranate paste. Stir-fry for 1 minute, remove from heat and set aside to cool.

3. Wet the palms and fingers of both hands before starting to shape the patties. Separate the dough into lumps the size of eggs. Make a hole with your forefinger in the center of each ball and stuff it with 1 teaspoon of the filling. With your wet finger and thumb pinch, seal and smooth the end closed. Using the palms of your hands, form the filled dough into a ball then flatten it into a round patty. Place the patties on an oiled baking sheet, 1/2 inch apart. Paint them with oil, cover with plastic wrap and refrigerate until you are ready to fry them.

4. For frying the patties, heat 4 cups of oil in a deep skillet over medium heat, until hot (330-375°F). Fry 3 patties at a time, for 4 to 5 minutes on all sides, turning frequently with a slotted spoon, until golden brown. Remove with a slotted spoon and drain on paper towels.

5. Arrange the patties on a platter, garnish with parsley, cilantro, basil or mint sprigs, and serve with warm flat bread, shredded lettuce, chopped tomatoes and tahini paste.

A TRADITIONAL KIBBEH

To make a traditional kibbeh, wet the palms of both hands before starting to shape the patties. Take 2 tablespoons of dough in the palm of your hand and roll it into a 3-inch oval-shaped ball. Using your forefinger make a hole in the center of the ball and continue to twist your finger until you have sculpted a thin shell with a large hole. Fill the hole by quickly placing 1 teaspoon of filling inside and pinch, seal, and smooth the opening with your wet hands.

VARIATIONS

PUMPKIN PATTIES
Substitute pumpkins, peeled and cooked for the potatoes.

LENTIL PATTIES
Substitute 1 cup lentils, boiled for 20 minutes and drained, for the cooked potatoes.

EGGPLANT PATTIES
Substitute 2 eggplants (about 1 pound), baked in a 350°F oven for 1 hour and then peeled, for the potatoes.

Istanbul Borek

Makes 24 boreks
Preparation time: 30 minutes
Cooking time: 35 minutes

DOUGH
2 packages yufka pastry leaves,* removed from packaging, covered with a dish towel to prevent drying

FILLING
1 pound zucchini, peeled and grated, all juice blotted out
1/2 pound feta cheese, grated
1 egg, lightly beaten
1 teaspoon salt
1 teaspoon freshly ground black pepper
1 teaspoon dried mint
2 tablespoons chopped fresh parsley
1 teaspoon cornstarch

YOGURT SAUCE
1 small cucumber, seeded and grated
1 clove garlic, crushed, peeled and chopped
1 cup fresh mint, or 1 teaspoon mint flakes
1 teaspoon salt
1/2 teaspoon freshly ground pepper
2 cups plain yogurt, beaten

Boreks are a family of Near Eastern filled pastries, so popular that at one time in Istanbul there were thousands of borek shops—many more than there were bakeries. The name seems to derive from the Turkish bobreg, meaning "kidney," a possible reference to one of the shapes of this pastry. Another indication of the importance of this pastry is a fourteenth-century Persian poem by Boshaq al Atameh, which describes a battle between the borek and the pilaf, personified as two kings.

Shells for borek may be most easily made using yufka leaves (sold under the brand name "Yoruk" at Middle Eastern groceries); if you use them, however, you should deep fry the boreks, as this dough is not best for baking. For baked boreks, use ready-made frozen filo dough.*

1. To make the borek filling, combine all the ingredients for the filling in a bowl and mix well with your hands until you have a thick paste. Cover and refrigerate for 20 minutes.

2. To make the borek, grease a baking sheet.

3. Place 1 yufka leaf vertically in front of you, place 1 teaspoon of the filling 1-inch from the end nearest to you and moisten the edges with a little water. Begin to roll up the borek, then tuck in both sides and finishing rolling (cigarette style). As you reach the end of the strip, dip both ends into a small bowl of water (to prevent the borek from unraveling while cooking). Place on the greased baking sheets, separated from each other. Cover with a lightly dampened towel and refrigerate until you are ready to cook.

4. To cook the boreks, heat 4 cups corn oil over medium heat in a wok or deep skillet, until hot (the temperature is important and should e between 330 to 375°F). Deep-fry in batches of 6 boreks at the time, on all sides, turning frequently with a slotted spoon, until golden brown. Remove and place on paper towels.

5. Mix all the ingredients for the yogurt sauce and serve with the boreks.

Pasta, Pizza & Bread / 210

Russian Pirozhki

Pirozhki is the diminutive plural of the Russian word for "pie," pirog, which comes from pir, meaning "feast."

1. Heat the oil in a large skillet over medium heat until very hot. Add the onion and stir-fry for 10 minutes, until golden brown. Add the mushrooms and garlic, and fry for 2 minutes longer. Add the dill, tomato and spices, and simmer over medium heat for 5 minutes longer, until all the liquid has evaporated. Remove from heat.

2. Add the sour cream, mix well and allow to cool. Cover and refrigerate for 20 minutes or until ready to use.

3. Preheat the oven to 350°F. On a cool surface, roll the dough out with a rolling pin to 1/4-inch thick. Using the open end of a glass dipped in flour, or a cookie cutter, cut the dough into 2 1/2-inch-diameter disks. Fill each disk with 2 teaspoons of the filling mixture. Fold each disk in half, and pinch and crimp the dough around the edges to seal.

4. Beat the egg yolk and yogurt to make the glaze.

5. Place the pirozhki on a baking sheet and paint each one with the glaze. Bake for 25 to 35 minutes, until golden brown.

6. Remove from oven and place on a serving platter with condiments.

Spanish Epanadillas

1. Heat the oil in a wok or deep skillet. Add the onion and fry for 15 minutes, stirring occasionally, until golden brown. Add the garlic and stir-fry for 1 minute. Add the spinach, salt and pepper, and cook, over medium heat, for 5 minutes, or until all the water has evaporated. Add the raisins and pine nuts, and stir-fry for 1 minute longer. Adjust seasoning to taste. Remove from heat and allow to cool.

2. Follow the above recipe from step 3 for baking.

Makes 24
Preparation time: 30 minutes, plus 20 minutes for refrigeration
Cooking time: 35 minutes f

1 package ready made frozen puff pastry, thawed for 1 hour
3 tablespoons vegetable oil, butter or ghee
1 medium onion, peeled and sliced
1 pound white mushrooms, finely sliced
1 clove garlic, peeled and chopped
1/4 cup chopped fresh dill
1 large tomato, peeled and chopped
1 teaspoon salt
1/4 teaspoon sugar
1 tablespoon fresh lime juice
1/2 teaspoon freshly ground black pepper
1 teaspoon hot curry powder
1/4 cup sour cream
1 egg yolk and 1 tablespoon yogurt to make a glaze

SPANISH EPANADILLAS
2 tablespoons olive oil
1 onion, peeled and thinly sliced
3 cloves garlic, crushed and peeled
2 pounds baby spinach, or 1 pound frozen spinach
1 teaspoon salt
1/2 teaspoon fresh ground pepper
2 tablespoons raisins
2 tablespoons toasted pine nuts

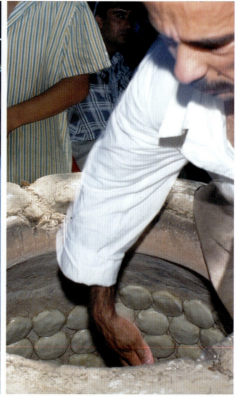

Uzbek Samsa

1. To make the filling, heat the oil in a wok or deep skillet. Add the onion and stir-fry for 10 minutes. Add the garlic and eggs, and stir-fry for 5 minutes. Add the chili, salt, pepper, cumin, coriander, rice and cilantro, and stir-fry for 1 minute. Remove from heat Adjust seasoning to taste and allow to cool.

2. Follow the pirozhki recipe on page 211. Wrap the samsa as shown in the photograph on the facing page.

3. Serve with vinegar.

Birjandi Sanbuseh (Noftieh)

1. Place the lentils in a medium-sized saucepan, cover with 6 cups water, add 1 teaspoon salt and bring to a boil. Reduce heat, partially cover and cook over medium heat for 15 minutes. Drain.

2. In a wok or deep skillet, heat 4 tablespoons oil over medium heat until very hot. Add the onion and fry for 15 minutes, stirring occasionally, until golden brown. Add the salt, pepper, turmeric, walnuts and lentils, and stir-fry for 10 seconds. Adjust seasoning to taste, remove from heat and allow to cool.

3. Follow the master recipe for the pirozhki on page 211 for stuffing the sanbuseh and cooking. Remove from the oven and brush with saffron water and melted butter.

Persian Barberry Sanbuseh

1. Combine all the ingredients in a bowl and set aside.

2. Follow the pirozhki recipe on page 211.

HOMEMADE WRAPPER FOR BAKING

Place 3 cups all-purpose flour in a food processor, add 1 egg and pulse. Add 1 tablespoon Crisco oil and pulse once more. With machine running, gradually add 1/2 cup warm water and knead for 5 minutes until you have a soft dough that does not stick to your hands. Cover and allow to rest for 30 minutes. On a cool surface, roll out the dough to a thin layer and generously and evenly paint it with Crisco oil. Form the dough into a tight, multi-layered cylinder by wrapping it around a thin rolling pin. Using a sharp knife, slit the dough, length-wise and divide into 12 multi-layered pieces. Roll out each piece into a 3-inch disk. Cover to prevent drying.

- 1 package ready-made frozen puff pastry, thawed for 1 hour or homemade dough
- 1 cup vegetable oil
- 1 large onion, peeled and thinly sliced
- 1 clove garlic, crushed and peeled
- 4 eggs
- 1 bird or serrano chili, sliced
- 2 cups cooked rice or chopped zucchini
- 1 teaspoon salt
- 1/2 teaspoon freshly ground pepper
- 1/2 teaspoon ground cumin
- 1/2 teaspoon ground coriander
- 1 cup chopped cilantro
- 1/2 cup rice vinegar

GLAZE
- 1 egg, beaten

BIRJANDI SANBUSEH
- 1 large onion, peeled and thinly sliced
- 2 cups brown lentils
- 1/2 cup vegetable oil
- 1 teaspoon salt
- 1 teaspoon freshly ground pepper
- 1/2 teaspoon turmeric
- 1 cup walnuts, finely ground
- 1/4 teaspoon ground saffron dissolved in 1 tablespoon hot water
- 2 tablespoons melted butter

IRANIAN BARBERRY SANBUSEH
- 1/2 cup vegetable oil
- 4 scallions, chopped
- 8 scrambled eggs, shredded
- 1 cup chopped fresh mint or 1 tablespoon dried mint
- 1 cup chopped fresh cilantro
- 1/4 chopped fresh parsley
- 2 tablespoon dried barberries, thoroughly washed and stir-fried with 1 teaspoon sugar
- 1 table spoon fresh lime juice
- 1 teaspoon salt
- 1/2 teaspoon freshly ground pepper

Indian Samosa

Makes 20
Preparation time: 30 minutes
Cooking time: 1 hour 15 minutes (15 minutes for each batch of 4 samosas)

FILLING
- 3 potatoes (2 pounds), boiled, peeled and diced into 1/4-inch pieces
- 1/4 cup oil, butter or ghee
- 1 teaspoon coriander seeds
- 1 teaspoon cumin seeds
- 1 large onion, peeled and chopped
- 1-inch fresh ginger, peeled and grated
- 1 hot green chili, seeded and chopped
- 1 cup fresh or frozen peas
- 1 1/2 teaspoons salt
- 1/2 teaspoon freshly ground pepper
- 1 teaspoon garam masala
- 1/2 teaspoon sugar
- 1/2 cup chopped fresh chopped cilantro
- 3 tablespoons fresh lime juice

DOUGH
- 2 cups all-purpose unbleached flour, sifted
- 1/2 teaspoon salt
- 3 tablespoons vegetable oil
- 1/2 cup ice water
- 1 teaspoon cumin seeds
- 4 cups corn oil for deep-frying

NOTE
To bake the samosas, place them on a greased baking sheet (1 inch apart), paint with vegetable oil and bake in a preheated 350°F oven for 20 to 30 minutes, until golden brown.
It's fun to use one package of frozen banana leaves (thawed and washed with warm water thoroughly, patted dry and cut into sections) as serving platters.

Samosas are sold throughout India at all hours of the day by street vendors. They are often served on leaves with a little cilantro relish and tamarind chutney on the side.

1. To make the filling, heat the oil in a wok or deep skillet over medium heat, until very hot. Add the coriander and cumin, and cook for 10 seconds, until aromatic (keep a cover handy to stop any seeds from flying out). Add the onion and fry over medium heat for 15 minutes. Add the

Pasta, Pizza & Bread / 214

ginger, potatoes, chili, peas, salt, pepper, garam masala, sugar, cilantro, and lime juice, and stir-fry for 1 minute. Adjust seasoning to taste. Remove from heat and allow to cool.

2. To make the wrapper, mix the flour, salt and oil in a food processor until crumbly. Pulse and gradually add the ice water until you have dough that is almost together. Turn out onto a floured surface. Gather the dough and knead in the cumin seeds. Shape the dough into a long cylindrical shape, cover with plastic and allow to rest for 30 minutes.

3. Divide the dough into 10 pieces. Roll out each piece into a 6-inch oval shape. Cut each in half.

4. Using your wet thumb and fingers, shape each half-oval into a cone.

5. Fill each cone with 1 tablespoon of filling.

6. Wet the top edges of the cone with water, close the cone, press together and seal. Repeat for all the dough. Place samosas on a greased baking sheet, separated from each other, and cover with a dish towel until ready to cook.

7. To cook the samosas, heat 4 cups corn oil in a wok or deep skillet over medium low heat (beware not to make the oil too hot, 330-375°F). Add 4 samosas at a time and deep-fry for 15 minutes, turning frequently until golden brown. Remove with a slotted spoon and drain on paper towels.

8. To make fresh cilantro relish, puree 3 cups chopped fresh cilantro leaves, 1/4 cup fresh mint, 1/4-inch fresh ginger (peeled), 1 bird or serrano chili (seeded), 3 tablespoons lime juice, 1 teaspoon cumin powder, 1 teaspoon salt, 1/2 teaspoon sugar, 1/4 cup almonds or yogurt and 1/4 cup water in a food processor. Adjust seasoning to taste and transfer to a small serving bowl.

9. To make tamarind chutney, mix 1 cup tamarind paste, 1/2 cup pitted dates, 1/4 cup water, 1/2 teaspoon salt, 1/4 teaspoon nutmeg, 1/4 teaspoon ground cumin, 1 teaspoon sugar and 1 bird or serrano chili in a food processor. Adjust seasoning to taste, cover and allow to rest for 30 minutes. This chutney keeps well in the refrigerator for 1 to 2 weeks.

10. Arrange the hot samosas on banana leaves or on a serving platter, and serve with the cilantro relish and tamarind chutney.

Pasta, Pizza & Bread / 215

Afghan Garlic Chive Boulani

Servings: 6
Preparation time: 20 minutes
Cooking time: 25 minutes

WRAPPERS

1 package ready-made, large sized egg roll skins, removed from the package and covered with a dish towel to prevent drying

FILLING

4 cups chopped scallions, or garlic-chives (gandana)
1/2 cup chopped fresh parsley
2 tablespoons vegetable oil
2 teaspoons salt
1 teaspoon freshly ground pepper
1 bird or serrano chili, finely chopped

YOGURT SAUCE

1 small cucumber, seeded and grated
1 clove garlic, crushed, peeled and chopped
1 cup fresh mint
1 teaspoon mint flakes
1 teaspoon salt
1/2 teaspoon freshly ground pepper
2 cups plain yogurt, beaten

NOTE

When using egg roll skins, frying the boulani gives the best results.

Boulani is a baked or fried, stuffed bread. It is made by filling a square piece of dough with a garlic-chive mixture and folding it diagonally into a triangle. Traditionally it is filled with gandana (similar to garlic-chives) and served with a yogurt sauce. Gandana is available at Middle Eastern markets; scallions, however, make a good substitute.

1. Combine all the ingredients for the filling using a rubber spatula (do not use a food processor as it makes it too liquidy) and set aside.

2. To make the yogurt sauce, combine all the ingredients for the sauce in a mixing bowl and set aside.

3. To fill the boulani, lay out a wrapper on your work surface. Place 2 heaping tablespoons of the filling in a diagonal corner of the wrapper and moisten the edge with a little water. Fold the wrapper over to form a triangle, and pinch and crimp the edges. Place the finished boulani, separated from each other, on a baking sheet lined with parchment paper. Cover with a dish towel to prevent them from drying out and place in the refrigerator until you are ready to cook.

4. To cook the boulani, heat 1/4 cup oil in a large nonstick skillet over medium heat, until hot (330 to 375°F). Fry for 1 minute, on each side, until they are a light golden brown. Remove and drain on paper towels.

5. Serve right away with the yogurt sauce on the side. Boulani is best eaten hot.

Beijing Crispy Rice Rolls

I ate this wonderful roll in a market in Beijing at a stand run by the young girl in the photograph (below), who made her pancakes in front of us. As I had bought a couple of her pancakes, she allowed me to photograph her.

1. To make the dipping sauce, combine all the ingredients for the sauce in a small saucepan and bring to a boil over medium heat. Remove from heat, transfer to a small serving bowl and set aside.

2. To make the rolls, divide the mushrooms, lettuce, carrot, cabbage, eggs, herbs, scallions and nuts into 8 equal portions.

3. To prepare the wrappers, fill a shallow container with warm water. Dip one of the wrappers in the water for 30 seconds and place it on a work surface, spread 1/2 teaspoon hoisin sauce over it and top it with the rest of the ingredients.

5. Roll up the wrapper halfway, tuck and fold in both the sides, and finish rolling into a cylinder. Continue for the remaining wrappers.

6. Heat 2 tablespoons oil over medium heat in a flat, non stick skillet until very hot and fry, 3 at a time, for 1 minute on each side.

7. Arrange on a platter and serve warm with the dipping sauce.

> Makes 8 wraps
> Preparation time: 30 minutes
> Cooking time: 15 minutes
>
> **DIPPING SAUCE**
> 1 clove garlic, crushed and peeled
> 1 teaspoon cornstarch, slaked in 1/4 cup water
> 2 tablespoons rice vinegar
> 1 tablespoon soy sauce
> 2 teaspoons sugar
> 2 tablespoons toasted sesame oil
> 1 teaspoon red hot chili paste
>
> **WRAPPERS**
> twenty-five 8 1/2-inch-diameter rice paper wrappers
>
> **FILLING**
> 6 mushrooms, washed and sliced
> 6 large leaves Boston lettuce, shredded
> 1 large carrot, peeled, julienned and sprinkled with 1/2 teaspoon sugar
> 2 cups napa cabbage, shredded (or bean sprouts, blanched)
> 6 eggs, scrambled and seasoned with 1/2 teaspoon salt and 1/4 teaspoon pepper
> 1 teaspoon chili paste
> 1 cup fresh cilantro leaves
> 1 cup fresh Thai basil leaves
> 1/2 cup fresh mint leaves
> 8 fresh scallions, shredded
> 1 cup coarsely chopped toasted peanuts or walnuts (optional)
> 2 tablespoons hoisin sauce

Pasta, Pizza & Bread / 217

Chinese Tofu Dumplings

Servings: 6 (32 dumplings)
Preparation time: 40 minutes
Cooking time: 1 hour

WRAPPERS
- 36 ready-made dumpling wrappers (pot stickers or gyoza); open the wrapper package and cover the wrapper with a dish towel to prevent drying (or use homemade wrappers*)

FILLING
- 1 pound firm tofu, shredded (to extract the excess water, wrap the tofu in a few layers of paper towels and let stand for 20 minutes)
- 1 head napa cabbage, shredded and sprinkled with 2 teaspoons salt (let stand for 15 minutes then squeeze out the liquid)
- 2 cloves garlic, crushed and peeled
- 1/4-inch ginger, peeled and shredded
- 5 dried Chinese mushrooms, soaked in warm water for 20 minutes, drained, stems removed and shredded
- 1 carrot, peeled and shredded
- 1 egg, lightly beaten
- 1 1/2 teaspoons chili paste
- 1/2 teaspoon sugar
- 3 tablespoons toasted sesame oil
- 2 teaspoons cornstarch
- 1/2 cup chopped fresh scallions
- 1 1/2 teaspoons salt
- 1/2 teaspoon freshly ground black pepper

DIPPING SAUCE
- 2 tablespoons soy sauce
- 1/2 cup rice vinegar
- 1 scallion, chopped

At a charming tea house near Xian's central gardens, we were served a marvelous breakfast of dim sum. A parade of carts piled high with dumplings, buns and other small dishes passed among the tables to tempt us. There were rice dumplings, some filled with sweet lotus seed paste and others with red bean paste. Peking-style dumplings were made of cabbage leaves stuffed with tofu, carrots and mushrooms. Such tender filled dumplings were served Shanghai style with vinegar. Delicate flower petal dumplings were first pan-fried, then steamed in broth. There was congee—a diluted rice pudding—as well. Tofu is a great source of protein and can stand in for meat, dairy products and even eggs. In this photo, which I took at the Xian market, a woman is making tofu dumplings.

1. To make the filling, combine all the ingredients for the filling in a mixing bowl and mix well until you have a thick paste. Cover and refrigerate.

2. To make the dipping sauce, combine all the ingredients for the dipping sauce in a mixing bowl and set aside.

3. To make the dumplings, place 1 heaping teaspoon of the filling in the center of a wrapper and moisten the edge with a little water. Fold the wrapper over to form a crescent, and pinch and crimp one side. Place the finished dumplings, separated from each other, on a baking sheet lined with parchment paper (they can also be frozen for later cooking, for up to 3 months).

4. To cook the dumplings (steam-fried method), heat 1 tablespoon corn oil in a large nonstick skillet. Add one layer of dumplings, seam side up, and pour 3/4 cup water over the dumplings. Cover and cook over low heat for 20 minutes without disturbing, until the water has evaporated and the dumplings are crisp and brown on the bottom. Remove dumplings and place on a warm plate. Repeat this process until you have steam-fried all the remaining dumplings.

5. Place the dumpling on a serving dish and serve with the dipping sauce on the side.

HOMEMADE WRAPPER

It is very easy to make this wrapper at home, and I prefer to do it in this way: Place 3 cups flour in a mixing bowl and gradually stir in 1 cup water. Knead for 5 minutes until you have a soft dough that does not stick to your hands. Cover and allow to rest at room temperature for 30 minutes. Roll the dough into a long cylinder and divide it into 32 pieces. Roll out each piece into a 3-inch disk. Cover the pieces to prevent drying while you prepare your filling.

Food for the Spirit

The countries that lie along the ancient Silk Road share a remarkable legacy of religious interchange, as archeology shows in such curiosities as these: In Baghdad, a bazaar built over a Buddhist temple that was built in turn over a Zoroastrian fire hall; in the highlands of Pakistan near Peshawar, the ruins of a rich Buddhist monastery complex designed in the style of classical Greece; in vast cave systems near Dunhuang in western China, scrolls bearing the prayers of a religion known as Manichaeism; in Xian (once Chang'an), a monument consisting of a Christian cross floating on a Taoist cloud above a Buddhist lotus; near Kaifeng, inscriptions that trace the presence of a Chinese Jewish community to the Han dynasty (202 BCE to 221 CE). Where the caravans traveled, ideas followed; as fields were sown and orchards planted, so philosophies grew and flourished.

Many of these ideas had their roots in what is sometimes called "the Axial Age"—the period between about 600 to 300 BCE when widely separated civilizations made independent spiritual leaps. This was the age of the prophets of Israel and the philosophers of Greece. Iranians had begun to follow the precepts of the philosopher Zoroaster, which focused on a single god, Ahura Mazda, and his evil opponent, Angra Mainyu. In China, the school of Confucius developed the ideas of hierarchy and filial piety that influence Asian thought to this day; at about the same time, the school of Lao-tzu offered the Tao, or Way, practices that led to an understanding of the ineffable universe. And in Hindu India, Siddartha Guatama, known as the Buddha, or "Enlightened One," found a way past Hindu belief in an eternal cycle of death, suffering and rebirth: Through self-control, self-sacrifice and charity, one could extinguish the ego and become part of a universal wholeness.

In the early centuries of our era, other religions appeared in this rich mix. One was Christianity, arising in the West among the Jews. Another was Manichaeism, which developed in Iran. And seventh-century Arabia gave birth to Islam.

All these religions—and with them ideas about food and spirituality—mingled along the trading routes. The great crossroads was the Kushan empire, which during the first 200 years of the common era had expanded until it reached south to the Punjab, north to the

Aral Sea and east to Khotan. At its heart, in the fertile valley of Sogdiana, between the Amu Darya and Syr Darya rivers, lived the premier traders of the Silk Road. A cosmopolitan people of Scythian, Iranian, Indian and Greek descent, the Sogdians welcomed deities of almost every persuasion and spread philosophies both west and east, so that, for instance, there were Buddhist, Jewish and Christian communities from Iran to China. Philosophies about food traveled with the religions. The most widespread were traditions of fasting. In almost every culture, fasting (not eating) and abstinence (not eating certain foods, usually meat) serve as means of commemoration, penance, or purification.

The Jews, for instance, followed a set of dietary laws based on passages in the Old Testament, the most noticeable probably being the restriction of meat to that from animals that both chew the cud and have cloven hooves: Jews ate no pork because the pig that has cloven hooves but does not chew the cud is an anomaly. Other customs, such as eating unleavened bread and destroying old grain during Passover in the spring, probably derived from ancient (and universal) farming traditions of sacrificing leftover grain from the old year to ensure a good harvest in the new. Jewish fasts, especially at Yom Kippur, the Day of Atonement, were periods of repentance and self-denial.

Some of these customs would appear in both Islam and Christianity. Muslims are forbidden to eat pork, for instance. During Ramadan—the ninth month of the Muslim lunar year, commemorating the first revelation of the Koran to the prophet Mohammed—most of the Islamic world fasts during the daylight hours, less as a penance than as a means of reaffirming belief and uniting the faithful. Christians fast for various commemorative or purifying purposes, abstaining (in early Christianity, from meat) during penitential periods before the great feasts of the Christian year. The best known is Lent, the 40 days before Easter, recalling Jesus' 40 days in the wilderness before the Crucifixion.

Such Christian fasting would have been most noticeable along the Silk Road among Nestorians, a sect that took its name from a bishop of Constantinople, who, unable to "imagine God as a little boy," believed that Jesus was not God Incarnate but a person of two natures, one human and one divine. The idea was declared heretical in 431 and Nestorians dispersed from Christendom to establish communities in Iran, from where traders and missionaries traveled as far as China. (Although the Nestorians tried to make their faith less alien by calling their texts "Sutras" and their saints "Buddhas," they had little success among the Chinese. Like Jews and Zoroastrians, they lived in isolated expatriate communities in cities like Changan.)

Complete abstention from meat—vegetarianism—seems to have originated in India, with the 4,000-year-old complex of rules, rituals and beliefs that make up Hinduism. Hindu regulations concerning food are dauntingly complicated and varied according to the individual's role in life, meaning which of the 3,000 Hindu castes or subcastes he is born into. Certain basic precepts are found everywhere, however. One is the belief, descended from prehistoric times, in the sanctity of the cow. Others are beliefs in the essential unity of all creation and in reincarnation. And while history would seem to refute the idea, Hinduism places great value on nonviolence. So Hindus generally are vegetarian; according to the sacred texts, the wisest and healthiest eat vegetables, milk, yogurt, and clarified butter, or ghee. At the low end of the spectrum is the diet of the ignorant and lazy, which includes meat, stale foods and other people's leavings. Two more religions that arose among the Hindus encouraged a vegetarian diet. One was Jainism, which asserts that every living thing, plant or animal, has a soul and must not be harmed. The emphasis on nonviolence is so strong that laymen cannot be fishermen; nor can they be farmers, lest they harm insects or animals in working the fields. Jains abstain not only from meat but, because a plant's soul resides in its root, from root vegetables like garlic or onions.

Jainism remained a small Indian sect; Buddhism, which appeared at about the same time, spread west with Sogdian merchants to Iran (where Merv was an important center) and east along the trade routes to China—the first known Buddhist missionary was actually a Parthian—and then to the rest of Asia. Buddhists believe in the reincarnation of souls and most emphatically in nonviolence. They are forbidden to kill any living creature. Except for monks and very devout laymen, however, they are not vegetarian. The sin lies in the killing, not in the eating.

The most noticeable vegetarians along the Silk Road were the Manichaeans, a sect formed by the Iranian prophet Mani in the third century. Mani's visions drew precepts from various sources. From his native Zoroastrianism he took a dualistic view of the universe: Good was equated with spirit and light, evil with matter and darkness. Life was essentially a battle between the body and the soul, reflecting the universal struggle of light to free itself from matter. The religion included an eclectic mixture of Iranian gods, the Christian Jesus and Buddhist doctrines such as the transmigration of souls. Although Mani either died or was executed in 273, his religion spread rapidly along the trade routes into Sogdiana, whose capital, Samarkand, had a thriving Manichaean community and whose translators rendered Mani's texts into Sogdian, Turkish and Chinese so that they might be understood far from home. Manichaeism required much of its believers, who were divided into an elect, who were missionaries and agents for freeing light, and lay supporters. Among other restrictions, the elect had to abstain from sexual intercourse because the light particles trapped in every human are divided when descendants appear. They could not prepare their own food because in doing so they might damage light particles in it. Their supporters, known as "hearers," supplied them. All Manichaeans ate vegetables, which thrived in sunlight and were therefore higher in light particles than any other food; grapes, melons and cucumbers were especially prized.

It was a demanding and austere religion, its adherents were persecuted in every culture, yet Manichaean dualism—and its ascetic practices—attracted the devout for centuries. Following a wild youth (when he famously prayed, "Give me chastity and continence, but not just now"), St. Augustine of Hippo became a Manichaean, although after his conversion to Christianity in 386 he bitterly attacked the faith. For about 70 years, in the eighth and ninth centuries, Manichaeism was the official religion of the Uighur Turks. It would survive as Catharism in southwest France until the Inquisition ruthlessly destroyed its followers in the fourteenth century. Still, the conflict it embodied between the spiritual self and the physical one continued to attract followers.

Opposite: A wall painting from the caves of Dunhuang, near the western end of China's Great Wall, shows a Buddhist monk with his walking staff. Such pilgrims traveled the Silk Road as early as the fourth century.

Above: A fragment of an eighth-century drawing depicting a church ceremony in memory of the prophet Mani. It features bread, grapes, and melons: The vegetarian Manichaeans believed that these foods were richest in light and goodness.

Prior leaf: Surrounded by spices, a grocer and his friend share a quiet moment in the bazaar at Tashkurgan, Afghanistan.

Neapolitan Pizza (Master Recipe)

Makes four 8-inch pizzas
Preparation time: 20 minutes, plus 30 for resting
Cooking time: 10 minutes

DOUGH
- 1 1/4 cup warm water
- 1 tablespoon active dry yeast
- 1/2 teaspoon sugar
- 3 cups unbleached all-purpose flour, sifted with 1 teaspoon salt
- 2 tablespoons olive oil

- 1 cup rice or corn flour for dusting

TOMATO TOPPING
- 4 tablespoons olive oil
- 1/4 cup grated Parmesan cheese
- 2 large tomatoes, peeled and sliced
- 4 cloves garlic, roasted, peeled and sliced
- 2 tablespoons fresh oregano leaves
- 2 cups shredded mozzarella cheese (about 1 pound)
- 1 teaspoon salt
- 1 teaspoon freshly ground pepper
- 1/2 teaspoon red chili flakes

Pizza is the Italian pronunciation for the word pitta, which the Greeks used to refer to flat bread from the Middle East. The Italians used the term pizza, pitta, petta, pizzela, *or* pizzeta *as early as the tenth century (though not for a dish with tomatoes, which did not arrive from the New World until much later). Today, of course, pizza has attained the status of an international food. It has been said that if Naples could have patented its pizza it would be one of Italy's wealthiest cities and not one of its poorest. The classic Neapolitan pizza is better known as marinara because the ingredients for its topping (oil, tomato, garlic, and oregano) could be stored on ships so that sailors* (marinai) *could have pizza away from home.*

MAKING THE DOUGH

1. Pour the warm water into a small bowl, sprinkle in the yeast and allow to rest for 10 minutes, undisturbed. Add the sugar, mix and set aside. Place the flour mixture in a food processor and pulse as you gradually add the yeast mixture and 2 tablespoons of oil. Knead for 7 to 10 minutes until you have a soft dough that does not stick to your hands and comes away easily from the sides of the mixing bowl. Gather the dough and place in a greased bowl. Cover with a dish towel and allow to rest for 30 minutes.

2. Place the dough on a floured work surface, punch down and divide it into 4 equal balls. Roll in olive oil and place on a greased baking sheet 6 inches apart. Cover with plastic wrap and allow to rise, at room temperature, for 30 minutes and up to 24 hours.

3. When you are ready to cook, place a baking stone on the lower rack of the oven and preheat oven to 500°F.

4. Divide the ingredients for the topping, for the 4 pizzas.

5. Form each ball into an 8-inch round piece of dough.

6. Dust a baker's peel with rice flour and place the dough on it.

7. Paint the dough with olive oil and dust with grated Parmesan.

8. Top with tomato slices, and sprinkle with garlic and oregano. Spread the mozzarella on top and sprinkle with salt, pepper and chili flakes. Drizzle a little olive oil on top.

9. Slide the dough onto the preheated baking stone and bake for 8 to 10 minutes, until golden brown on the edges.

10. Remove from the oven with the peel, cut into slices and serve. Repeat for the other dough rounds.

For an unusual experience, try some of the following Silk Road region toppings. Divide the ingredients for the 4 pizzas and add them as a topping in the following order: Parmesan cheese, olive oil, the remaining ingredients, except the mozzarella. Add the mozzarella (or goat cheese), top with olive oil, and sprinkle with salt, pepper and chili flakes.

Yemeni Fenugreek Topping

Prepare the dough per the master recipe for the Neapolitan Pizza on page 224 and make four 8-inch disks. Prepare the olive oil, Parmesan cheese, fenugreek seeds, garlic, cilantro leaves, tomato, mozzarella, chili flakes and salt topping for this recipe, divide into 4 and proceed with the master recipe for Neapolitan Pizza on page 224.

Caspian Olive, Pomegranate & Angelica Topping

Prepare the dough per the master recipe for the Neapolitan Pizza on page 224 and make four 8-inch disks. Prepare the olive oil, Parmesan cheese, onion, olives, caramelized walnuts, garlic, mint, cilantro, mozzarella, chili flakes, pomegranate seeds, salt and pepper topping for this recipe, divide into 4 and proceed with the master recipe for Neapolitan Pizza on page 224.

Syrian Zatar Topping

Prepare the dough per the master recipe for the Neapolitan Pizza on page 224 and make four 8-inch disks. Prepare the olive oil, Parmesan cheese, sumac berries, thyme, sesame seeds, mozzarella, salt, chili flakes topping for this recipe, divide into 4 and proceed with the master recipe for Neapolitan Pizza on page 224.

YEMENI FENUGREEK TOPPING
- 2 tablespoons olive oil
- 1/4 cup grated Parmesan cheese
- 2 teaspoons fenugreek seeds, soaked in 1/4 cup cold water overnight and drained
- 4 cloves garlic, roasted, peeled and sliced
- 1 1/2 cups chopped fresh cilantro leaves
- 1 large tomato, peeled, seeded and sliced
- 2 cups mozzarella (shredded) or goat cheese (crumbled)
- 1/2 teaspoon red chili flakes
- 1/4 teaspoon salt

CASPIAN OLIVE TOPPING
- 1/2 cup olive oil
- 1/4 cup grated Parmesan cheese
- 1 large onion, peeled, thinly sliced and caramelized*
- 1/4 pound (1 cup) green pitted olives
- 1 cup walnuts, caramelized
- 4 cloves garlic, roasted, peeled and sliced
- 1 cup chopped fresh mint or 1 teaspoon dried mint
- 4 strands fresh oregano or 1/4 teaspoon dried oregano
- 1/4 cup chopped fresh cilantro
- 2 cup mozzarella (shredded) or goat cheese (crumbled)
- 1/4 teaspoon angelica powder*
- 1 teaspoon chili flakes
- 1/4 cup fresh pomegranate seeds*(optional)
- 4 teaspoons pomegranate paste*
- 1/2 teaspoon salt
- 1/4 teaspoon ground pepper

SYRIAN ZATAR TOPPING
- 1/4 cup olive oil
- 1/4 cup grated Parmesan cheese
- 4 teaspoons ground sumac berries
- 1/4 cup chopped fresh lemon thyme (stems removed) or 2 teaspoons dried thyme
- 1/4 cup sesame seeds
- 2 cups mozzarella (shredded) or goat cheese (crumbled)
- 1/2 teaspoon salt
- 1 teaspoon red chili flakes

Caspian Olive, Pomegranate & Angelica Pizza

A Rumi Grape Story

In which we learn that a grape by any other name will taste as sweet

A Persian, an Arab a Greek, and a Turk, meeting at a Silk Road oasis, found a coin. They decided to buy some fruit with it that they could share. Almost at once, an argument broke out.

"I want angoor," said the Persian.

"What's that? I want enab," said the Arab.

"I don't want angoor or enab," said the Greek. "I want stafilia."

"I don't understand any of you," said the Turk. "I want uzun."

If a passing scholar familiar with languages had heard their quarrel, he could have put an end to it by saying, "Give me your coin and I will buy something to please you all." He would have bought a bunch of grapes, which would indeed have pleased them: It was just what each had asked for.

Saveh Sweet Saffron Bread (Shirmal)

In Iran, part of the Silk Road went from Rayy (Tehran) to Saveh and Hamedan (Ekbatan), all ancient cities. Saveh is reputed to have been built by the legendary Persian king Jamshid, well before the fifth century BCE. The city boasts a Jewish shrine dedicated to Ester and Mordecai. Ester, apparently, went to plead the Jewish cause in front of Xerxes I, and he married her. The Magi, the three wise men, are also said to have set off with their gold, frankincense and myrrh from Saveh for Jerusalem. And Marco Polo visited the city in the thirteenth century. This bread, which is easy to make and very tasty, is a Saveh specialty.

1. Preheat oven to 350°F. Oil 4 shallow 6-inch baking pans and dust generously with flour.

2. In a large mixing bowl, whisk the eggs, vanilla, sugar, milk, rose water, saffron water and ginger until creamy.

3. Sift the flour, baking soda and baking powder onto a sheet of wax paper. Blend these dry ingredients gradually into the egg mixture. Mix well for 1 minute to produce a smooth, thick batter.

4. Pour the batter evenly into the 4 prepared baking pans.

5. Brush the tops with the glaze and sprinkle with poppy seeds. Bake in the preheated oven for 25 to 30 minutes until the edges shrink from the sides.

6. Remove from the oven and allow to cool for 15 minutes. Loosen the breads from the pans using a knife around the edges, turn them out and allow them to further cool on a wire rack.

VARIATION

Kurdish Butternut Squash Bread

Substitute water for the milk in step 2. Also, substitute 1/2 pound butternut squash, peeled and chopped, 1 teaspoon ground cinnamon, and 1/4 teaspoon ground nutmeg for the saffron and ginger in step 2.

Makes 4 loaves
Preparation time: 15 minutes
Cooking time: 30 minutes

- 1/3 cup vegetable oil
- 5 eggs
- 1/2 teaspoon vanilla extract
- 1 cup sugar
- 1/2 cup milk
- 1 tablespoon cooking rose water
- 1 teaspoon ground saffron threads dissolved in 4 tablespoons hot water
- 2-inch fresh ginger, peeled and grated, or 2 teaspoons powdered ginger
- 3 1/2 cups all-purpose unbleached flour
- 1 teaspoon baking soda
- 1 teaspoon baking powder

GLAZE
- 1/4 cup melted butter, beaten with a drop of saffron water
- 2 tablespoons poppy, sesame or nigella seeds

Punjabi Flat Bread (Nan)

Makes 4 loaves
Preparation time: 25 minutes, plus 3 1/2 hours for the dough to rise
Cooking time: 4 minutes for each nan

1 cup warm milk or water
2 teaspoons active dry yeast
2 teaspoons sugar or honey
1/4 cup plain yogurt
1/4 cup vegetable oil
3 cups all-purpose unbleached or whole-wheat flour, mixed with 1 1/2 teaspoons salt and 1 teaspoon baking powder, sifted onto a sheet of wax paper
2 tablespoons nigella seeds
1/4 cup melted butter

AFGHAN BREAD

Follow the steps above but eliminate the yogurt and baking powder and glaze the dough with 1 egg, beaten, before placing in the oven.

The Punjab is a vast, semi-arid plain crossing northern India and Pakistan; its name, meaning "five rivers," comes from the Persian. It was home to an advanced civilization at Harappa as early as 2500 BCE, since when it has been settled, crossed or invaded by everyone from early Aryans, Scythians and Greeks to the Muslims of the eleventh century and the British of the nineteenth. It is perhaps best known as the home of the Sikhs, who ruled a kingdom there in the nineteenth century and whose holiest shrine is there, at Amritsar. With such a history, it is not surprising that the staple bread, nan, is common not only to the Punjab but throughout the Silk Road region. In the Punjab, this bread is cooked in a tandoor, or cylindrical clay oven. It is easy to make on a curved, hemispherical cast-iron surface set over an open flame, as is done in Iran, Armenia, and Turkey, where the implement is known as a saj; in other parts of India, where it is called a rumali; and in Afghanistan, where its name is tavah.

1. In a small bowl, sprinkle the yeast over the warm milk and leave for 10 minutes, undisturbed.

2. Add the sugar, yogurt and 2 tablespoons oil.

3. Place the flour, salt and baking powder mixture in a food processor and pulse to mix. Gradually add the dissolved yeast while the machine is running. Continue to mix until the dough forms into a ball (about 5 minutes). Allow the dough to rest in the machine for 5 minutes, then continue to mix for another minute.

4. Turn out the dough onto a lightly floured work surface and knead in the nigella seeds. Continue to knead for 3 to 5 minutes until you have a smooth and elastic dough.

5. Turn the dough in a well-oiled bowl to ensure it is coated evenly with oil. Cover with plastic wrap and allow it to rise at room temperature for 3 hours (or overnight), until double in size.

6. Turn out the dough onto a lightly floured work surface, punch down, cover and allow to rest for 30 minutes.

7. Divide the dough into 4 equal balls. Preheat the oven to 500°F.

8. Flatten one ball into an 8-inch circle and place it on a greased baking sheet. Stipe the dough using a fork. Bake for about 1 to 2 minutes on each side, until golden brown on top. Brush with melted butter. Repeat for the remaining dough.

9. Make a pile and cover with a clean kitchen cloth until ready to eat.

Persian Lavash Bread

Lavash is a crispy, paper-thin bread, one of the Silk Road region's oldest. It is perfectly suited to the nomadic life and lends itself well for scooping up sauce or dipping in soup or tea. It may be cooked in a tandoor or on any of the metal implements described for nan (see headnote page 228), but, as with nan, a wok inverted over a gas flame works just as well. Because lavash bread is so thin, it dries instantly, but that is also what makes it a perfect Silk Road bread, as in the dry form it is well preserved.

1. In a small bowl, sprinkle the yeast over the warm water and leave for 10 minutes, undisturbed.

2. Add the sugar and stir well.

3. Sift the flour, baking powder and salt onto a piece of wax paper, transfer to a food processor, and pulse to mix. Gradually add the dissolved yeast and 1/2 cup cold water while the machine is running. Continue to mix until the dough forms into a ball (about 5 minutes).

4. Turn the dough out onto a lightly floured work surface and continue to knead by hand for 3 to 5 minutes until you have a smooth and elastic dough.

5. Turn the dough in a well-oiled bowl to ensure it is coated evenly with oil. Cover the bowl with plastic wrap and allow it to rise at room temperature for 3 hours (or overnight), until double in volume.

6. Turn the dough out onto a lightly floured work surface, punch down and knead in the nigella seeds. Divide the dough into 6 equal balls. Cover and allow to rest for 30 minutes.

7. Flatten one ball and roll it out with a rolling pin as far as it will go. Allow to rest for a minute (once the gluten has stretched it can be rolled out further). Roll out further into a paper-thin sheet.

8. Heat a large wok (upside down over a high gas flame), or a saj (if you have one) until very hot. Lightly brush the top surface of the wok with oil. Pick up one piece of dough by partially furling it over a rolling pin, lay one end of the dough over the edge of the wok and unfurl the dough over the saj. Cook for 20 to 30 seconds, turn gently using tongs and cook the other side for another 20 to 30 seconds or until crispy. Repeat for the remaining dough.

9. Pile the sheets of bread and cover with a clean kitchen cloth, or wrap in plastic to keep soft, until ready to eat.

Make 6 loaves
Preparation time: 20 minutes, plus 3 1/2 hours for the dough to rise
Cooking time: 1 minute for each loaf

1 cup warm water
2 teaspoons dry yeast
1 teaspoon sugar
3 3/4 cups sifted unbleached or chapati flour
1 teaspoon baking powder
2 teaspoons salt
1/2 cup cold water
2 tablespoons nigella seeds

NOTE

To make the bread as thin as possible, use a long, thin rolling pin to roll out the dough.

Lavash bread dries quickly. It can be softened easily by sprinkling it with a little water and wrapping it in a cloth for a few minutes.

Tashkent Onion & Garlic Bread

Makes 4 loaves
Preparation time: 45 minutes,
plus 3 hours for the dough to rise
Cooking time: 25 to 35 minutes
for each loaf

- 3 teaspoons active dry yeast
- 2 teaspoons sugar
- 1 cup warm water or milk
- 3/4 cup vegetable oil or butter
- 3 cups all-purpose unbleached flour and 3/4 cup whole-wheat flour (chapati flour) mixed with 1 teaspoon salt and sifted onto a sheet of wax paper
- 2 tablespoons melted butter

TOPPING
- 1 large onion, peeled and grated
- 2 cloves garlic, peeled and grated
- 2 tablespoons cumin, nigella, sesame or poppy seeds
- 1/4 cup melted butter

GLAZE
- 1 egg, beaten

Tashkent, which means "stone castle or village," is the largest city in central Asia and was an important caravan town on the Silk Road for hundreds of years. The aroma of its famous, fragrant bread followed me wherever I went in the bazaar. Traditionally, the dough is slapped onto the side wall of a cylindrical clay oven or tandoor. When ready, the bread falls off the wall and is fished out by the baker using a hook on the end of a wooden pole. The round breads are then piled onto wooden pushcarts and sold in the bazaar or on the streets. I took the photographs (on these two pages) around midnight on my arrival in Tashkent, when some friends took me to their local bakery. I was very impressed, and it was both the fragrance of the bread and Uzbek hospitality that welcomed me.

1. In a small bowl, sprinkle the yeast and sugar over the warm water, and leave for 10 minutes, undisturbed.

2. Add the oil.

3. Place the flour mixture in a food processor and pulse to mix. Gradually add the dissolved yeast while the machine is running. Continue to mix until the dough forms into a ball (about 5 minutes). Allow the dough to rest in the machine for 5 minutes, then mix for another minute. Check the dough: It should not stick to your hands (add more flour if necessary).

4. Turn the dough in a generously buttered bowl to ensure it is coated evenly with butter. Cover the bowl with plastic wrap and allow the dough to rise at room temperature for 3 hours (or overnight), until double in size.

5. Turn out the dough onto a lightly floured work surface, punch down and divide the dough into 4 equal balls. Flatten each ball into a 7-inch disk, brush with water, cover and allow to rest for 30 minutes.

6. Preheat the oven to 350°F.

7. Grease a baking sheet and place a disk on it. With wet hands, make a 5-inch diameter indentation in the center of the disk and a 1-inch rim of crust. Prick all over the indented inner circle, paint with the glaze and sprinkle on the onion, garlic and cumin.

8. Bake for about 25 to 35 minutes, until golden brown on the edges. Remove from the oven and paint with butter. Repeat for the remaining dough.

Rayy Sweet Gingerbread (Nan-e Qandi)

Makes 6 loaves
Preparation time: 15 minutes, plus 20 minutes resting time
Cooking time: 7 to 10 minutes for each loaf

1 cup warm water
1/4 cup vegetable oil
1/4 cup molasses
1/4 cup honey
3-inch fresh ginger, grated
3/4 cup brown sugar
1 hot red chili, chopped. or 1/2 teaspoon chili paste
4 cups all-purpose unbleached flour
1 teaspoon baking powder
1/2 teaspoon baking soda
1/4 teaspoon salt
1/2 teaspoon ground cinnamon

DECORATION
1/4 cup sesame seeds

This gingerbread Persian biscotti dipped in a glass of sweet, hot tea was one of my favorite snacks when I was a child.

1. In a small bowl, combine the water, oil, molasses, honey, ginger, sugar and chili, and mix well.

2. Sift together the flour, baking powder, baking soda, salt and cinnamon onto a piece of wax paper and transfer to a mixing bowl. Gradually blend in the molasses mixture and knead until the dough forms into a ball (about 5 minutes).

3. Divide the dough into 6 equal balls, cover with a dish towel and allow to rest for 20 minutes.

4. Preheat the oven to 400°F and line a baking sheet with a piece of parchment paper.

5. Roll out one ball on a floured surface to form a 10-inch-by-5-inch-by-1/4-inch-thick oval loaf.

6. Immediately place the rolled out dough on the baking sheet, paint the dough with water, draw a stripe on it with a fork and sprinkle with sesame seeds. Bake for 7 to 10 minutes, until puffy. Repeat for all the dough.

7. Remove from the oven and allow to cool. This bread should be oval and brittle, and taste sweet and spicy.

Pasta, Pizza & Bread / 232

Armenian Festive Sweet Bread

One of the golden memories of my childhood was this sweet bread—piping hot—which we bought from Teresa's Armenian bakery in the heart of Tehran, and ate for breakfast with butter and fig preserves. Since the 1500s when Shah Abbas brought whole villages of Armenians from Armenia to Isfahan in order to encourage trade and building, there have been thriving communities of Armenians in Iran's major cities. With the Armenians came delicious pastries and the coffee break, for which they have a particular flair.

1. Place the warm water in a medium bowl, sprinkle on the yeast, and allow to sit for 15 minutes, undisturbed.

2. Sift the flour, salt and mahlab onto a sheet of wax paper, and transfer into a mixing bowl. Gradually, add the dissolved yeast and warm milk while the machine is running.

3. Beat in the eggs, one at a time. Add the butter, sugar, honey and orange zest. Mix well until you have a smooth, elastic, soft dough (about 5 minutes).

4. Place the dough in a greased bowl, turning to coat it evenly. Cover the bowl with a dish towel and allow the dough to rise at room temperature for 3 to 24 hours until it doubles in bulk.

5. Turn out the dough on a floured work surface, punch down, cover and allow to rest for 10 minutes.

6. Knead in the raisins. Shape the dough into a round 9-inch loaf and place it on a greased 12-inch-diameter baking pan. Cover with a dish towel and allow to proof (become light for cooking), at room temperature, for another hour.

7. Preheat oven to 375°F.

8. Paint the top of the loaf with the glaze and sprinkle with poppy seeds.

9. Bake in the preheated oven for about 40 to 50 minutes until the loaf is golden brown and a skewer inserted into the center comes out clean. Remove from the pan and allow to cool on a wire rack.

Makes 1 loaf
Preparation time: 20 minutes, plus 2 hours rising time
Cooking time: 50 minutes

- 1/4 cup warm water
- 1 package (1 tablespoon) dry active yeast
- 3 cups sifted all-purpose flour
- 1 teaspoon salt
- 1 teaspoon ground mahlab*
- 1/2 cup warm milk
- 2 eggs
- 3 tablespoons unsalted butter, ghee or vegetable oil
- 1/4 cup sugar
- 1 tablespoon honey
- Zest of 1 orange, grated
- 1 cup raisins

GLAZE & DECORATION
- 1 egg yolk (beaten) with 1 teaspoon water
- 2 tablespoons poppy or sesame seeds, or sliced almonds

NOTE
In step 8, you can divide the dough into 3 equal lengths of rope and braid them together before glazing.

Gujarati Pan Mung Bean Bread

Makes 6 loaves
Preparation time: 30 minutes, plus 20 minutes for resting
Cooking time: 3 minutes for each pan bread

- 1 cup mung beans
- 1 tablespoon olive oil
- 1 tablespoon sesame oil
- 3 cups water
- 1 teaspoon salt
- 1/2 cup rice flour mixed with 1/2 cup cold water
- 1 hot green chili, sliced
- 2 fresh scallions, shredded
- 1 clove garlic, peeled
- 1/4 teaspoon ground turmeric
- 1 tablespoon light soy sauce
- 1 tablespoon roasted sesame seeds
- 1/4 cup vegetable oil for cooking

DIPPING SAUCE
- 1/2 teaspoon chili paste
- 1/2 teaspoon sugar
- 1/4 teaspoon salt
- 1 teaspoon light soy sauce
- 4 tablespoons rice vinegar
- 1 tablespoon chopped fresh cilantro

NOTE
You may substitute 1 cup mung bean flour dissolved in 1/4 cup warm water for the whole mung beans.

1. Cover the mung beans with 3 cups water, add 1 teaspoon salt, bring to a boil, reduce heat, cover partially and cook over medium heat for 20 minutes, until tender. Remove from heat, drain and set aside.

2. In a food processor puree together the mung beans, olive oil and sesame oil, then add the rice flour, chili, scallions, garlic, salt, turmeric and soy sauce, and pulse until you have a soft dough.

3. Form the dough into a ball, knead in the sesame seeds, cover and allow to rest for 20 minutes. Place dough on a rice-floured surface and turn into a long log 2 inches in diameter. Divide it into 6 equal lengths. Cover with a moist towel to prevent drying. Using your hands, roll each dough into small balls, flatten in your hands and press into a plate of rice flour to coat it. Then use a rolling pin to roll the dough out into a 6-inch-round, thin disk. Repeat for all the balls of dough.

4. Heat an 8-to 10-inch, non stick skillet over medium heat until very hot (if you use an electric griddle, heat to 375°F). Paint the skillet with oil using a pastry brush.

5. Place one of the disks in the center of the skillet and cook for 30 seconds. Press down with a spatula until the dough forms pockets. Flip over and repeat. Flip over again and press down (the bread is ready when it is dry around the edges and the bottom is a light, reddish brown. Drip more oil on the skillet if it dries and repeat with the remaining disks.

6. Wrap all the loaves in foil and keep warm until ready to serve.

7. Combine all the ingredients for the dipping sauce and transfer to a small bowl. Cut the loaves into wedges and serve hot with the sauce.

Yemeni Pan Barley Bread

Yemen is strategically situated on the southern entrance of the Red Sea separating Arabia from Africa and at a crossroads of the trade routes. Its culture shows Greek, Persian, Roman, Indian, Indonesian and Chinese influences. In the glory days of the Silk Road, Yemen controlled the supply of frankincense and myrrh, and played an important role in the spice trade.

1. In a food processor, place the flour, barley flour, baking powder, baking soda, salt and sugar, and pulse to combine. Add 2 tablespoons oil and pulse to combine.

2. In a small bowl, combine the yogurt, milk, chili and garlic. Gradually add this mixture to the flour mixture and pulse as you do so, until you have a soft dough.

3. Form the dough into a ball, cover and allow to rest for 20 minutes.

4. Place the dough on a rice-floured surface and turn into a long 2-inch-diameter log. Divide into 6 equal pieces. Using your hands, flatten each piece and press into a plate of barley flour to coat it. Use a rolling pin to roll into a thin 6-inch-diameter disk.

5. Heat an 8- to 10-inch non stick skillet over medium heat until very hot (if you use an electric griddle, heat to 375°F). Paint the skillet with oil using a pastry brush.

6. Place one of the disks in the center of the skillet and cook for 30 seconds. Press down with a spatula until the dough forms pockets. Flip over and repeat. Flip over again and press down (the bread is ready when it is dry around the edges and the bottom is a light, reddish brown. Drip more oil on the skillet if it dries and repeat with the remaining disks.

7. Wrap all the loaves in foil to keep warm.

8. Cut the loaves into wedges and serve hot.

VARIATION

Gujarati Pan Millet Bread
Substitute millet flour for the barley flour.

Makes 6 loaves
Preparation time: 25 minutes, plus 20 minutes for resting
Cooking time: 3 minutes for each loaf

2 tablespoons unbleached all-purpose flour
1 1/2 cups barley flour
1/2 teaspoon baking powder
1/4 teaspoon baking soda
1 teaspoon salt
2 teaspoons sugar
1/4 cup vegetable oil for cooking
1/2 cup plain yogurt
2 tablespoons vegetable oil
1/2 cup plain milk
1 hot green chili, sliced
1 clove garlic, crushed & peeled

NOTE

You may cook 1 cup barley in 2 cups water for 20 minutes over medium heat, drain and substitute it for the barley flour.

Hindu Kush Pan Rice Bread

Makes 6 loaves
Preparation time: 15 minutes, plus 20 minutes for resting
Cooking time: 6 minutes for each loaf

- 2 cups rice flour
- 1 teaspoon salt
- 2 tablespoons vegetable oil for cooking
- 1/2 cup boiling water
- 3/4 cup plain yogurt
- 1/2 cup coconut milk
- 1 teaspoon freshly ground pepper
- 1 teaspoon mustard seeds, toasted
- 1 bird or Serrano chili, sliced
- 2 fresh scallions, chopped

GLAZE
- 1/2 cup coconut milk

The Hindu Kush are "the Alps" of Central Asia—500 miles long and 150 miles wide. The undulating eastern grasslands are emerald green oases full of small plots of wheat and rice, as well as orchards of mulberries, walnuts, almonds, jujubes and apricots irrigated by glacial snowmelt.

1. Place the rice flour and salt in a food processor, add the vegetable oil and pulse to combine. Add the boiling water and pulse to blend. Add the remaining ingredients and blend until you have a soft dough.

2. Form the dough into a ball, cover and allow to rest for 20 minutes.

3. Place the dough on a rice-floured surface and turn into a long 2-inch-diameter log. Divide into 6 equal pieces. Cover with a damp cloth to prevent drying. Using your hands, roll each piece into a small ball, press and coat each piece in rice flour. Using a rolling pin, roll out to a thin 6-inch-round dough.

4. Heat an 8- to 10-inch non stick skillet over medium heat until very hot (if you use an electric griddle, heat to 375°F). Paint the skillet with oil using a pastry brush.

5. Place one of the disks in the center of the skillet and cook for 30 seconds. Press down with a spatula until the dough forms pockets. Flip over and repeat. Flip over again and press down (the bread is ready when it is dry around the edges and the bottom is a light, reddish brown. Drip more oil on the skillet if it dries and repeat with the remaining loaves.

6. Remove from the skillet and paint each loaf with coconut milk. Wrap all the loaves in foil to keep warm.

Left: A woman makes rice flour bread in northeast Iran. This bread is also popular throughout India. On the Malabar coast in southern India, it is called Pathiri

Sichuan Pan Scallion Bread

> **Makes 6 loaves**
> Preparation time: 10 minutes, plus 30 minutes for resting
> Cooking time: 6 minutes for each bread
>
> **DOUGH**
> 3 cups all-purpose flour, sifted
> 1 1/4 cups boiling water
>
> **FILLING**
> 1/4 cup sesame oil
> 1 tablespoon salt
> 1 tablespoon raw sesame seeds
> 1 teaspoon toasted ground Sichuan pepper
> 2 scallions, shredded
> 1/4 cup olive oil for frying
>
> **DIPPING SAUCE**
> 1/2 cup vegetable stock
> 1/4 cup rice vinegar
> 2 tablespoons soy sauce
> 1 hot red chili, slit
> 1 scallion, chopped
> 1 clove garlic, crushed and peeled

1. To make the dough, place the flour in a food processor, gradually add the boiling water while pulsing for 5 minutes, until you have a soft dough. Remove the dough from the food processor, form it into a ball, cover with a damp dish towel and allow to rest for 30 minutes.
2. Form the dough into a long 2-inch-diameter cylinder and divide it into 6 equal pieces. On a lightly floured surface, roll out each piece into a 6-inch-round disk.
3. Paint each disk with sesame oil and sprinkle with a little salt, sesame seeds, Sichuan pepper and scallions.
4. Roll up each disk, jelly roll fashion. Coil each roll into a spiral circles and tuck in the end. Gently flatten the coil, edge side up, with your hands, place it on the working surface and gently roll out into a 6-inch-round dough.
5. Heat an 8- to 10-inch non stick skillet over medium heat until very hot. Add 2 tablespoons oil (if you use an electric griddle, heat to 375°F).
6. Place a round dough in the center of the skillet. Cook for 2 to 3 minutes without disturbing it, until it is dry around the edges and the bottom is reddish brown. Use a spatula to turn the bread to cook the other side. Add more oil to the skillet if it dries and repeat for the remaining loaves.
7. Stack the loaves, one on top of the other, between layers of paper towels.
8. For the dipping sauce, combine all the ingredients and transfer to a small bowl. Cut the bread into wedges and serve hot with the sauce.

Variation

This scallion bread is also cooked by steam-frying. This is done by adding 1 teaspoon of baking powder sifted into the flour in step 1. Then heat 1 tablespoon oil and 2 tablespoons water in a non stick frying pan, cover and cook over very low heat for 7 minutes on each side (this replaces steps 5 and 6).

Right: A girl sells scallion bread in the Xian market.

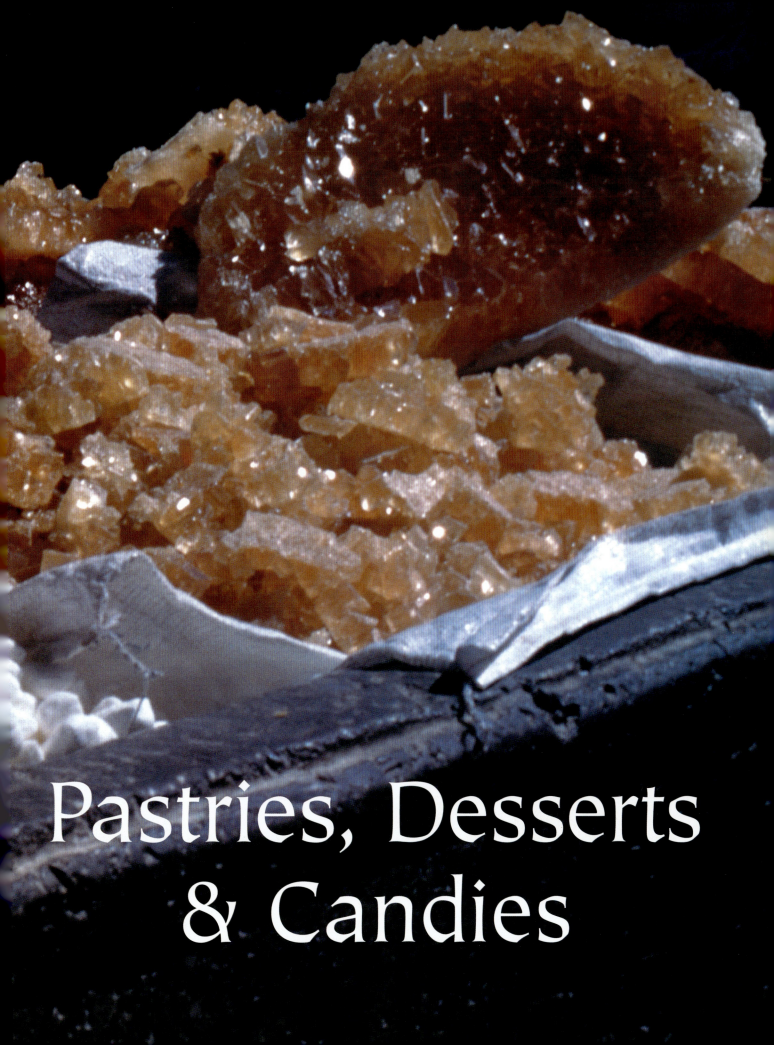

Pastries, Desserts & Candies

Spanish Orange Blossom Sponge Roll

Makes one 10-inch roll
Preparation time: 15 minutes
Cooking time: 12 minutes, plus 40 minutes in refrigerator

BATTER
5 egg yolks
1/2 cup sugar
Zest of one orange
1 vanilla bean, split and scraped, or 1/2 teaspoon vanilla extract
2 tablespoons cake flour
5 egg whites

FILLING
1 1/4 cups heavy cream
2 tablespoons confectioners' sugar
1 tablespoon orange blossom water

DECORATION
1/4 cup confectioners' sugar for dusting
2 organic orange blossoms and leaves

1. Oil a baking sheet and line it with parchment paper.

2. Preheat the oven to 400°F.

3. In a mixing bowl over a double boiler (or over a wok containing 2 cups of simmering water), beat the egg yolks with sugar, orange zest and vanilla for 5 minutes, until the mixture is creamy and pale.

4. Fold in the flour using a rubber spatula. Set aside

5. Whisk the egg whites in a mixing bowl until stiff but not dry. Fold the egg white into the mixture using a rubber spatula (mix in one direction only).

6. Spread the batter evenly on the lined baking sheet and bake for 10 to 12 minutes, until lightly golden.

7. Remove from the oven, cover the pastry in the baking sheet with a damp towel and allow to cool for 10 minutes.

8. Meanwhile, dust a large piece of parchment paper with sugar.

9. Turn the pastry sheet out onto the parchment paper. Peel off the lining paper from the top and allow the pastry to cool.

10. To prepare the filling, whip the cream, sugar and orange blossom water in a chilled mixing bowl, until thick.

11. Spread the whipped cream evenly over the pastry sheet. Very gently and carefully, using the parchment paper to help lift it, roll up the pastry sheet from one of the long ends and wrap it in the parchment paper. Chill for at least 40 minutes (it can also be frozen for later use).

12. Remove from the refrigerator and unwrap the parchment paper. Dust it with sugar and decorate with orange blossoms. Keep chilled until ready to serve.

Pastries, Desserts & Candies

East-West Almond Cookies

These cookies are made with varying flavors in many of the countries in the Silk Road region from China to Italy.

1. Preheat the oven to 425°F. Grease and line a cookie sheet with parchment paper.

2. Finely grind the almonds in a food processor and set aside.

3. Beat the sugar and oil in a mixing bowl until you have a soft paste.

4. Add the egg white and beat for 20 seconds. Fold in the flour, almonds, cardamom and rose water, and gently blend for 20 seconds, until you have a smooth batter.

5. Drop the batter by the spoonful onto the greased cookie sheet, leaving 2 1/2 inches between each piece for expansion. Decorate each piece with almonds and rose petals.

6. Place the cookie sheet in the center of the oven and bake for 5 to 10 minutes, until the edges of the cookies are lightly golden.

7. Take the cookie sheet out of the oven and immediately lift off the cookies using a spatula. Do this while the cookies are still hot; they won't peel off easily once cool.

Makes 15 cookies
Preparation time: 7 minutes
Cooking time: 10 minutes for each sheet of cookies

1 cup blanched almonds
1 cup granulated sugar
1/2 cup corn oil
5 egg whites, lightly beaten until foamy
1 cup all-purpose flour, sifted
1 teaspoon ground cardamom
2 tablespoons cooking rose water

DECORATION
15 blanched almonds or pistachios
2 tablespoons organic rose petals (optional)

Genoese Saffron & Rose Petal Biscotti

Makes: 15 biscotti
Preparation time: 15 minutes
Cooking time: 45 minutes

3 eggs, lightly beaten
1/4 cup butter or vegetable oil
1 cup sugar
1/4 cup rose water
1/2 teaspoon saffron threads, ground and dissolved in 1 tablespoon hot water
3 cups rice flour
1/2 cup unbleached all purpose flour
1 teaspoon cardamom powder
1 teaspoon baking soda
1 teaspoon baking powder
1/8 teaspoon salt
1/2 teaspoon ground cinnamon
1/2 cup unsalted pistachios, shelled*
1/4 cup dried organic rose petals

GLAZE
1 egg yolk, lightly beaten

Biscotto, from the Latin panis biscoctus, *means "bread twice cooked." A biscotto is perfect for travelers and sailors because it is dry and very hard, and therefore keeps well, often needing to be softened in liquid to be edible. Many an ancient mariner is said to have lost a tooth biting into a biscotto. A tenth-century Arab cookbook gives a recipe for a twice-cooked bread and attributes a Persian origin to it. And C. J. Wills, a British doctor working for the Telegraph Company in Persia in the 1860s wrote, "Rusks, biscuits, and a peculiar form of very dry bread, called 'twice-fired,' are specially made for travelers."*

This recipe is a blend of the Caspian, Uzbek and Genoese versions, and is perfect for dunking into tea.

1. Preheat the oven to 350°F. Line a baking sheet with parchment paper.

2. In a mixing bowl, beat the eggs, butter, sugar, rose water and saffron water until creamy.

3. Sift together all the flour, cardamom, baking soda, baking powder, salt and cinnamon onto a piece of wax paper, and gradually add it to the egg mixture. Blend until you have a smooth, soft dough that does not stick to your hands.

4. Turn the dough out onto a floured surface and, with your hands, knead the pistachios and rose petals into the dough. Shape it into a flat log about 10 inches long and 3 inches across. Place the log on the baking sheet.

5. Paint the log with the glaze and bake it in the preheated oven for 35 minutes, until lightly brown. Remove from the oven and cut it diagonally with a serrated knife into 15 slices. Turn the slices onto their flat sides, keeping them on the same baking sheet.

6. Reduce the heat to 325°F. Return the baking dish to the oven and cook 10 minutes longer.

7. Remove from the oven and allow to cool. Store in an airtight jar.

Yazdi Turnover Pastry with Cardamom & Rose Water (Sanbuseh)

Marco Polo called Yazd, a city in central Iran, a "noble city," and although it is an oasis in the dessert, at 1,200 feet elevation, its pastries are the finest, most delicate, and subtly flavored of all Iran.

1. To prepare the filling, mix the ground almonds and sugar together, and toast in a nonstick skillet over medium heat for 10 minutes until the sugar is lightly caramelized, stirring occasionally. Add the cardamom and rose water, and mix well. Set aside to cool.

2. On a cool floured working surface, roll the dough out very thin (about 1/8 inch) with a rolling pin. Cut the dough into 3-inch circles using a floured cookie cutter or the open end of a glass dipped in flour. Fill each circle with 1 teaspoon of the almond mixture. Fold the circles into halves and seal them shut, using a fork, around the outer surface.

3. Heat the oven to 350°F.

4. Carefully transfer the sanbusehs, one by one, onto a baking sheet lined with parchment paper. Do not crowd. Bake for 20 to 30 minutes, until golden brown.

5. Remove from the oven and allow to cool. When cool, roll them in confectioners' sugar and sprinkle with pistachios.

6. Arrange the pastries in a pyramid on a serving platter and serve immediately, or store in an airtight jar in a cool place.

Servings: 15 pieces
Preparation time: 1 hour plus 3 hours for dough to rise
Cooking time: 30 minutes

DOUGH
1 package frozen puff pastry, thawed for 1 hour before use

FILLING
1 cup unsalted, blanched almonds or pistachios, ground
1/2 cup sugar
1 tablespoon ground cardamom
1 tablespoon cooking rose water

GARNISH
1/2 cup confectioners' sugar
1/2 cup ground, unsalted pistachios

HOMEMADE DOUGH
You can make your own dough instead of using ready-made, frozen puff pastry. Beat 2 egg yolks until creamy. Add 1/2 cup yogurt and 1/2 cup oil, and mix well. Gradually blend in a sifted mixture of 2 cups unbleached all-purpose flour and 1 teaspoon baking powder. Knead well to produce a dough that does not stick to your hands. Place the dough in a plastic bag and refrigerate for 3 hours.

Sicilian Sour Cherry & Pistachio Crostata

Makes one 8-inch tart
Preparation time: 20 minutes
Cooking time: 50 minutes

HOMEMADE DOUGH
1 1/2 cups unbleached all-purpose flour
1/8 teaspoon salt
1/2 cup unsalted butter, diced
1 egg
4 tablespoons ice water

FILLING
1 egg
1/2 cup unsalted butter
1 cup sugar
1/8 teaspoon salt
2 tablespoons unbleached all-purpose flour
1 1/2 cups pistachios, unsalted
1/2 teaspoon baking powder
1/2 teaspoon ground cardamom
1/4 teaspoon ground cinnamon
1 tablespoon cooking rose water

TOPPING
3 cups pitted sour cherries, fresh, frozen or canned (two 24-ounce jars sour cherries in light syrup, drained)
1 tablespoon fresh lime juice

GARNISH
2 tablespoons confectioners' sugar
1 tablespoon unsalted pistachios

NOTE
You may substitute one package frozen puff pastry sheets, thawed for 1 hour and rolled out to a 1/4-inch thickness.

You may also substitute any one of the following fruits for the sour cherries: 10 red plums, pitted; 10 apricots, pitted; 10 dates, pitted; 8 apples, cored and sliced.

1. Place the flour and salt in a food processor, pulse, add the butter, pulse for 10 seconds, add the egg and pulse for 20 seconds. Gradually add the ice water and pulse until you have a dough that is just holding together. Gather the dough with your hands and form a ball.

2. Use a rolling pin to spread the dough out onto a floured surface. Transfer to an 8-inch pie pan and use the overhanging dough to create an edge. Prick the base of the shell with a fork. Place a large sheet of heavy-duty aluminum foil (heavy foil eliminates the need to weigh the dough down) over the shell, press down with the palms of your hands and wrap tightly with the foil. Chill for at least 30 minutes or until ready to use.

3. Preheat the oven to 400°F. Remove the shell from the refrigerator and bake for 15 minutes, still wrapped in aluminum foil.

4. Meanwhile, combine all the filling ingredients in a mixing bowl. Blend until you have a smooth batter.

5. Remove the shell from the oven and unwrap the aluminum. Spread the filling over the shell and top with the sour cherries and lime juice mixture.

6. Reduce heat to 375°F and bake for another 35 minutes until the edge is golden brown. Remove from the oven, transfer to a rack and allow to cool. Dust with confectioners' sugar and pistachios.

Pastries, Desserts & Candies / 244

Ardebil Quince Baklava

Servings: about 25 pieces
Preparation time: 35 minutes, plus 30 minutes resting time
Cooking time: 1 hour

ROSE WATER GLAZE
1 1/4 cups sugar
2/3 cup water
1/4 cup cooking rose water
2 tablespoons fresh lime juice

FILLING
2 cups almonds, blanched
1 teaspoon ground cardamom
1/2 teaspoon ground cinnamon
1 cup sugar

TOPPING
2 tablespoons butter or corn oil
3 pounds quinces (about 5 medium quinces), quartered, cored and cut into 1/8-inch-thick wedges and sprinkled with 2 tablespoons fresh lime juice
1/4 cup sugar

DOUGH
16 sheets filo dough (1 package), thawed for 1 hour in package before use, unrolled on a work surface and covered with a towel, or homemade dough*
1 cup butter (melted) or corn oil

GARNISH
2 tablespoons unsalted pistachios, ground
2 tablespoons dried organic rose petals

NOTE
You can use two pie pans to make two pies. You can also substitute cooking apples for the quince.

Ardebil, is in northwest Iran (near the Russian border). It gained importance both as a stopping place on the caravan route and during the reign of the Safavids in the sixteenth century, when the Italian traveler Pietro della Valle called it "little Venice." I adapted this recipe from Gholamali Ashbazbashi, a cook from Ardebil.

1. Prepare the glaze by combining the sugar and water in a saucepan. Bring to a boil, add the rose water and lime juice, and immediately remove from heat to prevent overboiling. Set aside.

2. For the filling, finely grind the almonds, cardamom, cinnamon and sugar together in a food processor. Set aside.

3. For the topping, heat 2 tablespoons butter in a deep skillet. Add the quince and 1/4 cup sugar. Cover and cook over medium heat for 20 minutes, stirring occasionally until the quince, turn pinkish. Remove from heat and allow to cool.

4. Preheat the oven to 350°F.

5. Paint a baking sheet with butter and lay 1 filo sheet over it. Generously paint the filo sheet with butter and repeat for up to 8 layers of filo dough, one on top of the other. Spread the almond filling evenly over the top of the filo dough layers. Arrange the quince evenly on top. Press down.

6. Cover the mixture with another 8 layers of buttered filo dough. Press down on the surface of the dough evenly with the palms of your hands.

7. Fold the overhanging edges of the top layers of dough over the edges of the bottom layer. Press and pinch them together, forming a rim around the baklava as you would form a rim to seal a pie.

8. Using a sharp knife, cut through the dough diagonally, 3 inches apart, to create a diamond pattern. Then paint the top and rim of the dough with 2 tablespoons of melted butter.

9. Bake for 35 to 40 minutes, in the middle level of the preheated oven, until the top is golden brown. Remove the pan from the oven and drizzle 1 cup of the glaze evenly over the top of the baklava.

10. Decorate the baklava with ground pistachios and rose petals.

11. Serve from the baking pan or, using a sharp knife, lift out the diamond pieces and arrange them on a serving dish.

Genoese Quince Paste with Pistachios

The quince, a native of the Caucasus, was beloved throughout the ancient world for its fragrance, astringency and delicate red color once cooked. It remains popular not only in the Caucasus, but also wherever sweet and sour dishes are favored—Turkey, Iran and Romania, for instance. In all of these countries and medieval Europe, quince pastes like this one were enjoyed as well—partly for their flavor; partly because quince, high in pectin, makes a paste that can be molded into fancy shapes (a French version is stamped with an image of Joan of Arc on a horse); and partly because the fruit was thought to be good for the digestion.

Then, too, this fragrant fruit has long been associated with love, which only adds to its attraction. The apples mentioned in the Song of Solomon are almost certainly quinces; the Greeks held it sacred to Aphrodite. Tenth-century Spanish poets called its distinctive flavor the "perfume of love."

Servings: 6
Preparation time: 15 minutes
Cooking time: 3 hours plus 3 days at room temperature to dry out

3 pounds quinces (about 5 medium quinces)
1 3/4 cups sugar
1 tablespoon fresh lime juice
1 teaspoon ground cardamom (optional)

GARNISH
1 cup ground pistachios (optional)

1. Wash and rub the fuzz off the quinces, core, grate, and place in a large nonstick pot. Cover (do not add water) and cook over low heat for 1 hour, stirring occasionally with a wooden spoon.

2. Add the sugar and lime juice. Cover and simmer over low heat for 2 1/2 hours, stirring occasionally with a wooden spoon, until tender. The quinces' color should change to dark pink.

3. Purée the quince, in a food processor and return to the pot. Add cardamom. Cook over medium heat for 30 minutes, stirring often with a wooden spoon. You should have a thick, reddish paste. Remove from heat and allow to cool for 10 minutes.

4. Transfer the quince paste to a greased 9-inch, square metal cake pan. Pack it firmly with a spoon and garnish with ground pistachios.

5. Leave it out at room temperature for a few days to set. Remove from the pan. Use a sharp, oiled knife to cut the paste into diamonds and arrange on a serving dish.

A Sweet & Sour Story

Consider the orange. At seventy million metric tons per year, it is the most widely produced tree fruit in the world, beating even the apple. It is now found everywhere, usually in the form of breakfast juice.

This common fruit has a most exotic and well-traveled past, however. The wild parent, *C. aurantium*, is native to southeast Asia; its name derives from the Sanskrit *nareng*. It seems to have been cultivated early in China and valued for the distinctive fragrance of its peel. Old Chinese texts describe warming oranges in the hands to release their scent.

This orange is a late traveler. Its first mention west of China doesn't appear until 100 CE, in an Indian religious text. It seems to have moved slowly west along overland trade routes and then north into Europe with the Arab diaspora. By the eleventh century the bitter orange was growing in Sicily, and by the end of the twelfth, in Spain.

As for the sweet orange, it was developed by the Chinese. It did not appear in the West until the end of the fifteenth century. While some seeds came through Genoa into Italy, most seem to have arrived in Portugal with Vasco da Gama following his discovery of the sea route to India. The Portuguese were soon exporting this delicious fruit both east and west, which is why it is called by a variant of the word "Portugal" in countries ranging from Greece to Iran, Turkey and Romania.

It is the older, sour orange, known to Iranians and Arabs as *narenj* and to westerners as the Seville or bitter orange, that most interests me in cooking. Westerners know this orange primarily as a component of marmalade. Cooks along the paths of the old Silk Road value it for its aromatic skin, flowers, leaves and juice.

The juice, for instance, serves as a subtle souring agent in many recipes. For more intense flavor, it may be reduced to a paste. It may also be cooked with sugar to make a syrup that is the basis for a tasty soft drink.

Seville orange leaves are particularly aromatic. They make an excellent tea, said to have both a digestive and calming effect.

As for the peel, when dried it may be combined with bay leaves to make another tea that is an excellent cold remedy. Or the peel may be candied for used in rice dishes, stuffings, and desserts (see Orange Peel, Candied, page 316).

Last there are fragrant orange blossoms. These may be distilled into orange flower water, widely available at specialty markets, for use as a flavoring. The distilling process also produces the much more intense orange flower essence, which is used to scent perfumes and liqueurs. The essence is called oil of neroli after a French princess who married an Italian duke (hence neroli), then became lady of the bedchamber to the queen of Spain, from which position she dominated Spanish government during the first decade of the eighteenth century. Why it is named for her we don't know.

Until recently, almost all Seville oranges in the West were made into marmalade: The fruit itself was quite hard to find. At least one English food writer was reduced to stealing oranges from the public parks in Seville; many Iranians had to take the same expedient in California. Today, however, Seville oranges are available during the winter months at Persian markets; the slivered and dried (or candied) peel is sold all year round, as is Seville orange paste.

Orange segments, candied orange peel and orange blossoms are ready to be combined with pomegranate seeds to make a salad (see page 236).

Persian Pomegranate & Orange Blossom Fruit Salad

Servings: 4
Preparation time: 20 minutes, plus 30 minutes for refrigeration

2 cups pomegranate seeds (about 2 pomegranates)*
4 large oranges, peeled and sliced (with membrane removed)*, chilled
1/4 cup candied orange peel*
1/2 cup fresh orange juice
1 teaspoon orange blossom water*

GARNISH
6 organic orange blossoms (optional)
6 organic orange leaves (optional)

1. Combine the pomegranate seeds, orange segments, candied orange peel, orange juice and orange blossom water in a bowl. Cover and chill in the refrigerator for at least 30 minutes.

2. Serve chilled in individual glasses, and garnish each glass with an orange blossom and an orange tree leaf.

Greek Sesame & Walnut Cake

Sesame, cultivated in Mesopotamia at least 3,500 years ago, is one of the oldest condiments and one of the first plants whose seeds were used for edible oil. Herodotus mentions that the Babylonians made sesame oil at least 2,500 years ago. There is even a much older depiction in an Egyptian tomb some 4,000 years old showing a baker adding sesame seeds to his dough. In fact, its name is one of the few to have entered modern languages from the ancient Egyptian (sesemt). The expression "open sesame" from the Ali Baba story in 1001 Nights might have come from the fact that once the sesame is ripe the pod suddenly bursts open. I have also heard that it might come from a pun: "open says me."

1. Preheat oven to 350°F.

2. Butter a 9-inch cake pan, dust with flour and line with parchment paper.

3. In a mixing bowl, combine the sesame paste, sugars and orange zest. Add the eggs, one at a time, and beat for about 5 minutes, until pale in color and creamy in texture. Add the orange juice and beat for another minute.

4. Use a triple-sifter to sift the flour, baking powder, baking soda, cinnamon, nutmeg, cloves and salt onto a piece of wax paper.

5. Fold the flour mixture into the egg mixture, then fold in the walnuts and raisins.

6. Pour the batter into the pan. Sprinkle the top with sesame seeds and bake in the preheated oven for 50 minutes or until a knife placed in the center comes out clean.

7. Remove from the oven and place on a rack to cool for 10 minutes. With mitts, tap the pan to release the cake. Turn the cake out onto the rack, peel off the parchment paper, turn the cake over, and allow to cool completely for about 8 hours, uncovered (to air-dry).

Servings: 6
Preparation time: 20 minutes
Cooking time: 50 minutes

1 cup sesame paste (tahini)
1/4 cup brown sugar
1 1/4 cups confectioners' sugar
zest of 1 orange
3 eggs
1 cup fresh orange juice
2 1/4 cups unbleached all-purpose flour
2 teaspoons baking powder
1/2 teaspoon baking soda
1/2 teaspoon ground cinnamon
1/4 teaspoon ground nutmeg
1/4 teaspoon ground cloves
1/8 teaspoon salt
1/2 cup walnuts, chopped
1/2 cup raisins
2 tablespoons raw sesame seeds

NOTE

You can also use this batter to make 40 individual cookies. Place 1 tablespoon dollops of batter, 2 1/2 inches apart, on a cookie sheet lined with parchment paper. Sprinkle sesame seeds over the top and bake for 20 to 25 minutes, until the edges are golden brown.

Susa Spiced Walnut & Date Scones (Kolucheh)

Servings eight 4-inch scones
Preparation time: 20 minutes
plus 4 hours resting time
Cooking time: 20 minutes

DOUGH
3 1/2 cups unbleached all-purpose flour, sifted with 1 teaspoon ground cumin, 1 teaspoon baking powder and 1/2 teaspoon baking soda
1 cup butter or oil
1/2 cup water
1/4 cup rose water

FILLING
2 cups pitted dates
2 cups walnuts
1 cup pistachios
1 teaspoon ground nutmeg
2 teaspoons ground cardamom
1 teaspoon ground cinnamon
1 tablespoon oil
2 tablespoons candied orange peel

NOTE
Wheat malt flour is made by allowing partial germination to modify the grains' natural food substances, making it softer and giving it a malty flavor.

These scones have been very popular among travelers along the Silk Road region since ancient times not only because they are soft, delicious and highly nutritious, but also because they keep very well. I have decorated these with a lotus flower rosette stamp, which is the flower in the hands of the Mede (bottom left photograph) found on a bas-relief at Persepolis.

1. For the dough, place the sifted flour mixture in a mixing bowl, gradually add the butter and mix until you have a crumbly dough. Cover the bowl with plastic and allow to rest for 3 hours and up to 24 hours.

2. Gradually add the water and rose water and knead well for 5 minutes, until the you have a soft dough. Cover and allow to rest at room temperature for 1 hour.

3. For the filling, combine all the filling ingredients in a food processor and mix until you have a soft paste.

4. Preheat the oven to 350°F.

5. Divide the dough into 16 balls. On a cool, floured surface, roll out each ball into a 1/4-inch-thick-by-4-inch disk.

6. Spread 1 tablespoon of filling over each of the 8 disks. Cover with another dough disk to make a sandwich. Gently roll over the disks to flatten.

7. Gently lift each sandwich up and pinch the edges to seal the filling inside. Use a stamp, according to your fancy, to decorate the top.

8. Lay the filled dough disks on a baking sheet, lined with parchment paper, 2 inches apart.

9. Place the baking sheet in the center of the preheated oven. Bake for 15 to 20 minutes, until the scones are lightly brown.

10. Remove from the oven and allow to cool. Arrange in a basket and serve with tea.

VARIATION

Kermani Wheat Malt Flour Scones (Kolombeh)
Substitute 7 cups wheat malt flour for the all-purpose flour.

Pastries, Desserts & Candies

Samarkand Baked Candied Quince with Walnuts

Servings: 4
Preparation time: 15 minutes
Cooking time: 1 1/2 hours

SYRUP
2 cups water
1 1/2 cups sugar
1 vanilla bean, split and scraped out, or 1/2 teaspoon vanilla extract
4 tablespoons fresh lime juice
2 medium-sized quinces (unpeeled)
Four 3-inch cinnamon sticks
4 bay leaves

GARNISH
1/2 cup fresh pomegranate seeds* or raisins
1/2 cup toasted walnuts, chopped
Vanilla ice cream (optional)

For the past 25 years I have been studying Persian miniature paintings, and when I first visited Bokhara with its white mosques and minarets, and Samarkand with its blues domes, it was as if I had walked into a work of art. Samarkand, in particular, took me back in time to the fabled city built by Tamerlane.

The market was enormous, with a splendid array of spices, fragrant and colorful. I was also struck by the fact that it was mostly women and children who were working, while the men dozed and chatted. The women were made up and bejeweled, dressed in boldly striped ikat gowns with brightly patterned scarves covering their heads. They sat in rows, breaking walnuts with great skill: Several precise, sharp blows opened each nut, leaving the flesh intact.

1. Preheat oven to 350°F.

2. In a saucepan, combine the water, sugar and vanilla, and bring to a boil over medium heat. Add the lime juice and remove from heat.

3. Wash and rub off the fuzz from the quinces. Core the quinces (do not peel) and cut into halves.

4. Place the quince halves face up in a deep, 9-inch baking dish.

5. Lay a cinnamon stick and a bay leaf inside the hollow of each quince.

6. Dribble the syrup over the quinces and bake for 1 1/2 hours, basting occasionally, until the quinces are pinkish-red.

7. Remove from the oven and transfer to individual serving dishes. Garnish with pomegranate seeds and walnuts, and serve with vanilla ice cream.

VARIATION

Baked Candied Apples

You may substitute full-flavored, firm apples, such as Rome or Empire, for the quinces, in which case reduce the baking time in step 6 to 45 minutes.

Yazdi Persimmon & Feta Cheese

1. Cut the tops off the persimmons and set them aside for later use. Scoop out the pulp inside the persimmons and place the pulp in a mixing bowl.

2. Add the cheese, honey, almonds and vinegar, and mix well. Adjust sweetness to taste by adding sugar if necessary.

3. Refill the hollowed persimmons with the cheese mixture, using a spoon, and chill for 30 minutes.

4. Just before serving, place 1 tablespoon of the persimmon puree on individual serving dishes and place a persimmon on top. Dust with confectioners' sugar and garnish with a bay leaf. Replace the tops.

Servings: 6
Preparation time: 15 minutes, plus 30 minutes for refrigeration
Cooking time: none

6 fresh Chinese persimmons, washed
1/4 pound feta cheese, rinsed with cold water and crumbled, or 2 cups cottage cheese
1 tablespoon honey or molasses
1/2 cup toasted almonds, walnuts or unsalted pistachios, chopped
1 teaspoon balsamic vinegar

GARNISH
Pulp of 2 persimmons, pureed in the blender
2 tablespoons confectioners' sugar
6 bay leaves

Amman Semolina Cake with Orange Blossom Glaze

Servings: 6
Preparation time: 20 minutes
Cooking time: 45 minutes

- 2 cups fine semolina
- 1 cup ground blanched almonds
- 1 teaspoon baking soda
- 1 teaspoon baking powder
- 1/8 teaspoon salt
- 1/4 cup butter, ghee or vegetable oil
- 1/4 cup tahini paste
- 1 vanilla bean, split and scraped out, or 1/2 teaspoon vanilla extract
- 1/2 cup sugar
- 1 teaspoon orange zest (1 orange)
- 3/4 cup plain yogurt

GLAZE
- Shredded rind of 1 orange
- 1 tablespoon cooking orange blossom water
- One 3-inch cinnamon stick
- 1 cup fresh orange juice
- 1 cup sugar

DECORATION
- 1/4 cup toasted almonds, sliced
- 2 organic orange blossoms (optional)

Semolina, made from hard durum wheat, can be finely milled to make pasta flour or more coarsely milled to make the semolina grains used here. Semolina cakes like this one are enjoyed everywhere from the Mediterranean to Central Asia. A Greek version includes eggs and flour; an Afghani one is flavored with rose water and made with pistachio and ghee (but no eggs). This Jordanian version is made with tahini and yogurt, and flavored with orange blossoms, as is common throughout the Arab world.

1. Preheat oven to 350°F.

2. Dust a greased 8-inch square cake pan with flour, tap out the excess flour and line with parchment paper.

3. Pour the semolina, almonds, baking soda, baking powder and salt into a triple-sifter, sift onto wax paper and set aside.

4. Combine the butter, tahini paste, vanilla, sugar and orange zest in a mixing bowl. Beat for 5 minutes until you have a soft paste. Add the yogurt and beat for 1 minute longer.

5. Add in the flour mixture and mix until you have a stiff, well-blended dough.

6. Spread the batter in the pan and bake in the preheated oven for 40 to 45 minutes, until a knife inserted in the center comes out clean. Remove the cake from the oven and place on a rack to cool in the pan for 10 minutes.

7. To prepare the glaze, combine all the ingredients in a small saucepan and bring to a boil over medium heat. Reduce heat and simmer over low heat for 5 minutes. Remove from heat.

8. Pour half of the glaze over the cake, leaving the cake in the pan until it has absorbed all the syrup. Tap the pan to release the cake and transfer it to a serving dish. Cut the cake into diamond shapes, decorate with almonds and orange blossoms, and pour the remaining glaze over them.

Persian Pistachio Cake

1. Preheat oven to 350°F.

2. Butter and dust an 8-inch spring form cake pan with flour and line the base with parchment paper.

3. Pulse the sugar and pistachios in a food processor until finely ground.

4. Beat in the egg yolks, gradually. Add the zest of orange, vanilla, rose water, yogurt and butter, and mix for about 5 minutes, until creamy.

5. Sift the salt, baking powder, baking soda and flour onto a piece of wax paper. Fold into the egg mixture.

6. In a separate mixing bowl, beat the egg whites until they form soft peaks and fold into the flour mixture using a rubber spatula.

7. Gently pour the batter into the cake pan and bake in the preheated oven for 35 to 40 minutes, until a tester comes out clean.

8. Remove from the oven and allow to cool on a rack for 10 minutes. Tap the pan to release the cake. Turn the cake out onto the rack and remove the mold, peel off the wax paper and turn the cake over. Sprinkle the top with ground pistachios and dust with confectioners' sugar. Allow to cool completely for about 9 hours, uncovered, to air-dry. Transfer to a serving platter.

Servings: 8
Preparation time: 20 minutes
Cooking time: 40 minutes

- 1 cup sugar
- 1 cup raw, unsalted pistachio nuts,* shelled (6 ounces)
- 4 eggs, separated (at room temperature)
- Zest of 1 orange
- 1 vanilla bean, split and scraped out, or 1/2 teaspoon vanilla extract
- 1 tablespoon rose water
- 1 cup plain yogurt
- 1/2 cup unsalted butter
- 1/8 teaspoon salt
- 1 teaspoon baking powder
- 1 teaspoon baking soda
- 2 cups unbleached all-purpose flour

GARNISH
- 1/4 cup unsalted pistachios,* ground
- 1/4 cup confectioners' sugar

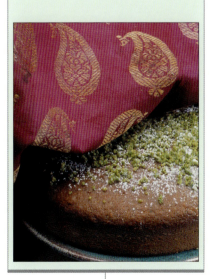

Georgian Sour Cherry Cake

Servings: 8
Preparation time: 20 minutes
Cooking time: 1 hour

1/4 cup butter, ghee or vegetable oil
1 cup sugar
1 cup strong tea (Darjeeling)
3 eggs, separated (at room temperature)
Zest of 1 orange
1 cup sour cherry preserve, drained
1/4 cup wine vinegar
1/4 teaspoon salt
1 teaspoon baking powder
1 teaspoon baking soda
2 1/2 cups unbleached all-purpose flour
1/4 cup walnuts, coarsely chopped

GLAZE & DECORATION
1 cup sour cherry syrup*
2 tablespoons fresh lime juice
1/2 cup pitted sour cherries, fresh, dried or canned (drained)

NOTE
You may substitute plums for the cherries.

Georgian mythology says that Georgians live in a paradise of plenty because as God was creating the earth he (wisely) took a dinner break, became a little tipsy, tripped over the high peaks of the Caucasus and spilled some of the food from his plate onto Georgia. His dinner must have included fruit and nuts, for which Georgian cooking is famous.

1. Preheat oven to 350°F. Generously butter and dust a 9-inch cake pan with flour, and line the bottom with parchment paper.

2. Melt the sugar in a saucepan over medium heat and cook for about 5 minutes until caramelized. Add the tea, cover and cook for 5 to 10 minutes until all the caramelized sugar has dissolved in the tea. Remove from heat.

3. In a mixing bowl, beat the egg yolks, remaining butter and orange zest for 5 minutes, until pale and creamy. Add the sour cherry preserve, vinegar and tea mixture, and beat for 1 minute.

4. Pour the salt, baking powder, baking soda and flour into a sifter, sift onto a piece of wax paper, and fold into the egg yolk mixture.

5. In a large bowl, beat the egg whites until they form soft peaks and gently fold in the flour mixture, using a rubber spatula, until you have a smooth batter.

6. Pour the batter into the pan and sprinkle with the walnuts. Place the pan in the lower third of the preheated oven and bake for 45 to 50 minutes, until a tester comes out clean.

7. Transfer the pan onto a rack and allow to cool for 10 minutes.

8. Meanwhile, prepare the glaze. Combine the sour cherry syrup and lime juice and bring to a gentle boil over medium heat. Remove from heat and set aside.

9. Tap the pan to release the cake and invert it onto the rack, remove the pan, peel off the parchment paper, and turn the cake face up. Glaze the top of the cake and arrange the sour cherries over the top. Allow to cool completely for about 2 hours, uncovered (to air-dry), so that the glaze is absorbed.

Chinese Eight Jewel Coconut Rice Pudding with Candied Orange Peel & Lotus Seeds

This Chinese rice pudding, popular for the New Year or Moon Dragon festival, is so named because it is traditionally made with eight preserved fruits. Classical recipes include sticky rice and red bean paste; my adaptation is based on rice flour and omits the paste.

1. Preheat oven to 400°F.

2. Combine the eggs, milk, sugar, vanilla, lime zest, orange peel, lotus seeds, coconut milk and salt, and beat for one minute, until pale and creamy. Fold in the rice flour and baking powder mixture.

3. Prepare 4 generously greased 6-ounce ramekins. Place a layer of mangos in each and pour the pudding into them. Place the ramekins in a large, deep baking dish lined with a few layers of paper towel, add boiling water to come halfway up the sides of the ramekins, cover them with a sheet of oiled aluminum foil, and bake for 35 to 40 minutes, until a knife inserted in the center comes out clean.

4. Remove the puddings from the oven, run a knife around the inside edge of the ramekins and allow to cool. Invert onto a serving dish and arrange the chilled mango slices on top.

Servings: 4
Preparation time: 5 minutes.
Cooking time: 40 minutes

- 2 eggs lightly beaten
- 1/2 cup milk
- 1 cup sugar
- 1 vanilla bean, split and scraped out, or 1/2 teaspoon vanilla extract
- Zest of 1 lime
- 1 teaspoon candied orange peel,* chopped
- 1 teaspoon candied lotus seeds* (optional)
- 1 1/2 cups coconut milk (two 14 fluid-ounce cans)
- 1/4 teaspoon salt
- 1 cup rice flour, sifted with 1/2 teaspoon baking powder
- 2 fresh mangos, peeled and chopped

GARNISH
- 1 mango, sliced and chilled

Left: Eight Jewel pudding sold at the market in Chengdu.

Turkish Delight with Rose Water (Rahat Lokum)

Servings: 20 pieces
Preparation time: 15 minutes
Cooking time: 1 1/4 hours, plus overnight setting

SYRUP
2 cups cold water
2 cups sugar
1 tablespoon fresh lime juice
2 tablespoons cooking rose water or 1 tablespoon orange blossom water

STARCH
1/2 cup wheat or cornstarch
1/2 teaspoon cream of tartar
1 cup cold water
1 drop red food coloring

FILLING (OPTIONAL)
1/4 cup toasted walnuts
1/4 cup toasted pistachios
1/4 cup toasted almonds

GARNISH
1 cup confectioners' sugar
1 teaspoon ground cardamom
3/4 cup cornstarch

NOTE
Although lokum is made in many of the countries along the ancient Silk Road, the best in the world is made by the Haji Bekir establishment in Istanbul which has been making it for over 200 years.

Lokum, meaning "rest for the throat" in Turkish, is the delicate, gummy jelly Westerners call Turkish Delight. It comes in many varieties, most flavored with lime or orange juice, but some with pomegranates, grapes or mulberries. The pink type is usually scented with rose water and the green with mint.

1. Oil a 12-inch-square, nonstick metal pan, dust with cornstarch, and set aside.
2. To make the syrup, combine the water, sugar, lime juice and rose water in a small heavy-based saucepan. Bring to a boil over high heat, reduce heat to medium and simmer for about 30 minutes, stirring occasionally, until the surface is full of bubbles and a candy thermometer reaches 250°F. Remove from heat.
3. To make the starch, combine the cornstarch, cream of tartar, and cold water in a large heavy-base saucepan. Blend well until smooth.
4. Place over medium heat and gradually add the hot syrup, stirring occasionally with a wire whisk. Cook for about 30 minutes or until the mixture has a thick texture and a pale gold color (it is ready when a little dropped into ice water forms a soft ball). Add a drop of the red food coloring to get the pink color. Remove from heat, add the nuts and continue to stir for another 15 minutes.
5. Spread the mixture in the oiled pan, pack and smooth the surface evenly.
6. Allow to set, at room temperature, overnight.
7. Mix the garnish ingredients and spread them on a work surface. Turn the jelly out on top of this mixture. Cut the jelly into 1-inch cubes with a sharp, oiled knife. Turn the cubes thoroughly in the sugar mixture to coat them.
8. Store in an airtight container and keep refrigerated (or even in the freezer).

VARIATION

Armenian Gelatin Lokum

Lokum can also be made using gelatin. Make the syrup as above. Remove from heat. Dissolve 1 ounce (4 envelopes) of unflavored gelatin powder in 1/4 cup cold water, 2 tablespoons rose water and 1/2 teaspoon vanilla extract. Let stand for 5 minutes, add to the syrup, and beat well until a smooth and creamy paste is created. Proceed from step 5 above.

Pastries, Desserts & Candies

Silk Road Sesame Brittle

Servings: 6 pieces
Preparation time: 10 minutes
Cooking time: 20 minutes, plus 30 minutes for cooling

3/4 cup sugar
3 tablespoons honey
1 tablespoon rose water
3/4 natural or raw (hulled) sesame seeds
1/4 teaspoon ground cinnamon
1/4 teaspoon ground nutmeg

This type of brittle—made with honey, sugar, oil, and various nuts and seeds such as pistachios, almonds and sesame—has been made throughout the Silk Road region since ancient times. In Italy, it is called croccant (crunchy) and made with almonds; in Iran it is called sohan asali (honey crunch); and in Afghanistan, it is called hasteh-ye shirin *(sweet kernel).*

1. Oil a nonstick baking sheet.

2. In a small, heavy-based saucepan, melt the sugar, honey and rose water over medium heat, stirring occasionally.

3. Add the sesame seeds, cinnamon and nutmeg, and stir constantly for 15 to 20 minutes, until the thermometer reaches 320°F.

4. Pour into the baking sheet and allow to cool. When the brittle has cooled, but before it is hard, use an oiled rubber spatula to ease it out of the pan onto a dish and allow it to harden for about 30 minutes. Break off into pieces, wrap in cellophane and store.

NOTE
Instead of using a baking sheet, you can use small, silver-dollar-sized individual nonstick molds.

Pastries, Desserts & Candies / 262

Persian Sequin Candy

Traditionally these candies are colored with saffron and served with tea, but you can also replace the saffron with various food colorings to make the candies more festive looking.

1. Melt the sugar in a small, heavy-bottomed saucepan over high heat, stirring constantly for 3 to 5 minutes until caramelized. Add the cardamom seeds and saffron water.

2. Spread some parchment paper on the counter.

3. Once the syrup has caramelized, use a spoon to drip 1-teaspoon sized dollops of syrup on the paper.

4. Allow to cool, peel off from the parchment paper, and serve with tea. These candies should be stored in an airtight jar.

Servings: 20 pieces
Preparation time: 5 minutes
Cooking time: 5 minutes

1 cup sugar
Seeds of 2 cardamom pods
1/8 teaspoon ground saffron threads dissolved in 1 tablespoon hot water

NOTE

To add a slightly sour flavor, 1 tablespoon of ground lime or sumac powder can be added with the saffron in step 1.

Viennese Cream Puffs with Rose Water

Servings: 24 pieces
Preparation time: 20 minutes
Cooking time: 30 minutes

FILLING
- 1 cup heavy cream (8 ounces)
- 1/4 tablespoon sugar
- 1 tablespoon cooking rose water
- Zest of 1/2 an orange

DOUGH
- 1 3/4 cups unbleached all-purpose flour
- 1 teaspoon baking powder
- 1 3/4 cups cold water
- 1/2 teaspoon salt
- 1/4 cup butter (unsalted), diced into small pieces
- 1 vanilla bean, split and scraped out, or 1/2 teaspoon vanilla extract
- Zest of 1 orange
- 4 eggs, lightly beaten, with 1 tablespoon cooking rose water

GLAZE
- 1 egg yolk
- 2 tablespoons milk

GARNISH
- 1 cup confectioners' sugar
- 1/4 cup ground pistachios
- 1 tablespoon dried rose petals

NOTE
You may substitute ice cream for the filling.

I ate this cream puff in Bokhara at Ismoil's Restaurant, after a long, hot drive from Samarkand. Walking into the restaurant garden was like stepping into paradise: a beautiful, shady place full of fruit trees, a vegetable and spice patch, a patio, and an arbor of vines, under which we sat. At the entrance of the garden was a big marble sink with hand towels for washing. When the owners, two brothers, found that I could talk to them in Tajiki, they were delighted. They treated my guide and me to a feast and gave me all their secret recipes, including this one. They took me to the house of the pastry chef, an 80-year-old Polish woman who had lived in Bokhara since the 1920s. This cream puff (in the photograph on the facing page) was her specialty. She had adapted and developed her recipe from one she had learned from her mother in Vienna.

1. To prepare the filling, combine the cream, sugar, rose water and orange zest, and refrigerate for at least 30 minutes. Then whip at high speed until soft peaks form. Keep chilled.

2. Lightly grease a baking sheet and dust with flour.

3. Preheat oven to 400°F and place a small pan of water on the lower tray of the oven to create a humid environment inside.

4. To prepare the dough, sift the flour and baking powder onto a sheet of wax paper and set aside.

5. In a heavy-based medium saucepan over medium heat, combine the water, salt and butter, and bring to a boil, stirring well with a wooden spoon. Add the vanilla and zest of orange. Reduce heat to very low and add the flour, all at once, stirring constantly until you have a stiff paste.

6. Remove from heat and transfer to a mixing bowl. Beat well for 5 minutes. The temperature of the mixture at this stage is very important; it should be around 150°F.

7. Mix the dough, at slow speed, while gradually adding the eggs until all the eggs have been absorbed and the dough is smooth, glossy and stiff.

8. Drop the dough (one heaping teaspoonful at a time) onto the prepared baking sheet, leaving 2 inches between each dollop to allow for expansion.

9. Prepare the glaze by beating together the egg and milk. Paint each puff with glaze.

10. Bake in the middle rack of the oven for 20 minutes.

11. Pull out the oven rack holding the sheet, and using a toothpick or wooden skewer, poke a hole in each pastry to release the steam. Push the tray back and close the oven. Continue to bake for another 5 minutes, until the puffs are golden brown and the interiors are dry.

12. Remove from the oven and allow to cool thoroughly.

13. A few hours prior to serving, use a pastry bag to squeeze the chilled filling into the pastry until full. Repeat for all the pastry.

14. Dust with confectioners' sugar, ground pistachios and rose petals. Refrigerate if not served immediately.

Photo left: A traditional tea setting in Bokhara is where the tea is drunk in small china bowls and served with flavored rock candy, and puff pastry here.

Photo below: Kalon Mosque in Bokhara.

Photo middle: A stall sells rock candy in the Bokhara market.

Photo bottom: The staff at Ismoil's poses for a photo just before closing for the evening.

Pastries, Desserts & Candies / 265

Shirazi Melon & Peach Sorbet with Crystallized Rose Petals

Servings: 4
Preparation time: 30 minutes
Cooking time: 10 minutes
Setting time: 40 minutes, varies depending on machine used

SYRUP
- 2 cups sugar
- 1 1/2 cups water
- 1/4 cup fresh organic rose petals, rinsed thoroughly, or 2 tablespoons dried rose petals

SORBET
- 1 (3 pounds) Persian melon or honeydew melon or cantaloupe, peeled, seeded and sliced
- 5 fresh peaches, peeled and sliced
- 1/2 teaspoon salt
- 2 tablespoons fresh lime juice

GARNISH
- 8 slices melon
- 8 slices peach
- 8 mint leaves
- 8 crystallized rose petals*

NOTE
While ice cream keeps well, sorbets are best served fresh.

You may substitute 2 cups persimmon pulp, pomegranate juice, blackberry pulp or quince for the melon and peach.

1. To make the syrup, combine the sugar and water in a heavy-based saucepan and bring to a boil over medium heat. Add the rose petals and simmer for 10 minutes over low heat. Remove from heat and allow to cool.

2. For the sorbet, puree the melon, peaches, salt, syrup and lime juice in a food processor.

3. Transfer to an ice cream maker canister and follow the manufacturer's instructions until you have a sorbet that holds its shape (about 40 minutes). Transfer to a covered freezer container and place in the freezer until ready to serve.

4. Twenty minutes before serving, transfer the sorbet to the refrigerator. Serve in individual fluted dishes. Garnish with slices of melon and peach, fresh mint leaves and crystallized rose petals.

Crystallized Rose Petals

Wash the rose petals thoroughly and pat dry. Line a cookie sheet with 1/4 cup super-fine sugar. Beat the egg white lightly with a fork until frothy. Use a brush to paint both sides of the rose petals with egg white. Arrange petals on a cookie sheet and coat both sides of the rose petals evenly with 1/4 cup sugar. Allow to dry on the bed of sugar at room temperature for at least 1 hour, until the sugar forms a crisp coat.

Turkish Quince Granita

1. Tie the quince slices in a cheese cloth and place in a large pot with 6 cups of water. Bring to a boil. Reduce heat to low, cover, and cook for 1 hour until tender. Drain and allow to cool. Lift the cheese cloth and squeeze out the juice into the pot (about 4 cups of juice). Discard the cheese cloth.

2. Add the lime juice, vanilla, sugar, and rose water to the pot. Stir well until completely dissolved.

3. Pour into a wide and shallow (about 1-inch deep), pyrex container, or metal pan and place in the freezer, for about 1 hour, until firm.

4. Using a spoon, break up the granita in the pan and replace in the freezer. Repeat, until all the juice has formed into ice crystals.

5. Scoop into individual dishes.

> Servings: 6
> Preparation time: 15 minutes
> Cooking time: 1 hour
> Setting time: 3 hours in freezer
>
> - 3 quinces (about 2 pounds), washed, cored and sliced
> - 2 tablespoons fresh lime juice
> - 1/4 teaspoon salt
> - 1 vanilla bean, split and scraped out, or 1/2 teaspoon vanilla extract
> - 1/2 cup sugar
> - 1 tablespoon cooking rose water (optional)

Iranian Granita with Rice Sticks & Sour Cherries

Servings: 6
Preparation time: 15 minutes
Cooking time: none
Setting time: 3 hours in freezer

2 cups water
2 cups sugar
2 ounces thin rice-stick noodles, snipped into 3-inch lengths using scissors, soaked in warm water for 20 minutes, drained and rinsed with cold water
1/4 teaspoon salt
2 tablespoons light corn syrup
1/4 cup fresh lime juice
1 tablespoon cooking rose water

GARNISH
2 tablespoons pistachios
1/4 cup fresh blackberries or sour cherry syrup*
4 tablespoons fresh lime juice

HOMEMADE RICESTICK NOODLES
These noodles can be made from rice or wheat starch.

1. Combine the water and sugar, and stir well until the sugar has completely dissolved. Add the remaining ingredients and stir well.

2. Pour into a wide and shallow (about 1-inch-deep) Pyrex, or metal pan and place in the freezer, for about 1 hour, until firm.

3. Using a spoon, break up the granita in the pan; replace in the freezer. Repeat, until all the juice has formed into ice crystals.

4. Scoop into individual dishes and garnish each with some pistachios, sour cherries syrup and lime juice.

Pastries, Desserts & Candies / 268

Iranian Pomegranate Granita

1. Mix all the ingredients until the sugar has dissolved.

2. Pour into a wide and shallow (about 1-inch-deep) glass or non-reactive metal pan and place in the freezer, for about 1 hour, until firm.

3. Using a spoon, break up the granita in the pan and replace in the freezer. Repeat, until all the juice has formed into ice crystals.

Servings: 6
Preparation time: 15 minutes
Cooking time: 1 hour
Setting time: 3 hours

4 cups pomegranate juice (juice extracted from 8 medium-sized fresh pomegranates)
1/2 cup sugar
2 tablespoons fresh lime juice
1 cup pomegranate seeds (about 2 pomegranates)
2 tablespoons light corn syrup

NOTE

To serve the granita in pomegranate shells, slice the tops off 4 medium-sized fresh pomegranates and set the tops aside for later use.

Remove the seeds from inside the pomegranates (using a spoon) and freeze the shells in the freezer for 30 minutes. Remove the pomegranate shells from the freezer and fill with the granita. Replace the tops and return to freezer for another 30 minutes.

Remove from the freezer and place in the refrigerator for 20 minutes prior to serving

Ready-made pomegranate juice is available at Iranian groceries in the U.S.

You may substitute 4 cups of a puree comprised of blackberries, barberries and sour cherries for the pomegranate juice.

Pastries, Desserts & Candies / 269

1001 Nights Chewy Saffron Ice Cream

Servings: 4
Preparation time: 25 minutes
Freezing time: 2 1/2 hours

1 cup whipping cream
4 1/2 cups milk
4 tablespoons salab mixture*
1/4 teaspoon salt
1/2 teaspoon ground saffron threads, dissolved in 1 tablespoon hot water
2 tablespoons cooking rose water
1 teaspoon ground cardamom
1/4 teaspoon mastic*
3 egg yolks
1 1/4 cups sugar
1/4 cup shelled, unsalted pistachios (blanched)

GARNISH
8 large organic rose petals, crystallized
Eight 4-inch-round ice cream wafers

NOTE
Traditionally this ice cream is made without egg yolks, but I prefer to use them because they add body and texture.

In my childhood in Iran, our favorite summer treat was a creamy, elastic, sweet ice cream flavored with rose water and saffron, and garnished with pistachios. After a siesta on a long hot summer afternoon, my three sisters and I were happiest when we could soak all our senses in an ice cream sandwich costing ten cents. We held in both hands a scoop of ice cream between two round crispy wafers. Eating it was an art we perfected with practice. We would begin by turning it around clockwise, gently and systematically, as we sucked and licked while squeezing the wafers with just the right amount of pressure. The idea was to make the ice cream last the longest amount of time possible without it melting or dripping. Each lick would bring to our mouths a cold, creamy, perfumed delight with chunks of solid, frozen cream. It was both delicious and sensuous. Once you know the taste of a Persian ice cream (bastany nuny) eaten in this way, you can never again see a good looking scoop of ice cream between two wafers without wanting to take a lick of it.

1. Pour the whipping cream into a 9-inch freezer proof pie dish and place in the freezer.

2. In a small bowl, dissolve the salab in 1/2 cup milk until quite smooth. Set aside.

Pastries, Desserts & Candies / 270

3. In a medium sauce pan, bring 4 cups milk to boil and reduce heat to very low. Add the salab mixture, salt, saffron, rose water, cardamom and mastic and bring back to a boil. Reduce heat to very low and simmer, stirring constantly, for 10 minutes.

4. Beat the egg yolks and sugar in a stainless mixing bowl placed over a wok with 2 cups boiling water (or a double boiler) for 5 minutes, until thick and creamy.

5. Pour the milk over the eggs and stir slowly and constantly for about 10 minutes, until the mixture coats the back of a spoon. Remove from heat and allow to cool to room temperature. Pour into a chilled ice cream maker. Freeze in an ice cream maker according to the manufacturer's instructions (about 1 hour).

6. Remove the whipping cream from the freezer. Remove it from the pan and break it into 1/4-inch pieces. Add it to the ice cream in the machine. Add the pistachios and continue to turn in the machine for another 20 minutes.

7. Pour the ice cream into a plastic container with a press-in-place lid. Cover tightly (uncovered ice cream develops an unpleasant taste). Freeze the ice cream for at least 1 hour to allow it to develop texture and flavor.

8. Twenty minutes before serving, remove the ice cream from the freezer and refrigerate.

9. Serve by placing three scoops of ice cream into individual glass containers and garnish with crystallized rose petals and two 4-inch wafers.

ICE CREAM SANDWICH
You can make round ice cream sandwiches, similar to those made in Iran and Turkey, using torte wafers available at Middle Eastern grocery stores. They come in 8 1/2-by-11-inch sheets. Use a cookie cutter to make 4-inch disks. You can also use a pizelle iron to make your own wafers (pizelles are thin, crisp Italian cookies).

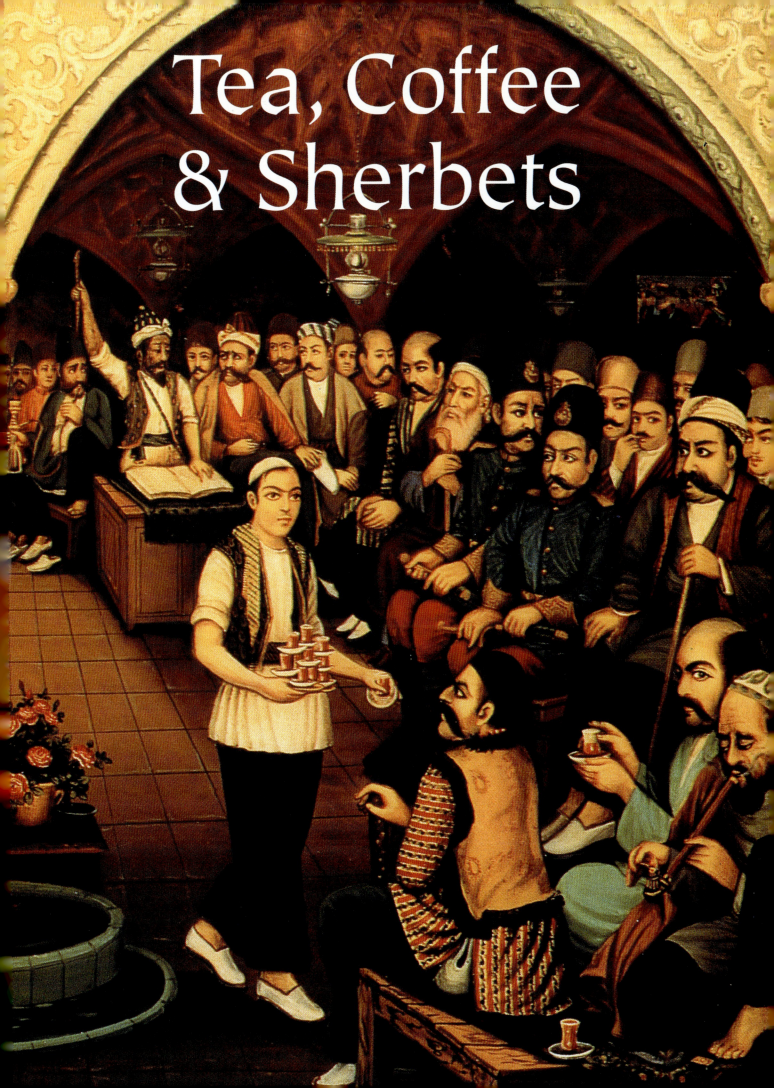
Tea, Coffee & Sherbets

TEA TIME

Early in the ninth century, an Arab Silk Road merchant named Soleyman reported that the Chinese infused a vastly expensive "sort of dried herb" in boiling water to make a drink that was an antidote to all ills. "It is a little more perfumed than clover," Soleyman reported, "but has a bitter taste." His was the first Western mention of tea, which over the next centuries would replace silk as the linchpin of East-West trade.

The Chinese had been cultivating tea since at least CE 350. They turned the judging, preparation and drinking of the drink into stylized rituals that, transplanted, would become the basis of the philosophical Japanese tea ceremony.

The pleasing beverage reached the West much more slowly—the first shipments arrived in Europe only in the seventeenth century—and until the nineteenth century, tea was a rare luxury. Then, however, tea plantations were established in the highlands of India, around the Caspian, in Iran, and in Indonesia, Sri Lanka and Africa, among other places. The result was that tea became almost a universal drink.

All teas are members of the camellia family; the differences among them arise not only from the soils and climates where they grow, but also from how the leaves are processed. Strong-flavored black teas such as pekoes and souchongs are fermented: The leaves are dried, bruised to release essential oils, and dried again in the open air. Oolong teas are semi-fermented—treated the same as black teas but for a shorter time—and tend to have a milder, smoother taste. Green teas are unfermented. Their pale color and slightly bitter taste are particularly valued in China and Japan.

In many countries along the old Silk Road today, tea houses (and private households) keep the Russian samovar steaming all day long to welcome guests. This is a large metal container with three stacked compartments—the top to keep a teapot warm, the middle for hot water and the bottom for a heating element.

As soon as guests walk in the door, the host offers them tea, usually in a small glass or ceramic cup. Except in Tibet and Afghanistan, where it is garnished with heavy cream called *qaymaq* (page 276) the tea usually comes without milk, although it may be flavored with nuts, saffron, flowers or herbs. A visitor may be offered sugar or rock candy, half a lime, honey, dates, raisins, cardamom or dried sweet mulberries for his tea. A spoonful of sour-cherry jam may be dropped into tea to give it a distinctive taste.

The traveller finds this pleasant welcome all along the old trading routes. In Xian, Tashkent, Bokhara, Tehran, or Istanbul, he will be invited to sit on colorful carpets in the market or on wooden benches around a stone pool, with the fountain gently spraying and the pomegranate trees in full bloom. There may be a vine trellis, with grapes hanging from it; the aroma will be of watered brick, mixed with the scent of jasmine. And the tea will be deliciously clear and very hot.

Making the Perfect Silk Road Tea

1. Bring water to a boil in a tea kettle. Warm a teapot by swirling some boiling water in it; pour out the water. Place 2 teaspoons of tea leaves in the pot, using half Earl Grey and half Darjeeling to get the effect of Persian, Uzbek, Turkish or Indian tea.

2. Fill the teapot half full with boiling water. Replace the lid, cover the pot with a cozy and let the tea steep for 5 to 10 minutes. Do not steep for more than 10 minutes: The quality will deteriorate and you will have to start over.

3. Pour a glassful of tea and return it to the pot to make sure the tea is evenly mixed.

4. Fill each glass or cup halfway with tea. Add boiling water from the kettle to dilute the tea to the desired color and taste: Some prefer their tea weak, some strong. Keep the pot covered with the cozy while you drink the first glasses.

Samovars *(above, right)*, originally imported from Russia, are to be found in every Central Asian house and café, keeping tea hot for any guests who might drop in.

Right: A couple have tea in a café in Tashkent. It was interesting for me, as a real tea lover, to note that everyone in every place in Central Asia was served tea in a china teapot and bowl. In China, however, I saw the appearance of Styrofoam cups and teabags—what a shame for a tea lover.

left: A young boy in Afghanistan dunks his cookie in a bowl of hot tea just poured from a well-used teapot.

Afghan Wedding Tea (Qaymaq Chai)

Servings: 4 cups
Preparation time: 30 minutes

4 cups water
3 tablespoons green tea
2 green cardamom pods, bruised, or 1/2 teaspoon powder
5 tablespoons sugar
1 cup hot milk
1/4 cup qaymaq* or heavy cream

*This is a tea served on special, festive occasions. During a wedding it is served at the bride's house along with sweets and pastries brought by the groom's family. A similar tea is made in Tibet and Kashmir where it is salted rather than sweetened. The name qaymaq refers to the thick cream, much like clotted or Devonshire cream, that is floated on top of the tea. You can find it ready made in Afghan stores or you can make your own.**

1. Bring the water to a boil in a saucepan, add the tea and continue to boil for 5 to 6 minutes, until the color turns dark yellow-green.

2. Remove from heat, strain and aerate the tea by pouring it from one pan to another (from a good height) until it becomes dark red.

3. Add the cardamom and sugar, and stir well. Reheat the tea, add the hot milk and bring back to a boil. Reduce heat and simmer over low heat until the tea becomes a beautiful purple-pink color (the color of Judas tree blossoms).

4. Fill each tea glass with tea and add a dollop of qaymaq on top.

To Make Qaymaq

Bring 4 cups whole milk and 1 1/4 cups heavy cream to a boil over medium heat, reduce heat to low and simmer for 2 hours, until the mixture is reduced to a clotted cream consistency. Remove from heat and sprinkle 1 teaspoon of cornstarch over the hot milk. Leave, undisturbed and at room temperature, for 6 hours until you have a thick layer of almost solid cream. Refrigerate for 3 hours and cut into segments using a knife.

Afghan Power Tea (Chaweh)

AFGHAN POWER TEA
4 cups water
4 teaspoons green tea
2-inch fresh ginger, sliced, or 1 teaspoon powder ginger
2 whole cardamoms, bruised
2 tablespoons ground walnuts
4-inch rock candy or 2 tablespoons brown sugar

1. Bring the water to boil in a saucepan, add all the ingredients, bring back to a boil, reduce heat, cover and simmer over very low heat for 30 minutes.

2. Adjust to taste with more sugar or boiling water.

Tea Time / 276

Armenian Spiced Rose Petal Tea

Servings: 4 cups
Preparation time: 25 minutes

4 cups water
One 3-inch cinnamon stick
2 whole cloves
1/2 teaspoon cardamom
1 tablespoon organic rose petals
2 teaspoons loose black tea
2 tablespoons sugar

1. Bring the water to a boil in a saucepan. Add the cinnamon, cloves, cardamom, and rose petals. Reduce heat to low, cover and simmer for 20 minutes. Remove from heat.

2. Place the tea leaves and sugar in a teapot.

3. Fill the teapot, through a strainer, with the boiling spice water and steep the tea for 5 to 10 minutes on top of a samovar, or simmering kettle or by using a tea cozy. Do not let the tea steep for more than 10 minutes—its quality will deteriorate.

4. Before serving, pour a glass or cupful of tea and return it to the pot to make sure the tea is evenly mixed.

5. Fill each glass with tea. Put the teapot back on top of the samovar or kettle or place the tea cozy on top of it to keep it hot.

Persian Saffron Love-Tea

Servings: 4 cups
Preparation time: 20 minutes

- 4 cups water
- 2 whole cardamom pods, bruised
- 1/2 teaspoon saffron thread, ground
- 1/2 cup cooking rose water
- 2-inch rock candy or 2 tablespoons sugar

This tea is traditionally served in parts of Iran by the bride-to-be to the groom's family after the bride and her family have accepted a marriage proposal: The serving of the tea is a subtle way of saying yes, no doubt because the tea is thought to have aphrodisiac qualities.

1. Bring the water to a boil in a medium saucepan. Add the cardamom, saffron, rose water and sugar. Reduce heat, cover and simmer for 15 minutes.

2. Before serving, pour a glassful of tea and return it to the saucepan to make sure the tea is evenly mixed.

3. Serve in a tea glass. Add sugar to taste.

PERSIAN BORAGE & VALERIAN NIGHTCAP

- 4 cups water
- 2 dried Persian limes,* pierced
- four 1-inch valerian roots
- 1 cup organic fresh borage flowers or 1/4 cup dried borage flowers
- 4 tablespoons sugar or 2-inch rock candy

Persian Borage & Valerian Nightcap

1. Bring the water to a boil in a medium saucepan. Add the limes, valerian root, borage and sugar. Bring back to a boil. Cover and simmer for 20 minutes over low heat. Keep warm over very low heat.

2. Before serving, pour a glassful of tea and return it to the saucepan to make sure the tea is evenly mixed.

3. Fill each glass with tea and adjust to taste by adding more sugar or lime.

Left: Saffron flowers, the dried stamens, the stamens ground with sugar, and dissolved saffron water.

Silk Road Jujube Panacea Tea

This tea, made with jujubes that were native to China, is a nice example of how good things spread along the Silk Road; it appears throughout Central Asia and is particularly popular in China and Iran.

1. Boil the water in a medium sauce pan. Add the jujubes and sugar, reduce heat, cover and simmer over low heat for 30 minutes. Keep warm over low heat.

2. Before serving, pour a glassful of tea and return it to the saucepan to make sure the tea is evenly mixed. Fill each glass or cup with tea. Add sugar to taste.

Servings: 4 cups
Preparation time: 30 minutes

4 cups water
1 cup fresh or 1/2 cup dried jujubes (Chinese dates)*
1 teaspoon sugar or 1/2-inch saffron rock candy

NOTE

You may substitute 1 cup fresh or 1/2 cup dried organic versions of any of the herbs or flowers below for the jujubes:

Mint (digestion), lemon verbena (relaxing), sage, linden, oregano, lavender flowers (aid sleep), jasmine flowers, orange blossoms (help circulation), rose petals, tamarind flowers (red tea), thyme or wild violet flowers.

You can also make this tea with the seeds or berries of the following fruits: 1 cup dried sour cherries, 1 cup jujubes, 1 cup barberries, 1 cup pomegranate seeds, 1 cup seville orange seeds, 1 cup quince seeds. These are very popular in various provinces throughout Iran.

Tea Time / 279

Baghdad Honey & Coriander Cold Remedy Tea

Servings: 4 cups
Preparation time: 25 minutes

4 cups water
3 teaspoons coriander seeds
6 black peppercorns
1 teaspoon loose black tea
2 tablespoons honey
1 tablespoon fresh lime juice

This is an excellent remedy for a cold. The Uzbeks make a similar tea but without the coriander.

1. In a medium saucepan, boil the water with the coriander and pepper corns. Simmer for 15 minutes over low heat.

2. Pour the spice water into the teapot. Add the tea leaves, honey and lime juice, and allow to steep over a simmering kettle, or by using a tea cozy, for 10 minutes. Keep the tea warm. Do not let the tea steep for more than 10 minutes.

3. Before serving, pour a glassful of tea and return it to the pot to make sure the tea is evenly mixed. Fill each glass with tea. Add sugar to taste.

Fertile Crescent Aromatic Almond Tea

FERTILE CRESCENT AROMATIC ALMOND TEA

Servings: 4 cups
Preparation time: 20 minutes

4 cups water
one 3-inch cinnamon stick
1 teaspoon caraway seeds
2 whole star anises
1/4 teaspoon ground nutmeg
1/4 cup Thai basil leaves
1 tablespoon organic dried rose petals
1/2 cup ground almonds
2 tablespoons sugar

1. Bring the water, cinnamon, caraway, star anise, nutmeg, basil and rose petals to a boil in a medium saucepan. Reduce heat, cover and simmer over low heat for 10 minutes. Add the ground almonds and sugar to a teapot and pour in the spice water. Steep the tea for 10 minutes over a simmering kettle or by using a tea cozy.

2. Before serving, pour a glassful of tea and return it to the pot to make sure the tea is evenly mixed.

3. Fill each glass with tea. Keep the tea warm.

Right: A tea setting with a samovar includes mulberry sweets, fresh figs and pomegranates.

COFFEE TALES

Coffee, a rich, enlivening drink, popular the world over, got its start in Ethiopia, home to a plant whose caffeine-rich berries could be mixed with fat and eaten or pulped and fermented to make wine. From Africa the berries traveled to Yemen—they are first mentioned by an eleventh-century Arab physician—where the practice of extracting, roasting, and grinding their beans seems to have appeared during the thirteenth century. Yemenis, who made an infusion from the drink, named it *qahwah*, a poetic word for wine; hence the botanical name for the most important coffee tree: coffea arabica.

Until the seventeenth century, Arabia kept coffee cultivation a closely guarded secret and other cultivators tried to do the same, because the monopoly on this instantly popular drink was extremely profitable. It was theft and intrigue that spread coffee cultivation around the world. Seeds stolen from Arabia by the Dutch were the source of the first plantations in Java, then a Dutch colony; from there, plants were taken to Europe. Cultivation of coffee in the Caribbean began with a French naval officer's abduction of a specimen tree from the Botanical Gardens in Paris in 1723. Brazil, now the world's leading coffee producer, got its start a few years later, when the wife of the governor of French Guinea gave some cuttings to her Brazilian lover.

By then, coffee houses had spread from Al Mukha (Mocha, to Westerners) in Yemen through the Middle East to Istanbul, where the first café had appeared in 1554; a few years later, the drink had arrived, via Venice, in Italy. Everywhere they appeared, coffee houses flourished as convivial meeting places for no doubt over-stimulated poets, writers, and revolutionaries, and as entertainment venues for storytellers, puppeteers and musicians. So popular were they, and such well-springs of sedition, that the authorities of every country, Christian or Arab, complained.

Nowadays, tea is the favorite drink in most countries along what was once the Silk Road. Nevertheless, the pleasant shops where it is served are called coffee houses. And if it is coffee you want, you can still get the thick, sweet drink unlike any other preparation in Europe. It is called Turkish coffee, but the same distinctive beverage is served in Greece, Cyprus, Iran, Yemen and Armenia. Sometimes, as in Armenia, it is served with pastry or fruit for happy festivals; in other places, such as Iran, it comes with halva and dates, and is usually a drink for funeral receptions.

In these countries, the coffee is made in a long-handled copper pan with a narrow top to hold the foam (known in Arabic as an *ibrik*). When making the coffee at home, you can use such a vessel, available at Middle East markets, but a small pan will produce equally good results. You will need very finely powdered coffee for the preparation. A coffee merchant can grind it for you or you can buy it in packages (often called Armenian or Turkish coffee) at specialty markets.

A PERFECT CUP OF SILK ROAD COFFEE

1. For each small (4-ounce) cup, put 1 teaspoon powdered coffee, 1 teaspoon sugar, and 1 Turkish cup (4 ounces) of water into a small pan or ibrik. Stir with a spoon.

2. Simmer over low heat until foam rises to the surface. If desired, add a dash of cardamom, saffron or rose water; for Yemeni-style coffee, add a dash of ground ginger. Remove from the heat. To make sure that every cup of coffee has the same consistency, fill each cup a little at a time, until each is full. Sip the coffee carefully so as not to swallow any grounds.

After drinking this coffee, remove the saucer and place it on top of the cup. Invert the cup and saucer away from yourself with your left hand (the hand of the heart). Then turn the cup over. A fortune teller—or just an insightful friend—can read your fate in the pattern of the grounds left behind in the cup.

Left: A Bedouin prepares coffee.
Above: A cup of Silk Road coffee complements some Armenian pastries.

HOW THE PERSIANS WENT FROM WINE TO SHERBET

As long ago as 7000 BCE, the inhabitants of Iran were wine drinkers, as archeologists investigating ancient sediments have attested. Outsiders like the Greek historian Herodotus, writing in the fifth century BCE, commented on the Persians' love of wine, and Persian poets then and later confirmed it in their verses.

> *I pressed my lip upon the winejar's lip*
> *And questioned how long life I might attain;*
> *Then lip to lip it whispering replied;*
> *"Drink wine—this world thou shalt not see again."*

With the advent of Islam, however, wine was forbidden, although courtiers (and poets) continued to enjoy it. They discarded the old Persian words for the drink (*badeh* and *mey*) and replaced them with *sharab*, Arabic for "sweet drink." That is the source of the English "syrup."

Renaming the forbidden was not enough. The Iranians needed a new, non-alcoholic drink, and *sharbat* was born. Its basis was the ice and snow that Iranians had learned to preserve during the hot summer months in spectacular domed ice wells on the edges of towns and along caravan routes. The flavorings were syrups, made by combining fruit or vegetable juice with honey, sugar, or date or grape molasses and boiling the mixture down to intensify the flavor. Sipped through a mound of crushed ice or snow, the syrup became a delightful drink.

Sharbats could be either sweet or savory. The Huguenot jeweler Jean Chardin, travelling in Iran, described a favorite of the Isfahanis: sugar, a pinch of salt, lemon or pomegranate juice, and a squeeze of garlic or lemon, all mixed with crushed ice. This sweet-sour mixture, he found, not only quenched the thirst but stimulated the appetite.

Such cool drinks traveled along the trade routes to become the sharbats of Turkey and Syria, the *sorbete* of Spain, the *sorbeto* of Italy, the sorbet of France and the sherbet of England. The European versions were iced mixtures, usually based on fruit, that one ate with a spoon—merely a difference in the degree of freezing.

Such frozen desserts in Iran are made with lime juice, sour cherries or black mulberries and served with sweet rice vermicelli. They have their own name: *paludeh* or *faludeh*. A Persian sharbat remains a fruit drink with plenty of ice, often perfumed with rose water or orange blossoms and served in summer.

Caspian Seville Orange Syrup

Servings: 2 pints
Preparation time: 5 minutes
Cooking time: 20 minutes

16 Seville oranges (2 cups Seville orange juice)
4 cups brown sugar
2 cups water

GARNISH
Fresh orange leaves
Orange blossoms

NOTE
You can use the seeds to make tea (page 255) and the skin for marmalade.

1. The peel of the Seville orange is quite bitter and will contaminate the juice if it comes into contact with it. To prevent the peel from coming into contact with the juice while juicing, wash the oranges and remove a 1/2-inch ring of orange peel from around the middle of each orange. Cut the oranges in half through the center of the strip where the peel has been removed. Remove the seeds and press the oranges in a juicer.

2. In a saucepan, bring the brown sugar and water to a boil over high heat. Pour in the orange juice and simmer over medium heat for 20 minutes, stirring occasionally. Remove from heat, allow to cool, pour into a clean, dry bottle and cork tightly.

3. In a pitcher, mix 1 part of this orange syrup with 3 parts water and add 2 ice cubes per person. Stir with a spoon and serve chilled. Decorate with orange leaves and blossoms.

Silk Road Yogurt Drink

This drink is popular in Turkey, Iran, Afghanistan, India, Uzbekistan and most of central Asia.

SILK ROAD YOGURT DRINK

Servings: 2
Preparation time: 10 minutes

1 cup plain yogurt, beaten
1 tablespoon chopped fresh mint or 1 teaspoon mint flakes, crushed
1/2 teaspoon salt
1/4 teaspoon freshly ground black pepper
1 teaspoon dried rose petals
1 1/2 cups club soda or spring water, chilled

1. Place yogurt, mint, salt, pepper and rose petals in a pitcher. Stir well.

2. Add club soda or spring water gradually, stirring constantly, until smooth. Add 3 or 4 ice cubes and mix again.

3. Serve chilled.

Qamsar Rose Water Syrup

Qamsar, a small desert town near Kashan in central Iran, is famous for its roses, which are harvested for their rose water in May. On the road to Qamsar from Kashan, there is a wonderful Safavid caravanserai said to have been built by one of Shah Abbas's generals. May is the time to go there and become intoxicated with the aroma of the roses as they are picked.

1. Bring the water and sugar to a boil in a medium saucepan. Simmer for 10 minutes. Add the lime juice and cook for 10 minutes longer, stirring occasionally.

2. Remove from heat, add the rose water and allow to cool. Pour the syrup into a clean, dry bottle; cork tightly.

3. In a pitcher, mix 1 part syrup with 3 parts water, and add 2 ice cubes per person. Stir with a spoon and serve well chilled.

VARIATION

Saffron Syrup

Add 1/4 teaspoon ground saffron threads dissolved in 2 tablespoons hot water, and 2 cardamom pods to the saucepan in step 1.

Lebanese Grape Syrup

1. To make the syrup, bring the grape juice, sugar and water to a boil. Reduce heat to low and simmer for 20 minutes. Remove from heat.

2. To make the drink, in a pitcher, mix 1 part syrup with 3 parts water, raisins, toasted pine nuts, and rose water. Pour into individual glasses full of ice and serve well chilled.

Servings: 1 pint
Preparation time: 5 minutes
Cooking time: 20 minutes

2 1/2 cups water
4 cups sugar
1/4 cup fresh lime juice
1/2 cup cooking rose water

LEBANESE GRAPE SYRUP (JALLAB)

6 cups grape juice
6 cups sugar
1 1/2 cups water
1 cup seedless raisins
1 cup toasted pine nuts
1 tablespoon rose water

Sherbets / 287

Bokhara Iced Melon Drink

Servings: 4
Preparation time: 15 minutes
Cooking time: none

1 large melon, cut, seeds removed, peeled and sliced
4 tablespoons sugar
1 teaspoon cooking rose water
10 ice cubes

DECORATION
1/2 teaspoon dried organic rose petals
8 fresh mint leaves

This very refreshing drink is also popular in Iran, where it is served during the summer at cafés and from street stalls.

1. In a food processor, puree the melon, sugar, rose water, and ice cubes.
2. Stir into a glass and serve with a spoon. Decorate with rose petals and mint.

Rayy Apple & Rose Water Iced Drink

RAYY APPLE & ROSE WATER ICED DRINK (FALUDEH)

Servings: 4
Preparation time: 15 minutes
Cooking time: none

1/2 cup sugar
4 cups ice water
1 teaspoon rose water
4 crisp apples, cored, peeled and coarsely grated

DECORATION
1/2 fresh lime, sliced
1/2 teaspoon dried organic rose petals
8 fresh mint leaves

In a pitcher, mix the sugar, water and rose water. Stir well with a spoon until the sugar has dissolved completely. Add the grated apple to the pitcher. Serve with a few ice cubes per glass, well chilled. Decorate with slices of lime, rose petals and mint.

Sherbets / 288

Isfahan Quince-Lime Syrup

> **Servings:** 1 pint
> **Preparation time:** 10 minutes
> **Cooking time:** 35 minutes
>
> 2 pounds quinces (about 2 cups juice)
> 4 cups sugar
> 2 cups water
> 1/2 cup fresh lime juice

1. Quarter the quinces and remove the cores with a knife. Do not peel. Wash, pat dry and process in a juicer.

2. Bring the sugar and water to a boil in a saucepan. Add the quince juice and boil for 20 minutes over medium heat, stirring occasionally; add the lime juice and cook for another 15 minutes or until the syrup thickens.

3. Remove the saucepan from the heat. Allow to cool. Pour the syrup into a clean, dry bottle and cork tightly.

4. In a pitcher, mix 1 part syrup with 3 parts water and add 2 ice cubes per person. Stir with a spoon.

> **NOTE**
> Another way to make Quince-Lime Syrup is to tie up the cleaned, sliced and washed quinces in doubled muslin or two layers of cheesecloth. Cover and cook in a pot with 4 cups water for 1 hour and 30 minutes over medium heat, until the quinces are tender. Drain and squeeze the juice from the quinces back into the pot. Discard the cheesecloth. Add 2 cups sugar to the juice, 2 cups water and 1/2 cup fresh lime juice; cover and cook over medium heat for another 30 minutes. Continue with step 3 above.
>
> Flixweed has yellow flowers that bear a reddish seed. The seeds can be bought at Persian groceries (page 326) where it is called khak-e shir; they are usually sandy and gritty, so wash them well. The washing of the seeds is an important step for making this syrup, said to be a remedy for sunstroke.

Persian Flixweed Drink

Place 1/2 cup flixweed seeds in a container, cover with cold water and then pour out the seeds into a second container, discarding any sediment. Repeat until you have clear water. Add 1/2 cup Sweet and Sour syrup from the recipe on page 290 and 1/2 cup ice water, stir well, and serve chilled. The seeds will go down very smoothly and do not need to be chewed.

Sherbets / 289

Persian Sweet & Sour Cucumber Iced Drink

Servings: 1 pint
Preparation time: 10 minutes
Cooking time: 30 minutes

6 cups sugar
2 cups water
1 1/2 cups wine vinegar
4 sprigs fresh mint

GARNISH
1 cucumber, peeled and grated
1 lime, thinly slices
8 fresh mint leaves

1. Bring the sugar and water to a boil in a medium saucepan. Simmer for 10 minutes over medium heat, stirring occasionally, until sugar has thoroughly dissolved.

2. Add the vinegar and boil for 15 to 20 minutes over medium heat, until a thick syrup forms. Remove the saucepan from the heat.

3. Wash the mint sprigs, pat dry and add them to the syrup. Allow to cool. Remove the mint and pour the syrup into a clean, dry bottle. Cork tightly.

4. In a pitcher, mix 1 part syrup with 3 parts water and add 2 ice cubes per person. Add the cucumber and stir well. Pour into individual glasses and decorate each with a slice of lime and a sprig of fresh mint. Serve well chilled.

Indian Tamarind Iced Drink

Servings: 1 pint
Preparation time: 15 minutes
Cooking time: 20 minutes

1 pound tamarind or 1/4 cup tamarind paste
4 cups water
1/4 cup sugar
1/4 teaspoon cardamom powder
1/4 teaspoon ground fennel
1/4-inch fresh ginger, peeled and thinly sliced, or 1/4 teaspoon ginger powder

GARNISH
4 slices lime
4 sprigs mint

1. To make tamarind paste, cover 1 pound of tamarinds with 4 cups water in a medium-sized heavy-bottom saucepan and bring to a boil. Reduce heat, cover and simmer for 20 minutes. Pass through a fine-mesh sieve. You can also find ready-made tamarind paste in Indian groceries.

2. In a pitcher, mix all the ingredients until the sugar has completely dissolved. Pour into individual glasses with 2 ice cubes per glass and decorate each with a slice of lime and a sprig of fresh mint. Serve well chilled.

Indian Nut & Spice Drink

INDIAN NUT & SPICE DRINK (THANDAI)

Servings: 4
Preparation time: 15 minutes
Cooking time: 2 minutes

SPICES
2 teaspoons fennel seeds
1 teaspoon cumin seeds
2 teaspoons coriander seeds
1/2 cup poppy seeds
1 teaspoon black peppercorns
5 whole cardamom pods

NUTS...
1 cup blanched almonds
1/4 cup walnuts
1/4 cup pine nuts
1/4 cup raw cashew nuts
1/4 cup raisins
1/4 cup sugar or honey
3 cups chilled water, soy milk, or plain milk

GARNISH
four 3-inch cinnamon sticks
4 sprigs fresh mint or lemon verbena
1 tablespoon organic dried rose petals

This famous summer drink specialty of the Uttar Pradesh province of northern India cools both body and mind. It is traditionally drunk with milk, but I prefer it without.

1. Heat a large skillet, and toast all the spices over medium heat for 1 minute, until aromatic. (Have a cover handy to stop any seeds from flying out.) Grind the spices in a spice grinder.

2. Reheat the skillet, and toast all the nuts for 1 minute and grind in a food processor. Add the ground spices and the rest of the ingredients, then puree until you have a smooth creamy mixture. Adjust seasoning to taste by adding more sugar or peppercorns. Serve in individual glasses with 2 ice cubes, stir with a cinnamon stick, and garnish with a sprig of mint and a few rose petals.

Sherbets / 291

Preserves, Pickles & Spices

CANNING

Local vegetables and fruits, harvested in spring and summer when their flavors are at a peak, make the finest pickles and chutneys. These delicious condiments will keep up to two weeks in the refrigerator. It is easy to preserve them by canning, however, so that you can enjoy them all year long.

Canning (which really should be called "jarring") means packing your newly made preserves in prepared jars and subjecting them to the high heat of boiling water. This is known as processing; it kills potentially harmful organisms and seals the jars against the air.

Equipment is simple and inexpensive. You will need jars made of heat-tempered glass, and fitted with flat lids and separate screw bands that keep the lids in place. These are called Mason jars after their inventor, and are sold in 1/2 pint pint, and quart sizes in hardware stores and supermarkets; extra lids are sold separately so that the jars can be reused. The same outlets provide the other canning necessity: a water bath canner, which is a large pot equipped with a rack to hold the jars.

A little advance planning makes the work go smoothly. Before you begin cooking, wash the jars, lids and bands, and sterilize them in boiling water for 10 minutes. Leave them in the water until needed. Also fill the canner with water and set it over medium heat to give it time to reach a simmer while you are making your preserves.

When the preserves are ready, remove the jars, lids and screw bands from the water, and drain them on paper towels. Pack each hot jar with the preserve, leaving 1/2-inch headspace to allow for the food's expansion. Wipe the jar rim clean, fit it with a lid and screw on the band, making it snug but not utterly tight.

Now you are ready to process the jars. The water in the canner should be at a strong simmer. Remove the rack from the canner, set the jars in the rack and lower it back into the canner so that the jars are covered by 1 inch of water. Cover the canner and raise the heat to high. When the water boils, begin timing the process, allowing 10 minutes for chutneys in pints or quarts, and 15 minutes for pickles.

When the time is up, use tongs to transfer the jars to a dry surface. Let them cool for 12 hours, during which time you will hear little popping noises indicating that air-tight seals are forming.

Iranian Pistachio Skin Preserve

Use pistachio skins that have no blemishes and are reddish pink.* This skin is so wonderfully delicate and subtly aromatic that there is no need to add any spices. If you can find them, this recipe is also excellent for whole, fresh baby pistachios.

1. To remove bitterness, place the pistachio skins in a pot and cover with cold water. Bring to a boil and simmer over medium heat for 15 minutes. Drain and rinse thoroughly with cold water.

2. In the same pot, bring the water, lime juice and sugar to a boil. Simmer over medium heat for 5 minutes. Return the pistachio skins to the pot and bring back to a boil. Simmer, uncovered, over medium heat for 45 to 55 minutes, until syrup has thickened and sticks to the back of a spoon. Remove from heat.

3. Jar per instructions on page 294.

Iranian Baby Walnut Preserve

Baby green walnuts* are harvested in early summer. They are made into a refined preserve, not only in Iran but in Egypt and Cypress as well.

1. To remove bitterness from the walnuts, place them in a medium-sized laminated pot with 1 tablespoon salt and cover with cold water. Bring to a boil and simmer over medium heat for 25 minutes until tender. Drain and rinse thoroughly with cold water. Taste and if there is even a trace of bitterness, soak in cold water and leave overnight.

2. In the same pot, place the walnuts, water, sugar, lime juice, honey, cinnamon stick and cloves, and bring to a boil. Reduce heat and simmer over medium heat for 35 minutes. Remove from heat, cover and allow to stand, at room temperature, for 8 to 24 hours.

4. Bring back to a boil and simmer over medium heat for another 15 to 20 minutes or until the syrup sticks to the back of a spoon. Remove from heat.

5. Jar and process per instructions on page 294.

NOTE

For a crisper preserve, dissolve 1/2 cup slaked lime* in 2 cups water and soak the parboiled walnuts for 4 hours. Drain and rinse thoroughly.

Makes a 1-pint jar
Preparation time: 15 minutes
Cooking time: 1 hour 15 minutes

1 pound fresh pistachio skins
3 cups water
3 tablespoons fresh lime juice
2 pounds (4 1/2 cups) sugar

IRANIAN BABY GREEN WALNUT PRESERVE
Makes a 1-pint jar
Preparation time: 25 minutes
Cooking time: 1 hour 10 minutes

2 pounds (about 25) unripe baby green walnuts, outer green shell removed and pricked with a kitchen needle
1 1/2 cups water
2 pounds (4 1/2 cups) sugar
3 tablespoons fresh lime juice
1/4 cup honey
1 3-inch cinnamon stick
4 whole cloves

Orange Blossom Preserve

Makes 1 half-pint jar
Preparation time: 35 minutes plus 1 day's soaking
Cooking time: 55 minutes

- 2 cups dried orange blossoms
- 3 1/2 cups sugar
- 3 cups water
- 1 cup Seville orange juice
- 2 tablespoons fresh lime juice
- 1 cup Seville orange seeds tied in a piece of cheesecloth
- 1 tablespoon orange blossom water

1. Carefully wash the orange blossoms, separate the petals and soak in a bowl of cold water. Set in refrigerator for a day, changing the water several times.

2. Bring 4 cups of water to a boil in a laminated pan over high heat. Add the blossoms, bring back to a boil, reduce heat and simmer for 10 minutes; drain in a colander and rinse with cold water. Taste and if too bitter, repeat. This step is essential to remove any traces of bitterness.

3. In a heavy saucepan, bring the sugar and 3 cups water to a boil. Add the seville orange juice and the cheesecloth with the seeds, reduce heat to medium and simmer for 15 minutes. Add the blossom petals and lime juice, cover and cook over medium heat for 30 minutes or until the syrup has thickened enough to stick to the back of a spoon. Add the orange blossom water.

4. Jar and process per instructions on page 294.

Variation

Rose Petal Preserve

Substitute 2 cups rose petals for the orange blossoms. Rose petals are more delicate than the orange blossoms so there is no need to cook them in step 2. Just blanche and drain. Prepare the syrup as above but cook for 35 minutes instead of 15 minutes. Add the blanched petals, cover and cook for another 20 minutes, until the syrup has thickened enough to stick to the back of a spoon. Finally substitute 1 tablespoon rose water for the orange blossom water, seville orange juice and the seeds.

Mesopotamian Date & Orange Peel Preserve

MESOPOTAMIAN DATE PRESERVE WITH CLOVES & ORANGE PEEL

Makes a 1-pint jar
Preparation time: 15 minutes
Cooking time: 55 minutes

- 2 pounds fresh, firm dates
- 4 cups water
- 2 pounds sugar (4 1/2 cups)
- 3 tablespoons fresh lime juice
- One 4-inch cinnamon stick
- 5 whole cloves
- 1/4 cup orange rind (1 orange)
- 1/2 cup blanched almonds or walnuts

NOTE
The traditional and more difficult method for making this recipe is to place the dates in a non-reactive pot, cover with water and bring to a boil. . Reduce heat and simmer for 15 minutes. Drain. This makes the dates tender and easy to pit, peel and stuff. Pit and stuff with almonds. Continue with step 2.

1. Remove the dates from the stalks, cut in half and pit.

2. In a medium non-reactive pot, bring the water and sugar to a boil over medium heat. Simmer for 10 minutes, until the sugar has dissolved completely.

3. Add the lime juice, cinnamon stick, cloves, orange rind, almonds and dates. Bring back to a boil. Reduce heat and simmer over medium heat for 45 minutes or until syrup has thickened and sticks to the back of a spoon. Remove from heat.

4. Jar and process per instructions on page 294.

Chinese Jujube Preserve

1. In a medium non-reactive pot, bring the water and sugar to a boil over medium heat. Simmer for 10 minutes, until the sugar has dissolved completely.

2. Add the lime juice, cinnamon and jujubes. Bring back to a boil. Reduce heat and simmer over medium heat for 45 minutes, or until syrup has thickened and sticks to the back of a spoon. Remove from heat.

3. Jar and process per instructions on page 294.

Makes a 1-pint jar
Preparation time: 15 minutes
Cooking time: 55 minutes

2 pounds fresh or dried jujubes
4 cups water
2 pounds (4 1/2 cups) sugar
3 tablespoons fresh lime juice
One 4-inch cinnamon stick
1 tablespoon rose water

NOTE
PERSIAN FIG PRESERVE
You may substitute 2 pounds firm yellow figs and 5 cardamom pods for the jujubes, orange rind and almonds.

Armenian Baby Eggplant Preserve

Makes a 1-pint jar
Preparation time: 25 minutes
Cooking time: 1 hour 10 minutes

- 2 pounds (about 20) fresh baby eggplants (pickling)
- 3 cups water
- 2 pounds sugar (4 1/2 cups)
- 3 tablespoons fresh lime juice
- 2-inch ginger, peeled and sliced
- 1/2 cup cooking rose water

1. Wash and trim the stems and peel the eggplants. Make a lengthwise slit on one side of each eggplant.

2. To remove the bitterness from the eggplants, bring 8 cups water and 1 teaspoon salt to a boil in a non-reactive medium sized pot. Add the eggplants and bring back to a boil. Immediately drain, rinse thoroughly, and allow to stand for 10 minutes.

3. In the same pot, bring the water, sugar, lime juice, ginger, and rose water to a boil over medium heat. Simmer for 15 minutes.

4. Place the eggplants in the syrup and bring back to a boil. Reduce heat and simmer over medium heat for 45 to 55 minutes, until the syrup has thickened and sticks to the back of a spoon. Remove from heat.

5. Jar and process per instructions on page 294.

Persian Baby Eggplant Pickles (Quick & Easy)

PERSIAN BABY EGGPLANT PICKLES

- 2 pounds (about 20) pickling eggplants
- 3 quarts (12 cups) wine vinegar
- 1 teaspoon salt
- 6 cloves garlic, peeled
- 1-inch ginger, peeled and grated
- 1/2 cup tamarind paste*
- 2 tablespoons black mustard seeds
- 2 tablespoons coriander seeds, toasted
- 2 tablespoons cumin seeds, toasted
- 2 hot red chilies, slit
- 2 teaspoons black peppercorns
- 1 tablespoon sugar
- 1 tablespoon salt

1. Wash the eggplants and remove the stems. Make a lengthwise slit on one side of each eggplant.

2. Place the eggplants in a large, non-reactive pot, cover with 4 cups of vinegar and 1 teaspoon salt, and bring to a boil. Immediately drain and let stand for 20 minutes.

3. In a food processor, puree together the garlic, ginger, tamarind paste, mustard seeds, coriander seeds, cumin seeds, chilies, peppercorns, sugar, and salt, until you have a paste.

4. Stuff each eggplant with the paste and press shut.

5. Arrange the stuffed eggplants in the same pot and cover with the remaining vinegar. Bring to a boil, reduce heat, cover and simmer over low heat for 30 minutes or until eggplants are tender. Allow to cool.

6. Serve immediately as a pickle or fill the sterilized jar with the eggplants. Fill the jars with vinegar to within 1/2 inch of the top. Cover and store in the refrigerator for up to 1 week.

Samarkand Golden Peach Chutney (Quick & Easy)

Servings: 8
Preparation time: 15 minutes
Cooking time: 10 minutes

- 2 tablespoons vegetable oil
- 1/4 teaspoon asafetida
- 1 teaspoon mustard seeds
- 2 tablespoons brown sugar or molasses
- 5 pounds firm peaches (about 10), peeled, pitted and sliced
- 2 serrano or bird chilies, chopped
- 1/4 teaspoon turmeric
- 2 teaspoons salt
- 1/2 teaspoon freshly ground black pepper
- 2 teaspoons corn starch dissolved in 1 cup water

1. Heat the oil in a wok or deep skillet over medium heat until very hot. Add the asafetida and mustard seeds, and stir-fry for 20 seconds until aromatic (keep a lid handy to stop the seeds from popping out of the wok).

2. Add the sugar, peaches, chilies, turmeric, salt, pepper and dissolved cornstarch and bring to a boil over medium heat. Reduce heat to low and simmer for 5 to 10 minutes until it thickens. Adjust seasoning to taste, adding salt or sugar.

3. Remove from heat and serve immediately as a chutney with rice or couscous. You can also cover and store in the refrigerator for up to 1 week.

VARIATION

Bombay Mango Chutney (Quick & Easy)

You may substitute 4 large unripe mangoes for the peaches.

Shirazi Lime Pickle (Quick & Easy)

SHIRAZI LIME PICKLE

Makes a 1-pint jar
Preparation time: 25 minutes
Cooking time: 30 minutes

- 2 pounds Persian limes (about 20)
- 1/2 cup salt
- 1 tablespoon toasted cumin
- 1 teaspoon black peppercorns
- 1 cup fresh lime juice

1. Wash and scrub the limes. Cut each lime vertically into 4 pieces and rub with salt.

2. Place the limes in a jar, and add the cumin, peppercorns and lime juice to within 1/2 inch of the neck.

3. Seal the jar and leave undisturbed for 10 days before serving. To speed up the process, place the jar upright in a large pot and fill the pot with water up to the neck of the jar. Bring to a boil, reduce heat and simmer for 20 to 30 minutes, until the limes are tender. Remove from heat and allow to cool in the pot. Serve immediately or store in the refrigerator for up to 1 week.

Persian Persimmon Chutney (Quick & Easy)

Makes a 1-pint jar
Preparation time: 25 minutes
Cooking time: 30 minutes

- 10 small persimmons (about 2 1/2 pounds)
- 2 tablespoons vegetable oil
- 2 tablespoons toasted black mustard seeds
- 2 tablespoons toasted coriander seeds
- 1 tablespoon toasted cumin seeds, toasted
- 2 cardamom pods
- Two 3-inch cinnamon sticks
- 5 garlic cloves, crushed and peeled
- 4 slices crystallized ginger, chopped
- 4 dried Persian limes* (limu Omani), pierced
- 2 red hot chilies, slit
- 2 teaspoons salt
- 1 teaspoon freshly ground black pepper
- 10 medjool dates, pitted and sliced
- 1/2 cup red wine vinegar

1. Wash the persimmons, remove the stems, and slice.

2. Heat the oil in a wok or deep skillet over medium heat until very hot. Add the mustard, coriander, cumin, cardamom and cinnamon, and cook for 20 seconds, until aromatic (keep a cover handy to stop any seeds from flying out).

3. Add the remaining ingredients, except the vinegar, and stir-fry for 5 minutes. Add the vinegar and bring to a boil. Reduce heat to medium and cook for 15 to 20 minutes, until most of the vinegar has evaporated. Remove from heat and adjust seasoning to taste.

4. You can serve this chutney immediately with rice or pasta, or cover and store in the refrigerator for up to 1 week.

Sichuan Cucumber Pickle (Quick & Easy)

A group of us entered the Li family's home restaurant in Beijing through an old wooden door that led to a small cobbled yard. On our left was a closed door that must have led to their private quarters; on our right there were two small rooms, behind which was a tiny kitchen. Mr Li, who who is shown below and who spoke fluent English, welcomed us with a wonderful generosity of spirit and very positive energies. He immediately made us feel quite at home. We were served an unbelievable array of small vegetable dishes that kept on coming (I was even more amazed after seeing how small the kitchen was). Our meal was concluded with an incredibly tasty jujube preserve. My favorite dish, however, was this cucumber pickle, the recipe for which Mr. Li gave me while we said our goodbyes.

Use only the freshest pickling cucumbers to produce a pickle that is properly light, crisp, crunchy and spicy.

1. Scrub and rinse the cucumbers, and pat dry. Cut each cucumber lengthwise into 6 slices.

2. To draw out excess juice from the cucumbers, place them in a large bowl, sprinkle with 1 1/2 tablespoons salt, and let stand for 20 minutes. Rinse, drain and pat dry.

3. To make the dressing, combine all the dressing ingredients and mix well.

4. Place the cucumbers in a large serving bowl, pour the dressing over them and toss well. For the best results, refrigerate for 30 minutes before serving.

Servings: 4
Preparation time: 25 minutes
Cooking time: none

2 1/2 pounds pickling cucumbers
1 1/2 tablespoons salt

DRESSING

2 cloves garlic, crushed and peeled
1-inch ginger root, peeled and grated
3 tablespoons rice vinegar
2 hot red peppers, seeded and sliced
3 tablespoons toasted sesame oil*
1 teaspoon toasted and ground Sichuan peppercorns*
1 tablespoon sugar
1/2 teaspoon salt

Preserves, Pickles & Spices / 301

SPICE MIXES

Chinese Five Spice Mixture (Wu Xiang Fen)

8 whole star anises
2 teaspoons Sichuan toasted peppercorns
2 teaspoons fennel seeds
1/2 teaspoons whole cloves
One 3-inch cinnamon sticks or cassia broken into pieces (yields about 1/4 cup).
Grind all the ingredients to a fine powder in a spice grinder. Keep in a sealed jar in a cool place.

This mix represents, wood, metal, water, fire and earth. Individually they are pungent, fragrant, hot, mild, slightly sweet.

Afghan Spice Mixture (Chahar Masala)

2 tablespoons cumin seeds
1 tablespoon whole cloves
One 3-inch cinnamon stick
4 tablespoons black cardamom
Grind all the ingredients together in a spice grinder. Keep in a sealed jar in a cool place (yields about 1/8 cup).

Caspian Herb Chutney (Dalar)

2 cups fresh mint leaves
1/4 cup fresh basil leaves
1/4 cup fresh parsley leaves
2 tablespoons fresh thyme
1 tablespoon fresh oregano leaves
2 tablespoons coarse salt
Puree all the ingredients in a food processor. Store in a sealed jar in the refrigerator (yields about 1/2 cup).

Azerbaijani Spice Mix for Rice (Advieh)

4 tablespoons organic dried rose petals
2 tablespoons cumin seeds
2 teaspoons black peppercorns
1/2 teaspoon ground nutmeg
Grind all the ingredients to a fine powder in a spice grinder. Store in an airtight container to preserve freshness. (Yields about 1/8cup)

Tunisian Spice Mix (Harrisa)

2 teaspoons cumin seeds
2 tablespoons coriander seeds
1 tablespoon caraway seeds
2 tablespoons fresh lime juice
4 tablespoons olive oil
1 teaspoon chili paste
2 hot red chilies, sliced
2 cloves garlic, peeled
1-inch fresh ginger, peeled
2 sundried tomatoes soaked in warm water for 25 minutes, then drained
1 teaspoon dried mint flakes
1/2 teaspoon salt

Heat a wok or deep skillet over medium heat until very hot. Toast the cumin, coriander and caraway seeds for 1 minute, shaking constantly, until aromatic. Grind the toasted seeds in a spice grinder. Place all the ingredients in a food processor and puree to create a paste. Transfer to an airtight jar and refrigerate (yields about 1/4 cup).

Georgian Spice & Herb Mix (Khmeli-Suneli)

1 teaspoon dried marigold
1 tablespoon dried basil
1 tablespoon dried parsley
1 tablespoon dried dill weed
1 tablespoon dried summer savory
1 teaspoon dried mint
1 teaspoon dried fenugreek flakes
1 tablespoon ground coriander seeds
1/2 teaspoon ground fenugreek seeds
1/2 teaspoon cayenne or paprika

Mix all the ingredients and store in a tight jar (yields about 1/4 cup).

North Indian Spice Mixture (Garam Masala)

1 1/2 tablespoons cumin seeds
1 1/2 tablespoons coriander seeds
1/4 teaspoon fennel seeds
One 3-inch cinnamon stick, broken into pieces
1 1/2 tablespoons black peppercorns
4 green cardamom pods
1/4 teaspoon whole cloves
4 small, dried red chilies, broken
1/2 teaspoon sesame seeds
1/4 teaspoon freshly grated nutmeg

Heat a wok over medium heat until very hot. Add all the ingredients except the nutmeg, reduce heat to low and toast for 5 to 8 minutes, tossing and turning constantly, until aromatic. Add the nutmeg. Remove from heat and allow to cool. Grind to a fine powder in a spice grinder. Store in an airtight jar (yields about 1/4 cup).

South Indian Spice Mixture (Sambar)

4 tablespoons coriander seeds
4 tablespoons cumin seeds
4 tablespoons black mustard seeds
1 tablespoon fenugreek seeds
1 tablespoon split yellow peas
6 hot, dried red chilies
20 curry leaves
2 teaspoons black peppercorns
4 teaspoons ground turmeric

Heat a wok over medium heat until very hot. Add all the ingredients except the turmeric, reduce heat to low and toast for 5 to 8 minutes, tossing and turning constantly, until aromatic. Add the turmeric. Remove from heat and allow to cool. Grind to a fine powder in a spice grinder. Store in an airtight jar (yields about 1/8 cup).

Persian Spice Mix (Advieh)

4 tablespoons dried rose petals
One 3-inch cinnamon stick, broken into pieces
2 tablespoons green cardamom pods
4 tablespoons cumin seeds

Grind all the ingredients to a fine powder in a spice grinder. Store in an airtight container to preserve freshness (yields about 1/4 cup).

Fertile Crescent Spice Mix (Baharat)

1 tablespoon ground nutmeg
4 tablespoons cumin seeds
1 tablespoon whole cloves
3-inch cinnamon stick, broken into pieces
2 teaspoons black peppercorns

Grind all the ingredients in a spice grinder. Store in an airtight container to preserve freshness (yields 1/8 cup).

Fertile Crescent Herb Mix (Zatar)

1/2 cup ground sumac berries
1 cup dried thyme
1/4 cup toasted sesame seeds
1 teaspoon salt

Grind all the ingredients in a spice grinder. Store in an airtight container to preserve freshness (yields 3/4 cup).

A Glossary of Silk Road Ingredients & Techniques

AGAR-AGAR (VEGETABLE GELATIN)

This gum, derived from seaweed, is widely used not only in Japan, where it was discovered in the 17th century, but throughout Asia for making jellies and for thickening sauces and soups. It is available in dry sheets, flakes, instant powder and crinkly white, red or green strands in long cellophane packages at Asian groceries. To make gelatin, soak 1 sheet (or 10 strands) of agar-agar in 1 1/2 cups of cold water for 15 minutes; strain out any lumps. For flakes, soak 3 tablespoons in 1/2 cup cold water until the flakes dissolve, then strain out lumps. For powder, bring 1 1/2 cups water to a boil, add 2 tablespoons powder and stir for 1 minute, until the mixture thickens. You may replace agar-agar in recipes with unflavored gelatin (which, unlike agar-agar, contains animal products). Dissolve the gelatin according to instructions on the packet.

ALMOND MILK

This delicious liquid takes about 10 minutes to make. This recipe produces about 1 cup, which may be stored in a tight jar in the refrigerator for up to 2 weeks.

1 cup finely ground almonds
1 1/2 cups boiling water

In a food processor, blend the almonds and water for 5 minutes, until creamy. Strain the mixture through 2 layers of cheesecloth into a bowl. Reserve the strained liquid and discard the solids.

ALMONDS, SWEET

Iran is the center from which almonds spread, on the one hand to Europe and on the other to Tibet and China. Almonds have long been favored for their delicate taste, which enhances both sweet and savory recipes.

For freshness, buy shelled, unblanched nuts. To blanch, drop the almonds into boiling water, boil for 1 minute, drain, and slip off the loosened skins. Then spread the nuts on a baking sheet and dry them for 5 minutes in a 350°F oven. Blanched almonds may be slivered or ground to powder in a food processor. Store whole or ground blanched almonds in airtight containers in the freezer. To roast, see "Nuts, Roasting"; to toast, see "Nuts, Toasting."

ANGELICA

This giant member of the parsley family is named after angels both in English and Persian: The Persian word, *gol-par*, is a compound of *gol*, or "flower," and *pari*, or "angel." According to folklore, the English name derives from the fact that angelica is best harvested around September 29, the Feast of St. Michael and All Angels. The Persian term honors the herb as a panacea. Its seeds, alone or burned with wild rue, defend against the evil eye; powdered seeds aid digestion; and the pungent roots and leaves are brewed for tea.

Western cooks know angelica in the form of decorative candied leaves. Persian cooks use the seeds and powder as souring agents for dishes containing pomegranates, and in soups and stews. Both seeds and powder are sold at Persian groceries.

ASAFETIDA

This spice, a dried gem resin obtained from the taproots of certain giant fennels, has been used since ancient times from the Mediterranean to Central Asia as a flavoring. The name comes from the Persian *asa,* or "mastic resin," and the Latin *foetida,* or "stinking," a reference to its pungent smell. It is available at Asian markets, usually in one of two forms. The best is "lump" asafetida, a mass of tiny pellets, or "tears." This may be powdered and mixed with such spices as turmeric in an attempt to reduce its odor; however, powdered asafetida produces a powerful, sulphurous smell that will pervade your kitchen. I advise buying the lump form shown below, which has little odor. Add asafetida to hot oil and allow it to fry for 2 seconds before you add other ingredients. The spice then acquires the scent of onions, for which it is often a substitute in Indian cooking, particularly among Jains, who do not eat root vegetables. Asafetida rounds out the flavor of other vegetables. It is also said to eliminate gas caused by legumes and help digestion.

ASHAK
Refers to boiled, filled pasta in Eastern Iran and Afghanistan. See "Wrappers" (egg roll, wonton).

BAHARAT
This Fertile Crescent spice—whose name is the generic term for "spice" in Arabic—is sold in Middle Eastern groceries. It is a blend of cloves, cinnamon, cumin, black pepper and nutmeg. You may replace it with equal amounts of allspice, which it closely resembles.

BANANA LEAVES

Banana leaves make a natural wrapper for steaming food. They keep the food moist and release a pleasant aroma. The leaves are also used as plates in much of south Asia, specially by street vendors and for large ceremonies.

The very large, broad, dark green frozen leaves are available, folded in packages, in Asian stores. Thaw thoroughly, carefully unwrap the leaves, soak in warm water for 30 minutes and clean each leaf thoroughly. Rinse with cold water, pat dry, fold and wrap in paper towels. Store in plastic bags in the refrigerator for up to 1 week.

BARBERRIES

These are the tart, red fruit, high in malic and citric acids, of a bush now only used for ornamental hedges in the West. In Iranian folklore, the thorny wild bushes are said to be the refuge of a gray partridge (white during a certain part of the season), whose wings are stained red by the fruit.

Barberries, usually too sour to be eaten raw (though as a child I often enjoyed them as a tart snack), are little appreciated in the West: In Europe, they were once pickled or made into syrups, jam or wine, and medieval Western recipes mention barberries. However, since the discovery that the barberry bush harbored the spores of a wheat blight, their planting has been prohibited in many areas in the West. In Iran, on the other hand, the berries' tart taste and bright, jewel-like color make the fruit a favorite for flavoring and seasoning. Fresh barberry juice (often sold by street vendors in Iran) is said to lower blood pressure and cleanse the system.

The berries usually are dried and stored, and you will find them at Persian groceries. Be sure to choose red ones: Dark berries may be elderly leftovers from earlier seasons.

Dried berries must be cleansed of sand before cooking. Stem the fruit, place it in a colander and partly immerse the colander in cold water. Let it rest for 20 minutes, while the sand sinks to the bottom of the colander. Then remove it from the water, run fresh cold water over the berries and drain them. Fresh barberries, if you should find them, need only be stemmed and rinsed.

BASIL, THAI
(OCIMUM BASILICUM MINIMUM)

Thai basil is similar to European sweet basil (which may be used as a substitute) but milder in taste. It has a distinctive, anise scent and a delicate, musty flavor with a touch of licorice and pepper, which make it good for eating raw, stir frying whole, or adding to curries and salads. It is sold at farmers' markets and Asian groceries.

BORAGE

This herb comes from the Middle East and grows throughout Europe and the U.S. The rather hairy leaves (when young and small) and the beautiful blue-purple flowers add a cucumber taste to teas, salads and ravioli stuffings. In Mediterranean countries, the stalks are sometimes cooked as a vegetable. The herb, which is said to have an exhilarating effect when eaten or mixed with wine, is easy to grow from seed.

In Iran, the purple flowers are used to make a tea, which is said to have a soothing effect. It can be found fresh in farmers' markets, and dried flowers are available in specialty stores and Persian groceries.

BROTH, VEGETABLE

The following recipe, which requires 20 minutes' preparation time and 1 hour of cooking, produces about 6 cups of broth. Because broth adds so much flavor to vegetarian recipes, it is an excellent preparation to have on hand. Make it in large amounts and freeze it in 1-pint containers. It will keep for up to 6 weeks.

1 teaspoon peppercorns
2 bay leaves
1 bunch dill, stalks and roots included
1 sprig fresh thyme
3 sprigs flat-leaf parsley
3 sprigs cilantro, stalks and roots included
1 teaspoon grated orange rind
2 large onions, peeled and thinly sliced
4 tablespoons olive oil
1-inch piece ginger root
5 dried mushrooms, such as shitake or porcini, diced
2 potatoes, peeled and chopped
2 carrots, chopped
2 celery stalks, chopped
1 large celeriac, peeled and chopped
2 leeks, cleaned and sliced paper thin
1 parsnip, chopped
1/2 teaspoon ground saffron threads dissolved in 2 tablespoons hot water
10 cups water

1. Bundle the peppercorns, bay leaves, dill, thyme, parsley, cilantro, and orange rind together, wrap them in a piece of cheesecloth and tie it shut.
2. In a large pot, stir-fry the onion in the olive oil.
3. Add all the remaining ingredients (including cheesecloth bundle) to the pot, cover with the water and bring to a boil. Skim off froth as it rises.
4. Reduce the heat to low, cover the pot and simmer for about 1 hour, adding more water if the level sinks so as to expose the vegetables.
5. Strain the broth through a fine sieve. Discard the cheesecloth bundle; the other solids may be pureed and served as a vegetable or used to thicken soups. Allow the strained liquid to cool, then store it.

BULGUR

Bulgur is wheat that is steamed whole, then dried and cracked into grits. The steaming makes it quick to prepare: Whether it is the coarse variety used in pilafs or the very fine type used in tabbouleh, bulgur needs only soaking. Do not confuse it with cracked wheat, which has not been steamed and must be cooked before eating.

BUTTER, CLARIFIED (SEE GHEE)

CARDAMOM

This widely available, highly flavored spice, a member of the ginger family, is native to India; travelling via caravan routes, it became a favorite in Iran, Greece and Rome by classical times.

There are two types of cardamom: The oval green variety (which may be bleached and sold as "white cardamom") is known in India as the "queen of spices." The larger, husky skinned, dark-brown type is called black cardamom. Green cardamom has a sweet, zesty taste with a hint of eucalyptus. Its pods contain about 20 small, round, black seeds. In many Silk Road countries, people suck the whole pods to sweeten the breath, especially after eating garlic; there is also a green cardamom tea, popular as a digestive. You will notice that some recipes call for using the whole pod (which gives a stronger flavor than the seeds alone); you should bruise the pod with the flat of a knife before adding it to a dish. Other recipes specify cardamom seeds alone: To get them, simply crack the pod and scrape out the seeds with the point of a knife. Black cardamom has a mellow, smoky taste and a nutty aroma. It is generally used as a whole pod, which should be bruised before cooking. While it is not used in sweet dishes—its peppery, medicinal flavor is not suitable for them—it is found in Afghan, Uzbek and Indian chutneys, rice dishes and masalas.

CASSIA (SEE CINNAMON)

CHEESE, WHITE

The recipe that follows takes about 20 minutes plus 3 hours' draining and setting time, and serves 6. You may spice the cheese by adding 1 teaspoon olive oil, 1 teaspoon rosemary or mint, and 1 teaspoon thyme to the reserved liquid in the final step.

1/2 gallon whole milk
1 cup plain yogurt
2 tablespoons salt (optional)
1/4 cup fresh lime juice
1/2 teaspoon salt
1 tablespoon plain yogurt

1. Bring the milk to a boil in a large, non-reactive pot set over low heat. Stir in the cup of yogurt, optional salt and lime juice, and simmer gently for 3 to 5 minutes, until the mixture turns yellow. Immediately pour it through a strainer lined with three layers of cheesecloth and set in a large container. Let the mixture drain into the container for several minutes. Strain the drained liquid and reserve it.

2. Pull the ends of the cheesecloth together over the mixture to enclose it, and return the bundle to the center of the strainer. Place a heavy weight on the bundle, and allow it to drain for 2 hours. Remove the weight, place the bundle in a bowl and refrigerate for 1 hour to set.

3. Unwrap the cheese and place it in a clean jar. Fill the jar with the reserved strained liquid, add 1/2 teaspoon salt and 1 tablespoon yogurt, and refrigerate until ready to serve.

CHERRIES, SOUR OR TART

Tart cherries are available fresh in the summer and dried, canned or frozen all year round in supermarkets or Persian groceries. The following are the ways each type can be prepared for use. These recipes require 5 minutes' preparation and up to 35 minutes' cooking, and produce enough cherries and syrup for a recipe serving 6 people.

For fresh tart cherries: Use 4 pounds of fresh tart cherries. Rinse them in cold water, remove the stems and pit the cherries over a stainless steel pot (you don't want to lose any of the juice). Add 1 1/2 cups sugar and cook over medium heat for 35 minutes. Drain, saving the cherries and the syrup separately for later use as instructed in the recipe.

For frozen pitted sour cherries: Combine 2 pounds of frozen pitted sour cherries with 1 cup sugar, bring to a boil over medium heat and cook for 35 minutes. Drain, saving the cherries and the syrup separately for later use as instructed in the recipe.

For tart, sour or Morello cherries in light syrup: Use three 1 1/2-pound jars. Drain the cherries, combine them with 1 cup sugar in a saucepan and boil over medium heat for 35 minutes. Drain, saving the cherries and the syrup separately for later use as instructed in the recipe.

For dried tart or sour cherries: In a heavy pot, combine 4 cups cherries with 1 cup sugar and 2 cups water. Bring to a boil over medium heat, cook for 35 minutes and stir in 2 tablespoons of fresh lime juice. Drain, saving the cherries and the syrup separately for later use as instructed in the recipe.

CHICKPEA FLOUR

Flour is one of the many products made from the chickpea, or garbanzo bean. It is sold at specialty and Iranian groceries. For the finest flavor, buy roasted chickpea flour.

CHILI, THAI BIRD OR SERRANO

Red or green Thai bird chilies (small, slender, extremely hot and flavorful) and serrano chilies (larger and usually green) are widely available in supermarkets and Asian markets. The two are interchangeable in recipes, although Thai bird chilies are a little more subtle in flavor.

CILANTRO (SEE CORIANDER)

CINNAMON

This spice, made from the bark of various Asian evergreen trees, is one of the oldest: It was first recorded in China in 2500 BCE. It is widely available as sticks (curled pieces of branch bark), chunks (pieces from more intense-tasting bark found low on the tree) and ground spice, which is the kind most frequently used. Chinese and Vietnamese cassia cinnamon are familiar varieties (sweet and aromatic). "True" cinnamon, from cinnamon trees in Ceylon, is milder, with more of a citrus scent. Either may be used for recipes in this book. Just be sure the spice is fresh: Even stored in tightly sealed jars, cinnamon deteriorates after a few months.

COCONUT MILK

Coconut milk is integral to the cooking of southern India and southeast Asia. It is sold in cans in supermarkets. Or you can make it yourself, using the shredded, unsweetened coconut sold in supermarkets or the meat from a fresh coconut. For fresh coconut meat, choose a heavy coconut with no cracks and shake it: If you can hear liquid moving inside, the coconut is ripe and fresh. Preheat the oven to 350°F. Pierce the eyes with an ice pick or corkscrew (*overleaf, steps 1 and 2*) and drain the coconut liquid. Bake the coconut for about 15 minutes or until the shell

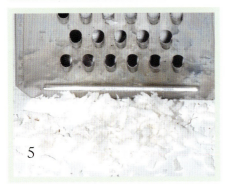

begins to crack. Remove from the oven and allow to cool. Using a hammer, whack the coconut around its circumference, making a full circle. Then use the hammer claw to pry the two halves apart *(left, step 3)*. Remove the flesh with a knife *(step 4)* and grate it *(step 5)*. For every cup of dry or fresh grated coconut, add 2 1/2 cups of boiling water and puree in a food processor for 3 minutes. Strain the puree through a sieve lined with three layers of cheesecloth, then gather the edges of the cheesecloth together and squeeze the bundle to extract all the juice. Discard the solids. The coconut milk will keep for up to 3 days in the refrigerator.

CORIANDER

Coriander is native to the central Silk Road region. It is sold in two quite different forms, both easy to find. Fresh leaves are known in America as cilantro, Chinese parsley or Mexican parsley, and have an intense, musky taste. They need only be rinsed and stemmed before use. Coriander seeds, which look like pale peppercorns, have a concentrated, fiery flavor. They are sold ground for use in cooking. However, it is best to buy whole seeds that can also be ground in a spice mill or small coffee grinder used exclusively for spices. Coriander seeds are an essential spice in Indian cookery and spice mixes. (They are always either fried in oil at the beginning of the cooking process, or toasted before grinding. See "Seeds and Peppercorns, Toasted). The fresh leaves are very popular in Chinese, Persian and Indian cooking.

COUSCOUS

Couscous is often mistakenly thought to be a grain, but is in fact a granular pasta made from semolina. It is traditionally steamed but can also be found in an instant variety. It is available in various pearl sizes: fine, medium and large.

CUCUMBERS

Throughout the Silk Road region, cucumbers are not only turned into pickles or added to salads, but eaten as a fruit. If you wish to try them as a fruit, choose the right variety: small, delicate, fine-skinned cucumbers that are juicy and succulent. These are available throughout the year at Middle Eastern and Persian groceries. Unless they are very young and delicate, peel them and sprinkle them with a little salt before eating.

CUMIN

Cumin is the dried seed of a plant in the parsley family. It is native to Iran, from where it was introduced to China in the second century. Pungent, hot, and rather bitter, a little adds complexity to many dishes.

CURRY LEAF

The curry plant, *Chalcas koenigii*,

comes from the same family as rue and lemons. Curry trees can be found growing throughout the foothills of the Himalayas, just as bay trees appear in every yard and park in the south of France, and Indian cooks use the glossy dark green aromatic leaves in much the same way French cooks use bay leaves. They add it for flavor during the early stages of cooking, then discard it, or they use it as a garnish for finished dishes. The curry leaf is an essential ingredient for south Indian vegetarian spice mixtures, or masalas. Fresh curry leaves are sold as plants in small pots or as cut leaves in Indian groceries. Cut leaves can be stored in sealed plastic bags in the refrigerator for up to two weeks. Dried leaves are also available, but they usually lack flavor.

CURRY POWDER

Commercial curry powder was a British invention and is rarely used in Indian cookery (they make their own). It can be found in a range of flavors and intensities from sweet to hot. All are mixtures of roasted, ground spices, generally including turmeric (the source of the yellow color), coriander, cumin, fenugreek, ginger, nutmeg, fennel, cinnamon, cardamom, various peppers and, of course, curry leaves.

In south Indian vegetarian cooking the curry leaf is an essential element in their masalas (spice mixtures), which also include: black mustard seeds, cumin, fenugreek seeds, dried chilies, black peppercorns, coriander seeds and turmeric. I recommend that you toast the spices and make your own mixture (see spice section on pages 302-305).

DAIKON

Also called white radish and lo pak,

daikon is a sweet, crisp, juicy member of the radish family. It is widely available most of the year but is tastiest in the fall and winter. Choose large, juicy daikons. It is best to peel the roots before cooking or adding to salads. If you are using daikon uncooked, soak it in ice water for about 15 minutes to add crispness.

DATES

The date palm has been cherished for millennia in western Asia for its succulent fruit, which is said to have 360 uses. Products made from dates include, flour, wine, soft drinks, syrup (dates are 50 percent sugar) and medicine for chest and other ailments. In addition, the pits can be ground to make a coffee substitute, and the sap can be fermented to make a toddy.

For eating and cooking, you will find three kinds of dates. Soft dates, harvested when unripe, are a delicious fruit just for eating; you will find them in specialty groceries. Semi-dry dates, from firmer varieties, are more syrupy and intense in flavor; the most widely sold U.S. variety is Deglet Noor. Dry dates are sun-dried on the trees, and are very firm and sugary. These hold their shape best—I prefer to use Medjool dates—in cooked dishes. Both semi-dry and dry dates are sold in supermarkets.

EGGPLANT

As many as 40 varieties of eggplant are

sold in supermarkets. They range from the familiar long purple eggplant to the Japanese and pale lavender Chinese species, which are narrow and as long as 10 inches. Whichever you choose, make sure the vegetable is firm and the skin smooth and shiny.

Chinese eggplants require no particular preparation before cooking and can be cooked with or without the peel. The flesh of other varieties, however, should be steeped before stewing, baking or frying to draw out its excess, sometimes bitter, juices. This is the best method: Peel the eggplants, slice them according to your recipe, place them in a colander in the sink and sprinkle them with salt, allowing 1 tablespoon of salt per 2 pounds of eggplant. Let the slices steep for 20 minutes, rinse them with cold water and pat them dry.

FAVA BEANS

Also known as broad beans, fava beans

are sold in the pod during the summer at specialty groceries and some supermarkets. Shelled beans are also available frozen. When shopping for fresh beans, choose those with tightly closed, bulging, dark-green pods. If stored in perforated plastic bags, they will keep for one or two days in the refrigerator.

To shell a bean, press down on the seam near the stem and split the seam with your thumbnail to pop out the beans. Each bean is covered with a protective membrane; split it with your thumbnail and pull it off in one piece.

Frozen, already shelled fava beans and dried yellow fava beans with membranes removed are both available in Persian grocery stores.

FENUGREEK

Although its English name—from the Latin *fenum graecum,* or "Greek hay"—refers to a Mediterranean origin, this herb actually is native to Iran, from where it was introduced to the classical world in antiquity and to China in the 2nd century.

Fenugreek seeds are very hard and therefore difficult to pulverize, so they are used whole and fried in oil at the beginning of the cooking. Some nomadic tribes in Iran, and in Yemen and Afghanistan, soak the seeds to make a jelly, which is said to be good for the digestion.

As for fenugreek leaves, which are sold at Indian and Middle Eastern markets, they are prepared according to their size and age. In all cases they are stripped from their stalks, which are tough. Young, oval, tender, 4- to 5-inch leaves appear in Indian salads, stuffings and breads. Older, larger (8-inch), rather bitter leaves are indispensable in certain Persian braises, such as the Elam Fenugreek, Kidney Bean and Lime Braise on page 178. Older leaves longer than 8 inches are very bitter: Before use, remove the bitterness by soaking them in salted cold water for 1 hour and rinsing them in several changes of water. Remember that fenugreek is a potent herb. It can be overwhelming, so you should be careful not to use more than specified in recipes.

FILO DOUGH
Filo refers to a paper thin dough. It is available frozen at the supermarket. It should be thawed for 1 hour just before using. Be sure to cover because it dries very easily. If you wish to make your own, use the following recipe:

1. Sift 4 cups all-purpose flour and 1 1/2 teaspoons salt into a mixing bowl.
2. Combine 1 1/3 cup warm water and 4 tablespoons oil, and gradually add to the flour. Knead for 10 minutes until you have a satiny dough. Cover and allow to rest for 2 hours.
3. Roll the dough into a long cylinder and divide it into 10 portions.
4. On a floured surface, roll out the dough as thin as possible, dusting with flour to prevent sticking.

GARLIC, SWEET FRESH BABY
This vegetable, which looks like large spring onions and has only the mildest garlic taste, is sold in Iranian groceries, farmers' markets and some supermarkets in the spring. If it is not available, use regular garlic.

GHEE
A staple in Persian, Indian, Afghan and Uzbek kitchens, ghee is clarified butter, which gives a delicious nutty taste to rice and pastries and has a higher scorching point than regular butter. It is sold in specialty-food stores, but it is easy to make at home: Melt 1 pound of unsalted butter in a saucepan. When it bubbles, cover and simmer over low heat for 15 to 20 minutes, until most of the froth subsides. Let it cool in the pan for 5 minutes. Then strain the liquid through one layer of muslin or three layers of cheesecloth to separate the clear butter fat from the milk solids. Discard the solids and store the ghee (the clear butter fat) in a tightly closed jar in your refrigerator.

GRAPE LEAVES
In America, fresh grape leaves are a rarity: Most of the commercial crop is canned. If you should find fresh leaves, choose the smallest and tenderest ones. Snip off the ends and wash thoroughly. Stack the leaves in bundles of 25, veins facing up, and tie them with a string. Blanch each stack in boiling salted water for 2 minutes, allowing 1/2 cup salt for 12 cups water. Drain the leaves in a colander, rinse with cold water, remove the strings and pat the leaves dry. To use canned grape leaves, simply drain the brine, unroll, rinse in cold water and pat dry.

GRAPES, UNRIPE

Unripe grapes (*ghureh* in Persian), used as a souring agent in many Iranian dishes, are sold at Persian groceries in various forms: fresh in season, whole frozen and canned; as unripe grape juice (*ab-ghureh*), also known as verjuice; and as powdered unripe grapes (*gard-e ghureh*). Although the taste will not be

312

quite the same, you can substitute fresh lime juice for them in recipes: Allow 4 tablespoons of lime juice per 1 1/2 cups unripe grapes, 1 cup grape juice or 1 teaspoon of powder.

HERBS, DRIED
If you must use dried herbs, use only one-quarter of the fresh herbs called for, to allow for the greater intensity of the dried product. For the best flavor, soak the dried herbs in a sieve set in a bowl of lukewarm water for 15 minutes, then drain them and proceed with the recipe.

HOISIN SAUCE
Hoisin sauce is a sweet, piquant paste made from fermented soybean paste, red beans, Chinese five-spice powder, vinegar, garlic, sugar and chili. It is used for stir-frying and marinades, and combined with onions, garlic, chilies, vinegar and crushed peanuts to make a very tasty dipping sauce for dumplings.

JUJUBE

Often called the "Chinese date," this fruit of small, spiny trees is popular from China (where it has been cultivated for at least 4,000 years) to Iran and the Mediterranean. Jujubes are available fresh at specialty markets in the autumn and candied in sugar or honey throughout the year.

The jujube is used in Chinese cooking in fillings and soups, and in Iran the tea is very popular and considered to be a panacea. Jujubes are also eaten whole, fresh or dried as snacks in both China and Iran.

LABNEH (SEE YOGURT)

LEMON GRASS
A grass family stalk with a bulb at the end, widely available lemon grass adds a delicate lemon taste to many south Asian soups. The bulb is best for cooking: Peel off its hard outer layers and chop it fine. If you use the large stalks, remove them at the end of cooking, as they are not good to eat.

LENTIL, RED

This legume, called *masoor dal* in India, is a wonderfully tasty, tiny, orange-red lentil that becomes yellow when cooked. Lentils add a creamy texture when pureed in soups. These lentils should be washed in several changes of cold water, until the water is clear, before cooking.

LIME, PICKLING
Pickling lime, also known as slaked lime, is food grade calcium hydroxide, sold without additives or preservatives. It has long been used (diluted with large amounts of water) as a preliminary treatment for vegetables, to make them greener and crisper. In Iran, for instance, all hard vegetables (such as zucchini, cucumber and pumpkin) are soaked in a pickling lime solution before frying or pickling. Pickling lime is sold as a paste called "White Magic" at Vietnamese and Korean groceries. It is also available through the Internet at http://www.mrswages.com/index.htm. Follow the package instructions for making soaking solutions.

LIMES, PERSIAN
The lime variety known as Persian lime has been grown in Iran for many centuries. These limes are widely available fresh. Persian groceries stock dried limes (*limu omani*) from California (which sometimes have seeds) and the dried lime powder (*gard-e limu omani*) made from them. This commercial powder is apt to be bitter, because it contains ground seeds, but it is easy to make your own from dried Persian limes: With a knife, crack open the limes, halve them and remove any seeds. Then grind the dried limes to powder in a food processor, and store in an airtight jar.

LOTUS SEEDS, CRYSTALLIZED
These seeds of the Asian or North American lotus are sold dried at Asian markets. You can also buy them in crystallized form, but crystallizing them at home takes just over an hour:

2 cups water
2 tablespoons sugar
1/2 cup dried lotus seeds, soaked in warm water for 1 hour and drained

1. In a small saucepan, bring the water and sugar to a boil.
2. Add the drained lotus seeds and return to a boil. Then reduce the heat and simmer for 20 minutes. Drain and use.

MAHLAB

Mahlab is a spice from the kernels found inside the pits of wild black cherries. Popular in Middle Eastern cooking, it gives an almondy taste to breads and pastries. It can be found in Middle Eastern groceries.

MASTIC

The Aegean island of Chios is the source of most mastic, the aromatic resin of a tree in the pistachio family. It may be chewed as gum, but it has a range of other uses throughout Greece and the Middle East, where it may be found in stews, breads, jams and ice cream. It is sold in Asian groceries as hard, translucent lumps and should be pulverized in a grinder with some sugar before it can be used.

MELOKHIYA

This Egyptian herb (*Corchorus olitorius*) is popular not only in Egypt but throughout the Levant. The leaves look something like spinach or sorrel, but their taste is unique. They are available fresh, frozen or dried at Middle Eastern markets. Do not substitute spinach, because you will lose the plant's distinctive flavor and also the special glutinous texture it gives to soups. The soup of the same name is very popular in Egypt.

MULBERRIES

Mulberries come in many varieties, the most important for eating being white and black. The white mulberry, native to the higher elevations of China, has been cultivated for at least 5,000 years for its leaves, which are the silkworms' only food, and for many centuries in other countries, notably Iran. Its sweet fruit, like that of the black mulberry, is delicate: It is not picked, but shaken from its tree onto a sheet. The fruit may be eaten fresh or incorporated in sherbet, jam, vinegar or wine. Dried white mulberries, available at Persian markets, are used as a sweetening agent or in stuffings as one would use raisins.

The black mulberry, known in Iran and Afghanistan as shahtut, or "King Mulberry," is special unto itself. It may be harvested in the same way as white mulberries and eaten fresh; it is not sweet, but tart, and full of a blue-black juice that stains everything it touches. It is said to cleanse the system, increase the appetite, and cure impotence. (The only U.S. mulberry that compares in taste is the red, *M. rubra*, which grows in the east.)

Shahtut berries may also be dried and powdered for use as a souring agent in cooking, as a flavoring in bread or, when mixed with walnuts, as a dip. The powder is sold at Persian markets.

MUSHROOMS, BLACK OR SHITAKE

Black or shitake mushrooms have a very rich, meaty flavor. They should be soaked in hot water for at least 30 minutes before using and the stems should be discarded.

MUSHROOMS, DRIED

Dried mushrooms, popular in south Asian cuisine, are also known as wood-ear, cloud-ear and tree-ear mushrooms. They are not very tasty but wonderfully crunchy. Buy the small black variety and make sure you rinse them well as they can be gritty.

NIGELLA SEEDS (NIGELLA SATIVA)

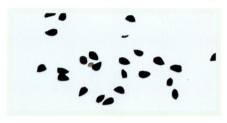

Nigella seeds are small, are black and have a spicy, oniony taste. They are used as a spice in Persian cooking and often sprinkled on Punjabi bread. They are sold at Asian markets.

NOODLES, ASIAN

Asian noodles, made from a range of starches, come in bewildering varieties. Here are the chief ones, all sold at Asian markets, and the methods for cooking them in 1-pound quantities.

Cellophane noodles (also called bean thread noodles): These translucent noodles made from ground mung beans. Before cooking, soak them for 30 minutes in cold water, drain them and cut them in half. Then drop them into boiling water and cook for 1 minute only—just until the water returns to a boil. Drain immediately in a fine-mesh colander, rinsing with water and shaking the colander to remove water and starch.

Rice noodles: These flat noodles, popular in China, Vietnam and Thailand, are made from rice and water and sold dried. To cook them, bring 8 cups water to a rolling boil in a large pot. Drop in the noodles, turn off the heat and let the noodles soak for 1 minute. Drain and rinse.

Rice stick noodles: These vermicelli-like noodles are sold dried. Soak them in warm water for 15 to 20 minutes, until soft; do not soak them longer. Drain them, snip them in half, and shake them to remove excess water and starch. They require no further cooking.

Wheat noodles (egg noodles): These noodles come in a variety of widths and are sold both fresh and dried. The Chinese curly noodles shown below,

excellent for soup, are just one type. To cook them, bring 5 quarts water to a rolling boil, add the noodles and cook for 2 minutes (for fresh noodles) to 7 minutes (for dried noodles). Cook only until the strands can be pulled apart with chopsticks; then drain.

NOODLES, PERSIAN

Persian flour noodles (called *reshteh*, from the Persian for "thread") are sold dried, or toasted and dried, at Persian groceries. They are made from water, flour and salt, and usually contain no eggs. Lacking Iranian noodles, you may substitute any flat, narrow, dried noodle, such as linguine. To toast noodles yourself, break them into pieces and toss them in a hot, ungreased skillet over low heat for a few minutes, until they are golden brown, or spread them on a baking sheet and broil them under high heat for 30 seconds. To cook 1 pound of dried noodles, bring 5 quarts of water to a rolling boil, add 2 tablespoons salt and the noodles, and cook for 2 to 12 minutes, depending on the width of the noodles. Test that the noodles have reached the texture you prefer by biting into one. Drain all the noodles. They are now ready for sauce.

NUTS, ROASTING

To roast nuts or seeds such as pumpkin seeds for appetizers, combine 1 pound nuts or seeds, 1 cup water and 1 tablespoon salt in a large skillet set over low heat. Cook, stirring occasionally, until the water evaporates. Then stir constantly until the nuts are dry and brown. Shake the nuts in a colander or sieve to remove excess salt, then spread them on a baking sheet and, if you wish, sprinkle them with saffron water, lime juice or spices to your taste. Shake the sheet to distribute the flavorings, and bake the nuts or seeds in a warm oven (250°F) for 1 to 1 1/2 hours, until completely dried. Store in an airtight jar.

NUTS, TOASTING

Heat a large skillet over medium heat and add nuts, but no oil. Cook over medium heat, stirring constantly, until the nuts are golden brown—5 to 10 minutes. Store in an airtight jar.

ONION JUICE

Onion juice for marinades should be made just before use (it turns bitter if left to stand). To make 1 cup of juice, puree 2 large peeled yellow onions in a food processor. Strain the puree through a fine-mesh sieve or food mill into a bowl, pressing to extract all the juice.

ORANGE, SEVILLE OR BITTER

The flesh of the Seville orange is too bitter to eat, but its juice is much used in Iranian cookery, and some recipes call for the intensity of Seville orange paste, made from the juice. Lacking Seville orange juice, you may substitute 1/4 cup fresh sweet orange juice plus 2 tablespoons fresh lime juice for every 1/2 cup of the Seville juice called for in a recipe. For treatments of orange peel and paste, see below.

ORANGE BLOSSOM WATER

A delicately scented distillation of orange flowers, this flavoring is sold in many supermarkets.

ORANGE PASTE, SEVILLE

Seville orange paste is sold in Persian groceries. You can also make it at home. This recipe requires 20 Seville oranges, 45 minutes' preparation time and 1 1/2 hours' cooking time, and produces 1 cup of paste.

1. Remove the peel in a 1-inch-wide strip around the middle of each orange (this reduces the bitterness). Halve each orange and remove the seeds. Juice each orange, and strain the juice.

2. Pour the juice into a non-reactive pot, bring it to a boil, reduce the heat to medium and simmer, uncovered, over medium heat for about 1 1/2 hours. As the juice thickens, you will need to stir constantly, to prevent sticking and burning, When it has reduced to a thick, soft paste, remove it from the heat.

3. Store the paste in a tightly closed jar in the refrigerator

ORANGE PEEL, BLANCHED

You may use either sweet or Seville orange peel for recipes. In either case, the peel should be blanched to remove the bitterness. To do so, peel the orange and cut the skin into slivers. Drop the slivers into boiling water and cook over medium heat for 7 to 10 minutes, then drain in a colander and rinse under cold running water. It saves time to blanch a good supply of orange peel. Stored in small 1-cup portions in plastic bags in the freezer, orange peel will keep for several months.

Seville orange peel has a unique perfume, but it is also extremely bitter. If you want to use it, then it should be soaked in water for 24 hours, drained and blanched 3 times, changing the water until all bitterness is removed.

ORANGE PEEL, CANDIED

Candied peel appears in supermarkets during the winter, but it is easy to make at home. The following recipe takes about 20 minutes' preparation time and 40 minutes' cooking time, and makes 1 cup of candied peel.

4 oranges
4 cups sugar
2 cups water
4 tablespoons fresh lime juice

1. Wash the oranges, peel them, cut the peel into slivers, and blanch (see "Orange Peel, Blanched" above).

2. In a saucepan, combine the blanched peel, sugar and water. Bring to a boil, reduce the heat to medium and simmer for 20 minutes. Add the lime juice and simmer 15 to 20 minutes more.

3. Drain the peel, spread it on parchment paper and let it dry for a few hours. Then sprinkle with confectioners' sugar if desired and store in a plastic bag in the refrigerator for weeks or in the freezer for months.

ORANGES, PEELING & SEGMENTING

To peel oranges neatly for salads or desserts, follow the simple procedure shown at left, top to bottom. First slice off the skin and bitter pith, cutting straight down (1). You should be able to do this in about four slices, to make a pentagon (2). Holding the orange over a plate or bowl to catch the juice, slice the knife down one side of a segment, inside the papery membrane, to loosen it (3). Then slice down the other side of the segment (4) to lift it neatly from the membrane. Repeat for each segment.

PEAS, SPLIT

Yellow split peas, the kind specified in recipes in this book, come in two main varieties, which are interchangeable. Those sold in supermarkets take 20 minutes to cook; however, those sold in Persian groceries take at least 40 minutes, and you should adjust recipe cooking times accordingly.

PERSIMMON

The persimmon (*Diospyros Kaki*) is native to China and traveled the Silk Road to the Middle East and the Mediterranean. There are two types of persimmons sold in the U.S. The large, round, dark orange variety, available at Middle Eastern markets, is often sold when hard and unripe. You should let the persimmon ripen at room temperature and eat it when it is soft. When it is ready, slice off the top and eat the flesh with a spoon. Or freeze it first, which gives the flesh the texture of a sorbet. (To enjoy them in this way, the Chinese sometimes let the fruit freeze on the tree.) At Chinese and Korean markets you will also find a smaller, flatter, light-orange persimmon, which is firm when ripe. Peel it and slice it for eating straight or for use in salads. Asian markets also sell dried persimmons, which may be eaten like any other dried fruit.

PINE NUTS

Pine nuts are the kernels from the cones of the stone or umbrella pine. They are widely available in supermarkets and specialty groceries.

PISTACHIO NUTS

These delicious nuts with their beautiful green color are native to Iran. Nicolaus of Damascus wrote in the 1st century BCE: "The youths of the Persians were taught to endure heat, cold, and rain; to cross torrents and to keep their armor and clothes dry; to pasture animals, to watch all night in the open air, and to subsist on wild fruit, such as pistachios, acorns, and wild pears." In Iran, pistachios are used for dishes ranging from soup to desserts.

Pistachios are widely available. At Middle Eastern markets you will find them shelled; these tend to be smaller than unshelled nuts. It is best to buy fresh pistachios unsalted in undyed shells. (Shells are sometimes dyed red to conceal imperfections.) After shelling, pistachios should be blanched to remove their papery skins: Drop the nuts into boiling water, boil for about 1 minute, and drain. Lay a towel on a work surface, fold it over the nuts, and rub your hands lightly back and forth over the top, rolling the nuts to dislodge the skins. Spread the nuts on a baking sheet and dry them for 15 to 25 minutes in a 250°F oven.

PLUMS

Fresh plums, in varieties ranging from purple to gold, are best bought during the summer months from local growers. In Iran, the small, round, green unripe variety known as *gojeh*—available in the U.S. in Persian groceries in the spring—is a favorite snack. This plum is also used as a souring agent in stews and braises. As a compote, for use throughout the year, different varieties of dried plums are sold at health food stores and Iranian groceries. They require only rinsing before use in a recipe. The syrup made from these plums is also sold at Persian groceries.

POMEGRANATE

The red pomegranate, native to Iran and cultivated there for at least 4,000 years, is considered the fruit of heaven; in fact, it was probably the real "apple" in the Garden of Eden. The ancients commended it. Among them were King Solomon, who had a pomegranate orchard. And the prophet Mohammed said, "Eat the pomegranate, for it purges the system of envy and hatred."

The fruit grows on large bushes or small trees, whose crimson flowers brighten the pale mud walls of villages in Iran, Spain, and Italy. In Persian folk medicine, every part of the plant is believed to have a virtue. The dried and powdered skin of the roots and fruit make a tea drunk to sweeten the breath, correct menstrual irregularity, kill parasites and relieve nausea. Another tea, made from young shoots and leaves, fresh or dried, is a good remedy for nausea, lack of appetite, anemia and headaches. The flowers repel insect pests—even honeybees avoid them—and provide yet a third tea, good for soothing uneasy stomachs.

Pomegranates, ranging in taste from sweet to sour-sweet, have a special place in cookery from Iran to China. The fresh seeds (the edible part of the fruit), sprinkled with angelica powder, make a tart appetizer, and they add a bright note to green salads. Puréed and strained, the seeds produce a refreshing juice for drinking or for flavoring soups and stews. Or the juice may be reduced to a paste, a favorite souring agent, particularly in central and southern Iran. Most recipes that include pomegranate, which is classified as a cold food, also include hot foods like walnuts or ginger for balance.

Pomegranates are available in supermarkets in the fall and winter. Choose deep red fruits without blemishes. They will keep at home for about a week at room temperature. I have been able to keep them fresh at the end of the season for three weeks or more by wrapping them individually in newspaper and keeping them in the refrigerator drawer.

POMEGRANATE, HOW TO SEED

To seed a pomegranate easily, follow the steps shown at left. After slicing off the crown with a sharp knife, make a superficial spiral cut in the skin around the pomegranate(1). Press both thumbs into the open crown (2) and pull the fruit apart (3). Hold each half seed side down over a bowl and tap the skin with a heavy spatula (4) to dislodge the seeds from the membrane that holds them (5).

POMEGRANATE JUICE

In Iran fresh pomegranate juice is a popular drink, like orange juice, and is sold by juice vendors on street corners. In the West this juice is sold in health food stores and Persian groceries. Or you can make your own, allowing 2 large pomegranates for 1 cup of juice: Seed the pomegranates (see "Pomegranate, How to Seed), purée the seeds in a food processor and strain the puree through a fine sieve. The juice will vary in sourness depending on the fruit; add sugar or lime juice to balance the taste to your liking.

POMEGRANATE, JUICED IN ITS SKIN

This is a favorite among Iranians, who call the process *ablambu*. It allows one to drink the juice of a pomegranate without fuss or mess. Choose a good-looking pomegranate with no blemishes or holes in the skin. Then, holding it in both hands with one thumb over the other, start by gently squeezing one of the raised parts of the fruit (there are usually four or five hills and valleys). The idea is to squeeze the seeds inside the skin without bursting the skin. This needs to be done gently and systematically, going around the pomegranate until the whole fruit is soft and squishy. Then press it to your mouth, make a small hole in the skin with your teeth while you suck with your mouth and squeeze gently with your hands. You will get a very refreshing burst of juice in your mouth that is both delicious and sensual. Continue working around the fruit, squeezing and sucking, until you have drunk all the juice. It is an art that you will perfect with practice, and once you know how you will never again see a good-looking pomegranate without wanting to *ablambu* it.

POMEGRANATE PASTE

Pomegranate paste is available in specialty stores and Persian groceries as a very sweet Persian brand and a very sour Arab brand. For Persian recipes, buy both types and mix them to achieve the proper sweet and sour taste. Or make your own paste. The following recipe requires 20 minutes' preparation and 1 hour's cooking, and yields about 1/2 pint:

1. Bring 8 cups fresh pomegranate juice (if the juice tastes sweet rather than sour, add the juice of 2 limes) to a boil in a non-reactive pot set over high heat.
2. Reduce the heat to medium, add 1 tablespoon salt, and simmer uncovered for 1 hour or more, stirring occasionally as the juice reduces. As it thickens to a paste, stir more frequently to prevent sticking and burning.
3. Let the paste cool. Then store it in a clean, tightly closed jar in the refrigerator, where it will keep for a month, or in the freezer, where it will keep for a year. Or can the paste as described on page 294 and store it in a cupboard.

PUMPKIN & OTHER WINTER SQUASH

Pumpkin or squash flowers *(above)*

make a delicious tempura. Round winter squashes such as pumpkin, and butternut and acorn squashes are all prepared the same way, as shown at right with a butternut squash. With a heavy cleaver, slice the squash crosswise into 2-inch rings *(1 and 2)*. Remove the seeds with a spoon *(3)* and use the cleaver to peel the squash *(4)*. Cut each squash into 1-inch cubes *(5)*, rinse and drain the cubes, and pat them dry.

QUINCE

This big tree, a relative of the rose, is native to Iran, and cultivation probably started there. The fruit's hard, astringent flesh, somewhere between an apple and a pear but with a special aromatic perfume, lends tartness to stews, jams, custards and sherbet drinks. Its blossoms are also used to make a popular jam. Although quinces are available in supermarkets during the late autumn and winter, the biggest and best ones are sold in Persian groceries. When shopping, choose firm, unblemished fruit. At the end of the season you can wrap individual quinces in newspaper and store them in the refrigerator drawer for 2 to 3 weeks.

Some varieties of Persian quinces can be eaten raw. The U.S. quince generally cannot. To prepare it for cooking, simply rub off the fuzz.

RHUBARB SYRUP

This recipe makes 1 pint of syrup, and requires 10 minutes' preparation and 20 to 30 minutes' cooking time:

2 pounds rhubarb, trimmed and rinsed
4 cups sugar
2 cups water
2 tablespoons lime juice

1. Bundle the rhubarb into a piece of doubled cheesecloth or muslin, and tie the ends securely with string to make a bag.
2. Bring the sugar and water to a boil over high heat. Reduce the heat to medium, drop in the bag of rhubarb, and simmer for 20 to 30 minutes. Remove the pan from the heat and let the contents cool.
3. Squeeze the cheesecloth bag over the cooled sugar water to extract every bit of rhubarb flavor. Discard the bag and the rhubarb. Add the lime juice.
4. Store the mixture in a jar in the refrigerator, where it will keep for several months.

RICE FLOUR

This delicate flour, made from rice grains, contains no gluten, so it cannot be used for bread making. However it is a fine thickener for braises, soups, puddings, and sweets such as the delicate rice cookies that are a favorite in Iran. The flour is sold in supermarkets.

RICE PAPER WRAPPERS
(SEE "WRAPPERS")

RICE STARCH

This is a fine powder thickener, much like cornstarch, which may be substituted for it.

ROSE PETALS

Dried rose petals (organic and without pesticides) suitable for use in cooking are sold in Persian groceries and specialty food stores.

ROSE PETALS, CRYSTALLIZED

Wash the rose petals thoroughly and pat dry. Line a cookie sheet with 1/4 cup super-fine sugar. Beat the egg white lightly with a fork until frothy. Use a brush to paint both sides of the rose petals with egg white. Arrange petals on a cookie sheet and coat both sides of the rose petals evenly with 1/4 cup sugar. Allow to dry on the bed of sugar at room temperature for at least

1 hour, until the sugar forms a crisp coat.

ROSE WATER
Rose water suitable for cooking is sold at Persian groceries. If it is kept cool, its aroma lasts for years.

SAFFRON
When buying saffron, choose threads rather than powder, which is too often adulterated with turmeric. Threads should be ground with a cube of sugar, which helps the grinding process, then dissolved in hot water. The saffron-water solution can then be stored and used as needed. Never use the unground threads.

SALAB (ALSO CALLED SALEP)
The powdered root of an orchid, which provides elasticity to ice cream, salab is sold in Middle Eastern markets in two forms: pure, and mixed with flour and cornstarch. Note that the pure form is four times as strong as the mixture; adjust recipe amounts accordingly.

SEEDS AND PEPPERCORNS, TOASTED
Add the seeds or peppercorns to a large skillet over medium heat without oil. Cook, stirring constantly, until the seeds begin to brown—5 to 10 minutes. The timing required for toasting will vary depending on the type of seeds. Be watchful once the seeds or peppercorns begin to brown to avoid burning them. Store in an airtight jar.

SESAME OIL, TOASTED
This aromatic oil is available at supermarkets and Asian groceries.

SESAME PASTE
Chinese sesame paste is made by grinding toasted sesame seeds. It is a grayish-brown color and is not to be confused with the light brown untoasted sesame paste of the Middle East called tahini. Chinese sesame paste is sold at Asian markets; tahini is sold at most supermarkets.

SICHUAN PEPPERCORNS
Sichuan peppercorns have a petal-like husk with a pleasant aroma, while the seeds inside are similar to, but perhaps a little more spicy than, black pepper. They are available in Chinese groceries and are best when toasted before use (see "Seeds and Peppercorns, Toasted)

SOY SAUCE
Chinese soy sauce is available in 3 weights: light, medium and heavy. Light soy sauce is more delicate and subtly flavored, and I recommend it for use with recipes in this book.

SPROUTS
1. Thoroughly wash and rinse 1 cup beans (alfalfa, wheat, mung beans or lentils) and place in a bowl, cover with 4 cups luke warm water and let stand at room temperature for 24 hours.
2. Drain the beans, bundle in a cheesecloth and replace in the drainer. Place in a dark, undisturbed spot (an off oven will do) and cover with a plate or lid. Allow to rest, undisturbed, for 24 hours.
3. The next day, the beans will have sprouted and will be ready to eat.

SUMAC
The red-berried sumac bush—*Rhus coriaria*, not to be confused with the poisonous white-berried species—provides one of the favorite flavorings for Persian and Central Asian cooking. To make sumac juice, the berries, along with, the leaves and branches, are boiled in water, then sieved. To make a powder, the berries alone are dried and crushed to a powder. The latter, sold in Persian groceries, is the more usual form of the spice; it is kept in the kitchen and on the table, along with salt and pepper.

Sumac is prized as a digestive, and even more prized as a pleasantly astringent souring agent: Iranians prefer its taste to that of lemon. It adds distinction to breads, marinades, soups and stews, among other dishes. It is also delicious when sprinkled on onion salads or mixed with yogurt.

SYRUP, SUGAR
An important ingredient in many Silk Road desserts, sugar syrup is easy to make at home. The following recipe takes about 10 minutes and produces about 1 cup of syrup. In a tightly closed jar, it will keep for 3 months in a cool place.

3 cups sugar
1 cup water
1 tablespoon lime juice
1 tablespoon rose water (optional)
1. Combine the sugar and water in a pot. Bring to a boil, reduce the heat and simmer for 4 minutes, being careful not to let the mixture boil over.
2. Remove the pot from the heat, stir in the lime juice and rose water, and set aside to cool. Then pour into a jar for storage.

TAHINI PASTE
This thick oily paste is made by grinding untoasted sesame seeds and used in Middle Eastern cooking. This paste should not be confused with the toasted sesame paste used in Chinese cooking.

TAMARIND
A native of tropical East Africa or perhaps India, now widely grown, the tamarind tree bears pods that are used to make a souring agent indispensable not only in Indian cuisine but in many Southern Iranian, Chinese, Thai, and Vietnamese dishes. The partly dried, seeded pods are sold in many specialty groceries. These stores also sell liquid

flavoring and paste made from tamarind. To make your own liquid or paste, see "Tamarind Paste" below.

TAMARIND LIQUID
Tamarind liquid is made the same way as tamarind paste (see "Tamarind Paste"). Simply add water to the finished paste to dilute it to the desired consistency.

TAMARIND PASTE

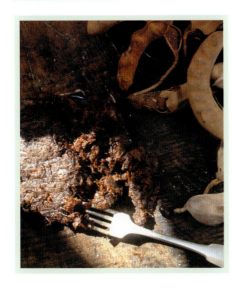

The following recipe, made from dried tamarind, requires 10 minutes' preparation and 40 minutes' cooking, and produces about 1/2 pint of paste.
1. Place 1 pound dried tamarind pods in a large saucepan, cover them with 8 cups water and bring to a boil. Reduce the heat to medium and simmer, uncovered, for 30 minutes, adding more water if the pan becomes dry.
2. Place a fine mesh colander or strainer over a bowl and pour in the softened tamarind pods with their liquid. With a masher, crush the pods to force out as much liquid as possible; you may pour a little boiling water over the pods to force more of their juice out. The strained juice will be thick and pasty. Transfer it to a dry jar, cap tightly and store in the refrigerator for up to a week.

TARKHINEH, TARKANA OR KISHK
These are patties or pellets made from a sun-dried fermented bulgur and yogurt dough. They are often eaten as is, but they also may be crumbled and mixed with milk to make a kind of breakfast cereal, or used as a thickener for soups.

TEMPEH
This high-protein food (cooked soybeans inoculated with a spore and then fermented) from Indonesia, is sold in firm, flat, spotted cakes at Asian markets. It is not usually precooked and should be steamed for 20 minutes before use. It then may be cut into strips, shredded, cubed or crumbled, and used as one would use ground beef. It has a great ability to absorb flavors.

TOFU
Tofu is the Japanese name for a high-protein white soybean curd invented in China (where it is called *dou fu*) and important to the cookery of much of Asia. In Asian markets you will find many varieties—plain, spiced, smoked and fermented among them. For the recipes in this book, buy the plain white, firm tofu sold in supermarkets.

TOMATOES, PEELING AND SEEDING
There is little to equal the taste of fresh ripe tomatoes in season; out of season, peeled, canned tomatoes make a good substitute. Most recipes require that fresh tomatoes be peeled. To do so, mark an X on the bottom of each tomato with a sharp knife. Plunge tomatoes into boiling water and blanch for 20 seconds, removing with a slotted spoon. Rinse with cold water. Drain, and slip off the skin. To seed, cut them open around the middle, and squeeze out and discard the seeds.

TURMERIC
Turmeric, a native of southeast Asia that is now grown in tropical climates throughout the world, comes from the rhizomes of a plant in the ginger family. Although the dried rhizomes are available, they are hard and difficult to grind at home. Store-bought ground turmeric is perfectly good. Turmeric has many nutritional properties, and keeps green vegetables green and crispy when cooked.

VALERIAN

Valerian, a small plant with pinkish or white flowers that grows throughout Europe and Asia, is known as "all heal" in English for the sedative qualities of its root. In China and Iran a small amount of the root—sold in health food stores and Persian groceries—is boiled with borage, dried lime and sugar to make a nightcap.

VEGETABLE BROTH (SEE "BROTH, VEGETABLE")

VEGETABLES, COOKING CHOICES
Different vegetables lend themselves to different cooking techniques. Here are a few tips:.

WATER COOKING: IMMERSION
Suitable vegetables include artichokes, asparagus, broccoli, cabbage, cauliflower, green beans, spinach, and all other green vegetables. These vegetables should be poached in water that is already boiling and salted. Starchy vegetables, including beets, dried beans, lentils and potatoes, should be placed in salted cold water, which you should gradually bring to a boil. Carrots, parsnips and turnips can be cooked either way. "Sun" vegetables such as bell peppers, eggplant, zucchini and tomatoes (except when part of a soup or sauce) should not be boiled or poached.

WATER COOKING: STEAMING
Almost all vegetables suitable for poaching can also be steamed, except for artichokes. Sprinkle the vegetables

with salt rather than salting the water. Do not chill steamed vegetables for serving later.

OVEN COOKING: GRILLING, BROILING AND BAKING

This is the best method for "sun" vegetables such as tomatoes. If grilling over an open flame, be sure that the flame does not touch the vegetables. Pour a little olive oil over the grilled vegetables before serving. You can also bake sun vegetables with a little water at very low heat (250°F to 275°F), which concentrates vegetable sugars and gives them a very sweet taste.

STOVE-TOP COOKING: BRAISING

Cooking firm young vegetables with a little water and butter gives them a particularly nice texture and flavor. Use a non-reactive casserole. In it place prepared young carrots, turnips, onions, asparagus tips, broccoli florets, beets, baby zucchini, butternut squash or snow peas; cover them with salted water, and add butter (or olive oil) and a pinch of sugar. Bring to a boil, reduce the heat, cover and simmer briefly, until tender. Then uncover, raise the heat to high, and boil off the liquid.

STOVE-TOP COOKING: DEEP-FRYING

A few tips on deep-frying: You will need a deep, heavy pan filled with enough oil that it remains at least 2 inches above the ingredients throughout the cooking process; a deep-frying basket is useful for lowering vegetables into and removing them from the oil. Before adding ingredients, heat the oil to a temperature between 330°F and 375°F (use a deep-frying thermometer to gauge the temperature). This is important: If the oil is too hot, the outsides of the ingredients will burn while their insides will remain uncooked; if it is too cold, ingredients will absorb the oil and become soggy and greasy.

STOVE-TOP COOKING: STIR-FRYING

Almost all firm vegetables are suitable for stir frying. Be sure to cut them into even pieces. Place an empty wok on high heat for a moment or two; when it is very hot, add about 2 tablespoons oil. Allow the oil to get hot (about 15 seconds) then add the ingredients and keep the pan moving at all times as you cook. If you are cooking large quantities, add the ingredients in batches to avoid over filling.

WALNUTS

The walnut is native to Northern Iran and spread to the West and China from there. Walnuts feature in many Persian, Georgian, and Central Asian dishes, especially those containing pomegranates. Peeled and salted, they make a delicious snack. In Iran they are sold fresh in season by street vendors, who spend the day picking and peeling them. They store them in brine in glass jars and then sell them in the evening in bags of four, as roasted chestnuts are sold in winter.

To make a similar snack from dried walnuts, wash the nuts, place them in very hot water with 1 teaspoon salt per pound of nuts, cover them and refrigerate overnight. The next day, rub off the loosened skin and drop the nuts into a bowl of cold water until ready to use. Then drain the nuts and sprinkle them with salt to taste.

WHEY, DRIED

In the West, whey means the thin liquid separated from milk curds during cheese making. In Iran and the Silk Road region, the term refers to drained, salted, sun-dried yogurt, used as a souring agent in many dishes. Whey is sold at Persian groceries. You may substitute sour cream.

WOK, HOW TO CLEAN

A wok is a wonderful cooking utensil and can be used for cooking almost anything, not just stir-fries. Always clean the wok right away (as soon after using as possible) with hot water—there is no need to use soap. Persistent burnt food can be rubbed off the wok by using a little salt, which is a natural abrasive. Dry your wok, over heat if you wish, after cleaning and rinsing.

WRAPPERS, DOUGH

Two interchangeable kinds of wrappers are sold at supermarkets and Asian groceries. Wonton wrappers are made from flour and water; they are the smaller and more delicate. Larger, tougher egg roll wrappers are made from a dough that is made of egg, water and flour. Either kind can be cut into various sizes and shapes to make wonton, ashak, crispy roll, boulani, manti, mantou, and other preparations shown in the recipes in this book.

WRAPPERS, HOMEMADE (FRYING)

For all fried stuffed pies, it is very easy to make your own wrapper at home: Place 3 cups flour in a mixing bowl and gradually stir in 1/2 cup boiling water. Add 2/3 cup cold water, knead for 5 minutes until you have a soft dough that does not stick to your hands. Cover and allow to rest at room temperature for 30 minutes. Roll the dough into a long cylinder and divide it into 32 pieces. Roll out each piece into a 3-

inch disk. Cover the pieces to prevent drying while you prepare your filling. You can also custom make your own wrappers. It is a very easy process, as the following recipe shows.

WRAPPERS, HOMEMADE (BAKING)

For pirozhki and sambuseh (and other baked stuffed pies), use ready-made puff pastry, or you can make your own from this recipe, which takes about 5 minutes to make (plus 30 minutes for resting) and produces 24 wrappers.

2 1/2 cups unbleached all-purpose flour, sifted with 1 1/2 teaspoons salt
1 egg
1 tablespoon vegetable oil
1/2 cup water

1. Place the flour mixture in a food processor, add the egg and pulse for 1 second. Add the oil and pulse 1 second more. With the machine running, gradually add the water; after about 5 minutes you should have a soft dough that does not stick to your hands. Cover and allow to rest for 30 minutes. On a floured surface, roll out the dough to a thin (about 1/8-inch) layer and paint evenly with oil. Form the dough into a tight cylinder.

2. Divide the dough into 24 pieces. On a cool, floured surface, roll out each piece into a thin disk. Cover the disks to prevent drying while you prepare any of the fillings.

WRAPPERS, RICE

Rice wrappers used for crispy rolls in this book are readily available at Asian groceries and some supermarkets. They are sold as large or small dried disks. To reconstitute them, dip the disks one by one into warm water, spread them out on towels and let them rest for 2 minutes.

WRAPPERS, YUFKA (BOREK)

Yufka is Turkish for a single leaf of pastry. Readymade Yörük brand pastry leaves, which are excellent for making boreks, are available at Middle Eastern and Turkish groceries.

YOGURT

Health-giving yogurt is one of the oldest foods. The well-known tale of its invention goes like this: A desert nomad carried milk in his goatskin canteen. During his journey, heat and bacteria (lactobacillus) transformed the milk into yogurt. Taking a chance, the nomad drank it and was astonished to find it creamy and pleasantly sour. Having survived the experiment, he shared the discovery.

Whatever the real origin, yogurt is mentioned in records of ancient civilizations from India to Iran; by 500 BCE, holy men on the subcontinent had labeled the delicious mixture of yogurt and honey "the food of the gods." It reached western Europe in the 16th century. The first American yogurt company was established in 1931 in Massachusetts by the Armenian Colombosians family, whose Colombo yogurt is still on the market.

Almost every power has been ascribed to yogurt: It has variously been said to prolong life, increase sexual potency, remedy baldness, calm the nervous system, and cure skin diseases and gastrointestinal ailments. Whether it does these things or not, it forms a fine enrichment for many of the sauces, stews and dips in this book. It is sold everywhere in low-fat and fat-free versions, or you can make your own (see "Yogurt, Homemade").

Any plain yogurt, store-bought or homemade, may be used in the recipes in this book. The choice depends on your taste and your diet. Creamy, homemade yogurt makes the richest, most tasty sauces, but it is high in fat. Plain homemade yogurt is the next richest, followed by low-fat and fat-free commercial products.

YOGURT, DRAINED

Many recipes call for drained yogurt, which is simple to produce. If you are using commercial yogurt, pour the yogurt into a bowl and place the bowl in a larger one to catch drips. Place three or four layers of paper towel on the surface of the yogurt, letting the edges overlap its bowl, and refrigerate for several hours. The towel will absorb excess moisture; discard it when the yogurt is thick.

If you are using homemade yogurt (see "Yogurt, Homemade" below), pour it into the center of a large square made of three layers of cheesecloth or muslin, draw the corners of the fabric together and tie them to make a bag (use a cotton jelly bag). Hang the bag over a large pot for 15 to 20 minutes. The liquid, which may be discarded, will slowly drain from the yogurt, leaving it thick and creamy.

YOGURT, HOMEMADE

When you prepare yogurt, make sure all your utensils are scrupulously clean: Dirty or greasy tools will not produce the desired result. This recipe requires 20 minutes' preparation and 12 hours' setting; it makes about 2 quarts of yogurt:

1. In a clean, non-reactive pot, bring 2 quarts whole milk to a boil over medium heat.

2. Immediately remove the milk from the heat and let it stand until cool but not completely cold. The temperature should be 115°F on a kitchen thermometer; the temperature is correct if you can just tolerate the heat on a finger for 20 seconds. (Temperature is important: If the milk is too cool, the culture will not grow; on the other hand, excess heat will kill the bacteria in the culture.)

3. Pour the milk into a square or rectangular glass dish. Pull out a rack in the center of the unheated oven and place the dish on it.

4. Place 1/4 cup plain low-fat or fat-free commercial yogurt in each of the four corners of the dish. Gently push the rack back into the oven, and close the door. Do not turn on the oven but leave the light in the oven on to get just the right amount of warmth: The yogurt must rest undisturbed for at least 24 hours. An alternative is to cover and wrap the dish in a large towel or blanket and let it rest in a non-drafty corner of your kitchen.

5. When the yogurt is ready, store it in the refrigerator and use as needed.

Variation: To make creamy yogurt, add 1 cup half-and-half to the milk.

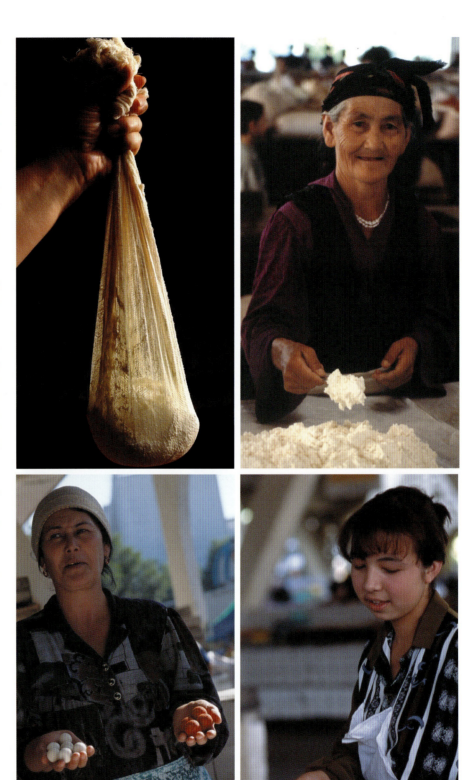

Clockwise from top left: Homemade yogurt drained in cheese cloth; a woman sells drained yogurt in the Tashkent market; a vendor holds rolled, drained plain yogurt in one hand and the red pepper spiced version in the other; a young girl sells the sun-dried final product.

Cooking Measurements

Note that all spoon and cup measurements used in this book are level. It is not easy to convert with absolute accuracy measurements for the kitchen, but absolute accuracy is usually not required (except for sauces, cakes and pastries). The tables below give the nearest convenient equivalents in both metric and British imperial measures while the formulas give a more precise conversion factor. British dry measures for ounces and pounds are the same as American measures. Liquid measures, however, are different.

LIQUID MEASURES

US	METRIC	UK (IMPERIAL)
1 teaspoon (⅓ tablespoon)	5 ml	1 teaspoon
2 teaspoons	10 ml	1 dessertspoon
1 tablespoon (3 teaspoons)	15 ml	1 tablespoon (½ fl. oz.)
2 tablespoons (⅛ cup)	30 ml	2 tablespoons
¼ cup (4 tablespoons)	60 ml	4 tablespoons
⅓ cup (5⅓ tablespoons)	80 ml	8 dessertspoons (2½ fl. oz.)
½ cup (8 tablespoons)	120 ml	scant ¼ pint (4 fl. oz.)
⅔ cup (10⅔ tablespoons)	160 ml	¼ pint
¾ cup (12 tablespoons)	180 ml	generous ¼ pint (6 fl. oz.)
1 cup (16 tablespoons)	240 ml	scant ½ pint (8 fl. oz.)
2 cups (1 pint, ½ quart or 16 fl. oz.)	480 ml	generous ¾ pint
2½ cups	600 ml	1 pint (20 fl. oz.)
3 cups (1½ pints or ¾ quart)	720 ml	1¼ pints
4 cups (2 pints or 1 quart)	960 ml	1½ pints (32 fl. oz.)
5 cups	1.2 liters	2 pints (1 quart, 40 fl. oz.)

LIQUID MEASURES

Cups x 0.24 = Liters
Liters x 4.23 = Cups

LINEAR MEASURES

US & UK	METRIC
¼ inch	6 mm
½ inch	13 mm
1 inch	2.5 cm
2 inches	5 cm
3 inches	7.5 cm
6 inches	15 cm
1 foot	30 cm

SOLID MEASURES

1 Pound = 16 Ounces
1 Kilo = 1000 Grams
Ounces x 28.35 = Grams
Grams x 0.035 = Ounces

US & UK	METRIC
1 oz.	28 grams
3½ oz.	100 grams
¼ pound	112 grams
⅓ pound	150 grams
½ pound	225 grams
1 pound	450 grams
2.2 pounds	1 Kilogram

OVEN TEMPERATURES

$°C = (°F - 32) \div 1.8$
$°F = (°C \times 1.8) + 32$

FAHRENHEIT	CENTIGRADE
200°	93°
250°	121°
300°	149°
350°	177°
400°	204°
450°	232°
500°	260°

Silk Road Groceries & Mail-Order Resources

The following are some good specialty stores in major cities in the U.S. and Canada. Also through the Internet and mail-order houses (in orange type) you can find every possible Silk Road region ingredient and much more.

WHOLE FOODS MARKET, INC.
Grains, nuts, herbs & spices; all cuisines"
www.wholefoods.com

CA

PARS MARKET
9016 W. Pico
Los Angeles, CA 90035
(310) 859-8125

FRIEDA'S
Exotic and specialty sauces
4465 Corporate Center Dr.
Los Alamitos, CA 90058
(800) 421-9477
www.frieda.com

SOOFER COMPANY/SADAF
2828 S. Alameda St.
Los Angeles, CA 90058
(800) 852-4050
(323) 234-2447
www.sadaf.com
info@sadaf.com

TEHRAN MARKET
1417 Wilshire Blvd.
Santa Monica, CA 90403
(310) 393-6719

BANN THAI AT SAFFRON
3735 India St.
San Diego, CA 92103
(619) 574-0322
www.sumeiyu.com

ARIA INTERNATIONAL MARKET
2710 Garnet Ave. #205
San Diego, CA 92109
(781) 274-9632

ATTARI DELI
582 S. Murphy Ave.
Sunnyvale, CA 94086
(408) 773-0290

VANILLA SAFFRON IMPORTS
949 Valencia Street
San Francisco, CA 94110
(415) 648-8990
(415) 648-2240
www.saffron.com

VIVANDE
2125 Fillmore Street
San Francisco, CA 94115
(415) 346-4430

FARM FRESH PERSIAN GROCERY
10021 S. Blaney Ave.
Cupertino, CA 95608
(408) 257-3746

GA

SHAHRZAD INT'L
6435 Roswell Rd Suite A
Atlanta, GA 30328
(404) 257-9045

IL

ARYA FOOD IMPORTS
5061 N. Clark St.
Chicago, IL 60640
(773) 878-2092

PARS PERSIAN STORE
5260 N. Clark St.
Chicago, IL 60640
(773) 769-6635

THAI GROCERY
5014 North Broadway St.
Chicago, IL 60640
(773) 561-5522
www.uwahimaya.com

ORIENTAL FOOD MARKET
Chinese products and spices
2801 West Howard St.
Chicago, IL 60645
(773) 274-2826

THAI GROCER
3161 North Cambridge St. Ste 507
Chicago, IL 60657
(773) 477-6268
www.thaigrocer.com

MA

ORIENTAL PANTRY
423 Great Rd. (2A)
Acton, MA 01720
(800) 828-0368
(978) 264-4576
www.orientalpantry.com

SUPER HERO'S MARKET
509 Mt. Auburn St.
Watertown, MA 02172
(617) 924-9507

MD

YEKTA GROCERY
1488 Rockville Pike
Rockville, MD 20852
(301) 984-1190

INT'L HOUSE INDIAN FOOD
765-H Rockville Pike
Rockville, MD 20852
(301 279 2121

MI

ZINGERMAN'S
422 Detroit St.
Ann Arbor, MI 41104
(734) 663-3354
www.zingermans.com

RAFAL SPICE COMPANY
2521 Russell St.
Detroit, MI 48207
(800) 228-4276
(313) 259-6373
www.rafalspicecompany.com

NC

CASPIAN INT'L MARKET
2909 Brentwood Rd.
Raleigh, NC 27604
(919) 954-0029

NJ

FILLO FACTORY, INC.
Fresh filo
56 Cortland Ave.
Dumont, NJ 07628
(800) OK-FILLO

NM

THE COOKING POST
chiles, wild rice
The Puebla of Santa Ana 2 Dove Rd.
Bernalillo, NM 87004
(888) 867-5198
www.cookingpost.com

THE CHILE PEPPER EMPORIUM
Chiles and chile products
89 Winrock Center
Albuquerque, NM 87110
(800) 288 9648

Left: An early 1500s miniature painting shows a grocery shop window and right: A grocer's wares are displayed in Bokhara.

AIKO'S ORIENTAL FOODS
781 Granada Center
Alamogordo, NM 88310
(505) 434-1040
www.neonwok.com

NV

MEDITERRANEAN MARKET
4147 S. Maryland Pkwy.
Las Vegas, NV 89119
(702) 731-6030

NY

ADRIANA'S CARAVAN
Spices & ethnic ingredients, grains & seeds"
78 Grand Central Terminal
New York, NY 10017
(800) 316-0820
www.adrianscaravan.com

DEAN & DELUCA
560 Broadway
New York, NY 10012
(800) 221-7714
(212) 999-0306
www.deananddeluca.com

KIM MAN FOOD PRODUCTS
200 Canal St.
New York, NY 10013
(212) 571-0330

Fax: (212) 766-9085

KALUSTYAN'S
123 Lexington Ave.
New York, NY 10016
(212) 685-3451
(212) 683-3888
www.kalustyans.com

KATAGIRI
Japanese noodles
seasonings, spices, & pickles
224 East 59th St.
New York, NY 10016
(212) 755-3566
Fax: (212) 752-4197
www.katagiri.com

NADER INTERNATIONAL FOOD
1 East 28th St.
Flushing, NY 10016
(212) 686-5793

PARS INTERNATIONAL PRODUCE
145 West 30th St.
New York, NY 10021
(212) 760-7277

ZABAR'S
2245 Broadway
New York, NY 10024
(212) 787-2000
(800) 697-6301
www.zabars.com

SULTAN'S DELIGHT
Med. & Middle Eastern products
P.O. Box 090302
Brooklyn, NY 11209
(800) 852-5046
(718) 274-2826
www.sultansdelight.com

OR
KOLBEH MEDITERRANEAN
11830 SW Kerr Pkwy.
Lake Oswego, OR 97035
(503) 246-8227

TN
INT'L FOOD MARKET
206 Thompson Ln.
Nashville, TN 37211
(615) 333-9651

TX
MOZZARELLA COMPANY
Fresh mozzarella and ricotta
2944 Elm St.
Dallas, TX 75226
(800) 798-2954
www.mozzarellacompany.com

ANDRE IMPORTED FOODS
1478 W. Spring Valley
Richardson, TX 77036
(972) 644-7644

GARCONS
2926 Hillcroft
Houston, TX 77036
(713) 781-0400

SUPER VANAK
5692 Hillcroft
Houston, TX 77036
(713) 952-7676

WY
SPICE MERCHANT
P.O Box 534
Jackson Hole, WY 83001
(307) 733-6343
stirfry@compuserve.com

VA
IRANSARA
6039 Leesburg Pike
Falls Church, VA 22041
(703) 578-3232

AFGHAN MARKET
5709 Edsal Rd.
Alexandria, VA 22304
(703) 212-9529

WA
PARS MARKET
2331 140th Ave. NE
Bellevue, WA 98005
(425) 641-5265

SUR LA TABLE
84 Pine St. Pike Place
Farmers' Market
Seattle, WA 98101
(800) 243-0852
www.surlatable.com

THE SPANISH TABLE
Spanish, Portuguese, &
Moroccan products"
1427 Western Avenue
Seattle, WA 98101
(206) 682-2827
tablespan@aol.com

UWAJIMAYA
519 6th Avenue South
Seattle, WA 98104
(800) 889-1928
(206) 624-6248
(206) 624-6248

PACIFIC SUPERMARKET
12332 Lake City Way NE
Seattle, WA 98125
(206) 363-8639

WI
PENZEYS SPICES
Spices and flavorings
19300 Janacek Ct.
Brookfield, WI 53045
(800) 741-7787
(414) 574-0278
www.penzeys.com

SPICE HOUSE
Spices from around the world
1031 N. Old World Third St.
Milwaukee, WI 53203
(414) 272-0977
www.spicehouse.com

OK
TRAVEL BY TASTE
4818 N. McArthur
Warr Acres, OK 73122
(405) 787-2969

Canada
AKHAVAN MARKET
5768 Sherbrooke W.
Montreal PQ H4A 1X1
(514) 485-4887

AYOUB'S MARKET
322 Sommerset St. E
Ottawa, ON A1L 6W3
(613) 233-6417

BIJAN SPECIALTY FOOD
1461 Clyde Ave.
W. Vancouver, BC V7T 1E9
(604) 925-1055

MAIN IMPORTING GROCERY
1188 St. Laurant
Montreal, PQ H2X 2S5
(514) 861-5681

PARS DELI MARKET
1801 Lonsdale Ave.
N. Vancouver, BC V7M 2J8
(604) 988-3515

SOUTH CHINA SEAS TRADING COMPANY
1689 Johnston St.
Granville Island Market
Vancouver, BC V6H 3R9
(604) 681-5402

Credits

Photography

All photographs are by Serge Ephraim and Najmieh Batmanglij ©, except as otherwise noted for the pages listed below:

Roland and Sabrina Michaud © / Rapho: 2–3, 33, 112–113, 220–221, 229
Hulton-Deutsch Collection © / Corbis: 6–7
Keren Su © / Stone: 8, 22–23,
Aldo Tutino / Najmieh Batmanglij ©: 12–13, 81, 248–249
Ric Ergenbright © / Corbis: 9 (top)
The British Library, OR 2265, 157v: 9 (bottom)
Michelle Garret © / Corbis: 15 (top)
Yann Layma © Stone: 18–19, 38–39
The Metropolitan Museum of Art, Gift of the Dillon Fund, 1973 (1973.120.3) Photograph © 1994, The Metropolitan Museum of Art: 25, 26–27
Freer Gallery of Art, Smithsonian Institution, Washington, DC, F12946.12.253a: 28–29
Mehdi Khonsari ©: 30–31, 252
Manoocher © / Webistan: 35 (bottom)
Daniel Nadler ©: 37 (top)
Paul Almasy © / Corbis: 44–45
David Ball © / Stone: 46–47
Reza © / Webistan: 49, 274
National Gallery of Art, Giovanni Bellini & Titian, The Feast of the Gods, Widener Collection, Photograph © 2002 Board of Trustees, National Gallery of Art, Washington: 50–51
Jonathan Blair / Woodfin Camp & Associates: 172-173
Carl and Ann Purcell © / Corbis: 54
Owen Franken © / Corbis: 57 (left)
Arthur M. Sackler Museum, Harvard University ©: 58, 59
Jonathan Blair © / Corbis: 67
Afshin Bakhtiar ©: 75
Liley Franey © / Rapho: 110
Will Curtis © / Stone: 113
Owen Franken © / Corbis: 126 (top & bottom), 127 (right)
James Stanfield © / National Geographic: 134-135
Maryam Zandi / Mage Publishers ©: 146–149, 158, 188–189, 201, 267, 292–293

Gérard Sioen © / Rapho: 196-197
Sassan Afsoosi ©: 236
Michele Kay ©: 273
Marie-Claire Bordaz © / Rapho: 282
Collection Prince Sadruddin Aga Khan ©: 326

Map

Karen E. Rasmussen, Archeographics, Washington, DC

Translation

Dick Davis © (poems): 7, 9, 10, 112, 149, 285
Husain Haddawy (text): courtesy of W.W. Norton © 1990: 66–67
Stephen H. West © (text): 91
Reynold A. Nicholson (poem): 111
Edward FitzGerald: 146

Acknowledgments

I am indebted to too many people to name them all here: family, friends, guides, students, teachers, editors, photographers and cooks. Writing a cookbook is a collaborative effort and, like raising children, it takes a village and many years to do it.

Nonetheless, there are those who have given me invaluable support to realize this book. I would like to thank my husband Mohammad who is my editor-in-chief and who also looked after everything, including the kids, dogs, house and office while I traveled; my son Zal for his artistic suggestions in designing the book; and my son Rostam for putting up with my cooking experiments, being patient and supporting me in difficult times. Most of all, I would like to thank my family for not making me feel guilty (for the most part) for being consumed by this project.

I am indebted to my long-time photographer Serge Ephraim, who dropped everything he was doing in the sunny south of France to come to travel with me whenever I needed him. Most important, he was able to calmly handle the chaos in my house during the weeks-long photo shoots and create beautiful photographs that brought my cooking to life, and for that, I thank him.

I would like to thank George Constable for his guidance and astute editorial suggestions. I am also very grateful to my cookbook editor Ellen Phillips who made the text flow and whose enthusiasm, great knowledge, good questions and hard work brought together the various aspects of the book. Her passion kept me going even when I was exhausted and didn't want to do any more work. I would also like to thank Robin Bray for his artist's eye and help on the design of the book, Harry Endrulat for copyediting the manuscript and making it consistent, and Tony Ross for his help in the very first draft of the recipes.

I would like to thank Dick Davis for his masterful translations of my favorite Rumi and Khayyam poems. He is not only a wonderful poet in his own right but also the best translator of Persian.

In China my guide in five cities was the late Barbara Tropp, author of *The Modern Art of Chinese Cooking,* and Zhu Yanam (Jo), who not only introduced me to cooking schools, but also to great restaurants, markets and wonderful home cooks throughout China. I would also like to thank my neighbors Alison and Bo Jia, and my sister-in-law Xiapo who lent me their Chinese treasures. For Uzbekistan, Khosrow Zamani was a great help in getting me there, and once there his assistant Firouzeh became a good resource and my guide. Also in Uzbekistan, I would like to thank Christopher Sahakian, and his assistant Anahita who guided me throughout the country. I would have been completely lost there without them.

My sisters have always been a great help to me, but for this book I would like to especially thank Ezat, a great cook in her own right, who turned up with everything I needed and assisted me during the photography shoots. Shirin was always there for me, and her love and emotional support kept me going; and Faezeh offered me her resourcefulness while I was working on this book.

I would also like to thank all those who have guided me through the intricacies of the various cuisines along the Silk Road: Gülumay Selamet, Turkish; Olga Bounias, Greek; Seyyed Ali, Afghan; Josette Yenkomenshian, Lebanese; Janet Haratounian, Armenian; Marie Louise Pellegrini, Genoese and Sicilian; Atul Kochhar, Savitra Chand, Shoppa Shah, Yasaman Radji, Indian. I wish to thank my Les Dames d'Escoffier colleague Ann Yonkers for bringing about Fresh Farms Market in Dupont Circle (a modern Silk Road open air market right next door); and Sheila Saleh for lending me her wonderful samovar collection. Thanks are also due to my international student assistants; Radka; Monia; Ambica; Sophia; and my assistants in the kitchen: Marlene, Rosie and Maria-Corinna.

Index of Recipes & Special Ingredients

A

agar-agar (vegetable gelatin) 306
almond milk 306
angelica 306
asafetida 306
ashak 307

B

banana leaves 307
barberries 307
basil, Thai 307
borage 308
BREADS
   Armenian Festive Sweet Bread 233
   Gujarati Pan Millet Bread 235
   Gujarati Pan Mung Bean Bread 234
   Hindu Kush Pan Rice Bread 236
   Kurdish Butternut Squash Bread 227
   Persian Lavash Bread 229
   Punjabi Flat Bread (Nan) 228
   Rayy Sweet Gingerbread (Nan-e Qandi) 232
   Saveh Sweet Saffron Bread (Shirmal) 227
   Sichuan Pan Scallion Bread 237
   Tashkent Onion & Garlic Bread 230
   Yemeni Pan Barley Bread 235
broth, vegetable 308
bulgur 308
butter, clarified (see ghee) 308

C

CAKES
   Amman Semolina Cake with Orange Blossom Glaze 256
   Georgian Sour Cherry Cake 258
   Greek Sesame & Walnut Cake 251
   Persian Pistachio Cake 257
   Susa Spiced Walnut & Date Scones (Kolucheh) 252

CANDIES
   Persian Sequin Candy 263
   Silk Road Sesame Brittle 262
   Turkish Delight with Rose Water (Rahat Lokum) 260

canning 294
cardamom 308
cassia 308
cheese, white 308
cherries, sour or tart 309
chickpea Flour 309
chili, Thai bird 309
cilantro 309
coconut milk 309
Coffee Tales 282
   Silk Road Coffee 283
cooking measurements 325
coriander 310
couscous 310
cucumbers 310
cumin 310
curry leaf 310
curry powder 311

D

daikon 311
dates 311
DESSERTS
   Chinese Eight Jewel Coconut Rice Pudding 259
   Genoese Quince Paste with Pistachios 247
   Persian Pomegranate & Orange Blossom Fruit Salad ... 250
   Viennese Cream Puffs with Rose Water 264
   Yazdi Persimmon & Feta Cheese 255
DUMPLINGS & PATTIES
   Beijing Crispy Rice Rolls 217
   Birjandi Sanbuseh (Noftieh) 213
   Chinese Tofu Dumplings 218
   Indian Samosa 214, 216
   Mosul Bulgur Patties (Kibbeh) 208
      Eggplant Patties 209
      Lentil Patties 209
      Pumpkin Patties 209
   Persian Barberry Sanbuseh 213
   Pirozhki 211
   Spanish Epanadillas 211
   Uzbek Samsa 213

E

Eggplant 311

EGGS
    Alexandrian Chickpea Patties (Falafel, Tameya) 132
    Bokhara Pancake 124
    Caspian Fresh Herb Kuku Rolled in Lavash Bread 130
    Delhi Curried Potato & Egg Patties 127
    Fava Bean Patties (Falafel) 132
    Persian Cauliflower Kuku 128
    Persian Omelet with Saffron & Rose Water 121
    Sicilian Eggplant with Saffron Soufflé 126
    Silk Road Onion & Tomato Omelet 124
    Simply Silk Road Eggs 120
    Solomon's Apple Omelet 125
    Sumerian Quince Omelet 125

F

fava beans 311
fenugreek 311
filo dough 312

FRUIT & VEGETABLE BRAISES
    Athenian Artichoke & Pearl Onion Braise 175
    Bombay Mushroom Curry 183
    Caspian Eggplant & Aromatic Herbs Braise 195
    Caspian Fava Bean Braise with Garlic & Dill 174
    Elam Kidney Bean & Lime Braise 178
    Gilani Jujube, Walnut & Pomegranates Braise 184
    Gujarati Potato Braise 182
    Horn of Africa Okra & Eggplant Braise with Unripe Grapes . 181
    Indian Cauliflower & Potato Curry 192
    Indonesian Stir-Fry Tempeh 194
    Isfahani Green Bean & Tomato Braise 176
    Isfahani Quince & Pomegranate Braise 185
    Kurdish Rhubarb Braise with Aromatic Herbs 186
    Persian Butternut Squash Braise 190
    Samarkand Golden Peach Braise 191
    Sichuan Spicy Stir-Fry Tofu 194
    Uzbek Apple & Tart Cherry Braise 180
    Uzbek Sweet & Sour Carrot & Raisin Braise 187

G

garlic, sweet fresh baby 312
ghee 312
grape
    leaves 312
    unripe 312
groceries & mail-order resources 326

H

herbs, dried 313

I

1001 Nights Chewy Saffron Ice Cream 270

J

jujube 313

L

labneh (see yogurt) 313
lemon grass 313
lentil, red 313
lime
    Persian 313
    pickling 313
lotus seeds, crystallized 313

M

mahlab 313
mastic 314
mulberries 314
mushrooms
    black or shitake 314
    dried 314

N

nigella seeds (nigella sativa) 314
noodles
    Asian 314
    cellophane 314
    Persian 315
    rice stick 315
    wheat (egg noodles) 315
Nuts
    almonds, sweet 306
    pine 317
    pistachio 317
    roasting 315
    toasting 315
    walnuts 322

O

onion juice 315
orange
    blossom water 315
    paste, Seville 315
    peel, blanched 316
    peel, candied 316
    Seville or bitter 315
    peeling & segmenting 316

P

PASTAS
    Afghan Garlic Chive Ravioli with Yogurt Sauce (Ashak) 204
    Afghan Spicy Yogurt Sauce (Shurba) 202
    Afghan Yogurt & Bread Sauce (Qoruti) 202
    Birjandi Cucumber & Pistachio Sauce 200
    Birjandi Whey Sauce 200
    Greek Garlic & Almond Sauce (Skorthalia) 202
    Greek Spinach & Leek Pie in Filo Pastry (Spanakopita) 205
    Kurdish Bulgur Sauce (Tarkhineh) 202
    Neapolitan Pasta with Tomato Sauce (Master Recipe) 198
    Persian Pistachio Sauce 200
    Sicilian Fava Bean, Garlic & Dill Crostata 206
    Sicilian Mushroom, Saffron Cream Sauce 199
    Silk Road Noodle Sauces 200
    Syrian Tahini Sauce (Tarator) 203
    Thai Stir-Fry Coconut Sauce (Pad Thai Sauce) 203
    Vietnamese Peanut Sauce (Nuocleo) 203

PASTRIES
    Ardebil Quince Baklava 246
    East-West Almond Cookies 241
    Genoese Saffron & Rose Petal Biscotti 242
    Sicilian Sour Cherry & Pistachio Crostata 244
    Spanish Orange Blossom Sponge Roll 240
    Yazdi Turnover Pastry with Rose Water (Sanbuseh) 243

peas, split 316
persimmon 317

PICKLES & CHUTNEYS
    Bombay Mango Chutney (Quick & Easy) 299
    Persian Baby Eggplant Pickles (Quick & Easy) 298
    Persian Persimmon Chutney (Quick & Easy) 300
    Samarkand Golden Peach Chutney (Quick & Easy) 299
    Shirazi Lime Pickle (Quick & Easy) 299
    Sichuan Cucumber Pickle (Quick & Easy) 301

PIZZA
    Istanbul Borek 210
    Neapolitan (Master Recipe) 224
        Caspian Olive, Pomegranate & Angelica Topping 225
        Syrian Zatar Topping 225
        Yemeni Fenugreek Topping 225

plums 317
pomegranate 317
    how to seed 318
    juice 318
    juiced in its skin 318
    paste 318

PRESERVES
    Chinese Jujube Preserve 297
    Iranian Baby Walnut Preserve 295
    Iranian Pistachio Skin Preserve 295
    Mesopotamian Date & Orange Peel Preserve 296
    Orange Blossom Preserve 296
    Rose Petal Preserve 296

pumpkin & other winter squash 318

Q

quince 319

R

RICE
    Afghan Qabeli Pilau 153
    Afghan Turnip Pilau 158
    Armenian Vermicelli Pilavi 161
    Armenian Wedding Pilavi 156
    Astara Barberry & Cumin Polow 162
    Baghdad Bulgur & Lentil Pilaf 155
    Bulgur with Noodles & Dates 161
    California Brown Rice Pilaf 144
    Caspian Dill & Fava Bean Polow with Baby Garlic 165
    Damascus Sweet Rice 136
    Delhi Mustard Seed & Yogurt Pullao 152
    Fertile Crescent Bulgur & Mung Bean Pilaf 155
    Genoese Dill & Fava Bean Risotto 154
    Georgian Pilaf with Tart Cherries 163
    Gilani Smothered Rice (Kateh) Master Recipe 136
    Herat Noodle & Date Pilau 161
    Indian Millet & Mung Bean Pilaf 155
    Japanese Rice 140
    Kanu Festival Tamarind & Coconut Pullao 143
    Kermani Polow with Saffron & Pistachios 150
    Levantine Pilaf in Pastry 168
    Minnesota Wild Rice 145
    Persian Polow with Green Beans & Tomatoes 164
    Persian Rice (Dami) Rice Cooker Method 137
    Persian Saffron Rice with Golden Crust (Chelow) 138
    Persian Wedding Polow with Orange Peel 166

Punjabi Pilaf 136
Shirazi Baked Saffron Polow with Spinach 160
Steamed Brown Basmati Polow (Rice Cooker Method) 137
Stir-Fried Rice Noodles 151
Susa Polow with Lentils, Currants & Dates 156
Thai Soft Sweet Sticky Rice in Banana Leaf 141
Uzbek Carrot Palov with Cumin 153
Uzbek Mung Bean & Apricot Pilau 155
Uzbek Quince Palau 166
Vietnamese Sticky Rice 140
Xian Stir-Fried Rice 151
Yazdi Polow with Eggplant & Pomegranate 158

RICE CRUSTS
Rice with Bread Crust 139
Rice with Eggplant & Garlic Crust 139
Rice with Lettuce Crust 139
Rice with Potato Crust 139

rice flour 319
rose 146
   petals 319
      crystallized 319
   water 320

S

saffron 45, 51, 56, 122
salab 320

SALADS
Alexandrian Spicy Dried Fava Bean Spread 65
Alexandrian Stir-Fried Celery Roots 83
Amoli Rice Salad with Barberries & Orange Peel 74
Armenian Bulgur & Pomegranate Stuffed Grapevine Leaves .84
Baalbek Chickpea & Sesame Spread (Hummus) 79
Beijing-Style Bok Choy with Mushrooms 85
Bekaa Valley Bulgur Salad with Tomato & Parsley (Tabbouleh) 69
Bengali Chickpea Vegetable Fritters 82
Caspian Olives with Pomegranate & Angelica 60
Chinese Noodle Salad 71
Fertile Crescent Young White Turnips with Dates 87
Georgian Rice Salad with Eggplant & Tart Cherries 72
Georgian Tomatoes Stuffed with Walnuts & Pomegranates ..64
Indian Five Spice Eggplant 92
Konya Eggplants with Onion & Garlic (Imam Bayaldi) 93
Kurdish Chickpea, Cilantro & Cumin Salad 68
Levantine Roasted Eggplant & Sesame Dip (Baba Ghanoush) 90
Mesopotamian Rice Salad with Green Lentils 76
Persian Eggplant Borani 90
Rayy Eggplant & Sun-Dried Yogurt in Lavash Rolls 62
Samarkand Mung Bean Salad 86
Shirazi Cucumber & Pomegranate Salad 80
Sichuan Toasted Sesame & Cabbage Salad 70
Sicilian Roasted Pepper & Eggplant Salad 61
Tashkent Daikon & Pomegranate Salad 88
Tunisian Couscous Salad with Pine Nuts & Barberries ... 77
Uzbek Carrot Salad 89
Uzbek Potato Salad 78
Xian Eggplant & Pomegranate Salad 92

seeds & peppercorns, toasted 320
sesame paste 320

SHERBETS 285
Bokhara Iced Melon Drink 288
Caspian Seville Orange Syrup 286
Indian Tamarind Iced Drink 291
Isfahan Quince-Lime Syrup 289
Lebanese Grape Syrup 287
Persian Flixweed Drink 289
Persian Sweet & Sour Cucumber Iced Drink 290
Qamsar Rose Water Syrup 287
Rayy Apple & Rose Water Iced Drink 288
Saffron Syrup 287
Silk Road Yogurt Drink 286
Rhubarb Syrup 319

Sichuan peppercorns 320

SORBETS & GRANITAS 266
Iranian Granita with Rice Sticks & Sour Cherries 268
Iranian Pomegranate Granita 269
Shirazi Melon & Peach Sorbet with Crystallized Rose Petals 266
Turkish Quince Granita 267

SOUPS
Azerbaijani Pomegranate & Spinach Soup 104
Balkh Brown Lentil Soup 99
Beijing Hot & Sour Noodle Soup 97
Caspian Butternut Squash, Bulgur & Wild Orange Soup 98
Catalan Almond Soup 105
Chinese Tofu Wonton Soup 96
Damavand Yogurt & Cucumber Cold Soup 100
Genoese Minestrone with Pesto Sauce 103
Gujarati Carrot & Yogurt Soup 107
Homemade Tarkhineh 115
Kermani Pistachio & Barberry Soup 105
Kurdish Bulgur & Yogurt Soup (Tarkhineh) 115
Madras Red Lentil Soup 108
Mesopotamian Barley, Lentil & Tahini Soup 109
Oxus Tamarind & Coconut Soup 116
Susa Noodles Soup with Fresh Herbs 102
Tusy Mung Bean, Tarragon & Kohlrabi Soup 106

Soy sauce 320

SPICE MIXES
    Afghan Spice Mixture (Chahar Masala) 303
    Azerbaijani Spice Mix for Rice (Advieh) 303
    Caspian Herb Chutney (Dalar) 303
    Chinese Five Spice Mixture (Wu Xiang Fen) 303
    Fertile Crescent Herb Mix (Zatar) 305
    Fertile Crescent Spice Mix (Baharat) 305
    Georgian Spice & Herb Mix (Khmeli-Suneli) 304
    North Indian Spice Mixture (Garam Masala) 304
    Persian Spice Mix (Advieh) 305
    South Indian Spice Mixture (Sambar) 305
    Tunisian Spice Mix (Harrisa) 304
sprouts 320
sumac 320
syrup, sugar 320

T

tahini paste 320
tamarind 320
    liquid 321
    paste 321
tarkhineh 321
TEA
    Afghan Wedding Tea (Qaymaq Chai) 276
    Armenian Spiced Rose Petal Tea 277
    Baghdad Honey & Coriander Cold Remedy Tea 280
    Fertile Crescent Aromatic Almond Tea 280
    Persian Borage & Valerian Nightcap 278
    Persian Saffron Love-Tea 278
    Silk Road Jujube Panacea Tea 279
tempeh 321
tofu 321
tomatoes, peeling and seeding 321
turmeric 321

V

valerian 321
vegetable broth 321
vegetables, cooking choices 321
    oven cooking
        grilling, broiling and baking 322
    stove-top cooking
        braising 322
        deep-frying 322
        stir-frying 322
    water cooking
        immersion 321
        steaming 321

W

whey, dried 322
wok, how to clean 322
wrappers
    dough 322
    Homemade 218, 322, 323
    Rice 323
    Rice paper 319
    yufka (borek) 323

Y

yogurt
    drained 323
    homemade 323

Index of Headnotes, Introduction, Poems & Stories

HEADNOTES

Alborz Mountains, 60; Alexandria, 65; Amol, 74; Amu Darya and Syr Darya, 78; Anatolia, 208; Ardebil, 246; Astara, 162; Baalbek, 79; Balkh, 99; Bekaa Valley, 69; Biscotti, 242; Bok choy, 97; Bokhara, 264; Boreks, 210; Boulani, 216; Buddha, 41; Bulgur, 155; Cantonese, 97; Caucasus, 247; Chinese Date, 184; Clavijo, 104; Cyprus, 128; Damavand Mountain, 100; Fertile Crescent, 76; Genoese Specialty, 103; Georgian Cuisine, 72; Georgian Mythology, 258; Gilan, 136; Gujarat, 107; Haroun al-Rashid, 62; Herat, 161; Herodotus, 132; Hindu Kush, 99, 236; Kanu Festival, 143; Kerman, 105; Lavash Bread, 229; Levant, 90; Lokum, 260; Manichaean Dualism, 223; Marco Polo, 154; Mashhad, 106; Moon Dragon Festival, 259; Mosul, 208; New World Food, 124; Okra, 181; Peking-Style Dumplings, 218; Pirozhki, 211; Pizza, 224; Portuguese Traders, 182; Punjab, 228; Rayy, 62; Rhubarb, 186; Samarkand, 86; Saveh, 227; Semolina, 256; Sesame, 251; Shiraz, 80; Sicilian Crostata, 206; Sicily, 61; Song of Solomon, 125; Susa, 156; Tabriz, 104; Tarkhineh, 115; Teresa's Armenian Bakery, 233; Tunisia, 77; Uzbekistan, 153; Vegetarian Persia, 68; Wenshu Monastery in Chengdu, 194; Wonton, 96; Xian, 92; Yazd, 158; Yemen, 235

INTRODUCTION

Afghanistan, 12, 16, 20, 27–28; Albania, 20; Amu Darya, 28; Arabs adopted the braises, salads, breads, cheeses and omelets of Iran, 45; Bactrian camels, 32; Buddhists, 37; Chang'an, 24; China, 12, 14, 16, 20, 24, 41–42, 54; China and culinary imports, 41; Christians, 37; collection of 150 vegetarian recipes from countries touched by Silk Road trade, 54; Confucian analects; 41; Cuneiform recipe for turnip soup, 45; Emperor Wu, 24; European Renaissance, 51; Ferghana, 27; For both vegetarians and non-vegetarians, 54; Genoa, 12; Great Wall, 24; Han dynasty, 24; Hindus, 37; Indian food, 12, 48; Italy, 12, 14, 16, 20, 51, 54; Kitab al tabikh va islah al-aghdhiya al makulat, 14; Lady Wen-chi, 25; Layli and Majnun, 28; lokantas, 14; Manicheans, 37; Modern Silk Road, 56; Mongolian hot pot, 41; New Foods—East & West, 38; New World, 47; Pamirs, 25; Pasta probably originated in Persia, 14; Persia, 9, 12, 14, 16, 20, 28, 37, 41–42; Silk Road trade flourished, its culinary treasures entered Europe in the same ways as they moved between China, Mesopotamia and the Levant: with armies, emigrants and merchants, 51; Secret of silk making remained in China for centuries, 28; Song dynasty, 42; Spain, 12, 51; Taklimakan, 37; The Era of Caravans, 31; Timeless nomad traditions, 54; Towards a Silk Road Cuisine, 53; Turkey, 12, 20; Upanishads, 48; Uzbekistan, 12, 16, 27; vegetarian focus, 14; Wu and Parthian Persia, 28; Wu Di, 24; Xian, 12, 21, 41; Zhang Qian, 24, 27; Zoroastrians, 37

POEMS

Khayyam, Omar 146
   Look to the rose that blows about us 146
Li Ho
   A Tartar horn tugs at the north wind 32
Rumi, Jalal al-Din
   I have put duality away 111
   If wheat springs from my dust 112
   In anguished tales of separation's pains 10
   Oh listen to the flute as it complains 9
   Our guest's the sun that rises in the east 7
   When the rose is withered 149
Song of Solomon
   As an apple tree among the trees of the wood 125

STORIES

A Rumi Grape Story 226
A Rumi Tale of Dreams 142
A Rumi Tale of Sufi Hospitality 114
A Sweet & Sour Story 248
Food for the Spirit 221
Fruits on Sticks 91
Grocery Shopping from 1001 Nights 66
Saffron 122
Tea Time 274
The Poet of Journeys 111
The Rose 146
The Stranger at the Gate 188

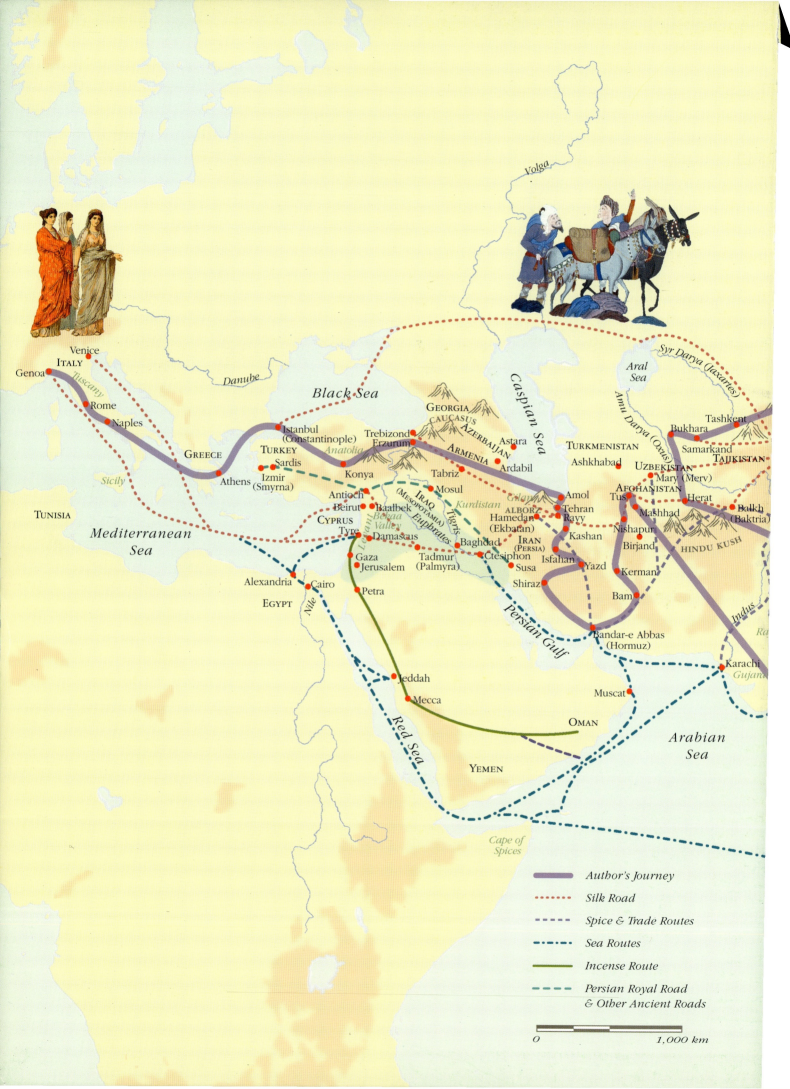